Fictional Points
of View

Fictional Points of View

PETER LAMARQUE

Cornell University Press

ITHACA AND LONDON

First published 1996 by Cornell University Press.

Library of Congress Cataloging-in-Publication Data

Lamarque, Peter.
    Fictional points of view / Peter Lamarque.
      p. cm.
    Includes bibliographical references and index.
    ISBN 0–8014–3216–2
      1. Point of view (Literature)   2. Literature—Philosophy.
I. Title.
PN3383.P64L29   1996
801'.953—dc20   96–81

Printed in the United States of America

To
MARY, TOBY, AND HUGH

CONTENTS

Contents

PREFACE

This book is addressed to all those with a philosophical interest in foundational questions about the nature of fictionality and the institution of literature and literary criticism. It offers an analytical study of certain basic concepts relating to literary criticism: fiction, character, reference, truth, intention, author, emotion, knowledge, tragedy, mind, autonomy, and more besides.

Richard Rorty has said, apparently without irony or disapproval, that nowadays all that literary critics (including par excellence literary theorists) do is "spend their time placing books in the context of other books, figures in the context of other figures."[1] I hope this book achieves a little more than that, but what is notable is that the books and figures holding center stage here are not those (or not many of those) whose names have acquired canonical status in more familiar literary theoretical investigations. The perspective or "point of view" on offer here is not that of standard textbooks in literary theory. The dramatis personae are different. The key figures under discussion include Iris Murdoch on truth and art, Stanley Cavell on tragedy, Roland Barthes and Michel Foucault on "the death of the author," David Lewis on "truth in fiction," Kendall Walton on fearing fictions, Freud on psychoanalysis and literature, and Rorty himself on literary criticism. There is also a discussion of a somewhat less well known "literary theorist," the fifteenth-century Japanese playwright and drama teacher Zeami Motokiyo (1363–1443), the founding father of the Noh theater.

Thus both the figures and the topics are somewhat off the beaten track. Furthermore, the book is not principally a "books and figures" sur-

---

1. Richard Rorty, *Contingency, Irony, and Solidarity* (Cambridge, 1989), p. 80.

vey so much as a study of ideas or concepts, many of which, as we shall see, have been at the center of heated controversy. What is perhaps most unusual in the treatment of the topics is the analytical or logical methodology. It is this philosophical contribution that I hope will serve to illuminate the subject matter at least to the extent of casting both familiar and less familiar issues in a new and helpful light.

It is tiresome to replay the old antagonisms between "analytic philosophy" and "continental philosophy," and although the book's general approach can be readily identified as "analytic," it is not offered in a combative spirit, nor does it seek to disparage the other "side." While I do believe that clarity of expression, the use of reasoned argument, and the making explicit of theses being defended or attacked are important virtues in philosophy, I do not believe that analytic philosophers have a monopoly on those virtues. What I hope to promote is the common and laudable goal, shared by theorists of all schools, of seeking deeper understanding of the deceptively simple concepts that underlie our ordinary critical and interpretive processes, all the time resisting the easy option of falling back on unreflective received opinion. I hope this book is able to make a small contribution toward attaining that goal.

Much of the work on this volume was carried out during my Visiting Fellowship in 1994 at the Humanities Research Centre of the Australian National University. It is hard to imagine more congenial surroundings for research, and I thank all the staff, notably Graeme Clark, Iain McCalman, Stephanie Stockdill, Jodi Parvey, and Leena Messina, for their help in so many ways, and also the other Fellows whose "work in progress" lectures, coffee-time conversations, and suggestions for reading were such a valuable stimulus.

It is a particular pleasure to be publishing the book with Cornell University Press, because of a long personal connection with Cornell University. I first went there, on sabbatical leave, in 1976 and have returned, on visits of varying lengths, most years ever since. Friends in the Sage School of Philosophy, notably Carl Ginet, Norman Kretzmann, Sydney Shoemaker, Richard Boyd, and Nick Sturgeon, have been constantly supportive, and I thank them for their kindness, generosity, and philosophical inspiration over the years.

I also thank, once again, Stein Haugom Olsen, of the University of Oslo, with whom I coauthored an earlier book on related topics, *Truth, Fiction, and Literature: A Philosophical Perspective* (Oxford, 1994), for his

Preface

help and advice over a great many years. His influence on my thinking will be obvious to anyone who knows his work.

Former colleagues at the University of Stirling have heard me discourse on these topics for more years than I care to remember. I am grateful to them for the high standards of argument they always promoted. I thank my new colleagues at the University of Hull (where I moved in 1995) for giving me time during my first term to complete this work.

Although most of the chapters have as their basis previously published articles of mine, the volume is less a "collection of essays" than a sustained treatment of closely interwoven problems in the philosophy of literature and criticism. All the previously published pieces have been revised, some extensively, and much new material has been added (Chapters 1, 9, and 12 are entirely new, as are the lengthy appendixes to Chapters 6 and 7). Also I have chosen to draw only on work that fits into the fairly narrow scope of topics defined in Chapter 1.

I thank the original publishers for permission to reprint parts of this material: Chapters 2 and 3 are from "Fiction and Reality," in *Philosophy and Fiction: Essays in Literary Aesthetics*, ed. Peter Lamarque (Aberdeen, 1983), pp. 52–72, and "Bits and Pieces of Fiction," *British Journal of Aesthetics* 24 (1984): 53–58; Chapter 4 is from "Reasoning to What Is True in Fiction," *Argumentation* 4 (1990): 333–346 (© 1990 Kluwer Academic Press; reprinted by permission of Kluwer Academic Publishers); Chapter 5, "Expression and the Mask: The Dissolution of Personality in Noh," *Journal of Aesthetics and Art Criticism* 47 (1989): 157–178; Chapter 6, "Truth and Art in Iris Murdoch's *The Black Prince*," *Philosophy and Literature* 2 (1978): 209–222; Chapter 7, "How Can We Fear and Pity Fictions?" *British Journal of Aesthetics* 21 (1981): 291–304; Chapter 8, "Tragedy and Moral Value," *Australasian Journal of Philosophy* 73 (1995): 239–249; Chapter 10, "The Death of the Author: An Analytical Autopsy," *British Journal of Aesthetics* 30 (1990): 319–331; Chapter 11, "On the Irrelevance of Psychoanalysis to Literary Criticism," in *Mind, Psychoanalysis, and Science*, ed. Peter Clark and Crispin Wright (Oxford, 1988), pp. 257–273 (by permission of Blackwell Publishers). Material from the *British Journal of Aesthetics* appears by permission of Oxford University Press.

PETER LAMARQUE

Bishop Burton, East Yorkshire

*Fictional Points
of View*

Introduction: Points of View

'And what are you reading, Miss____?' 'Oh! it is only a novel!' replies the young lady; while she lays down her book with affected indifference, or momentary shame.— 'It is only Cecilia, or Camilla, or Belinda;' or, in short, only some work in which the greatest powers of the mind are displayed, in which the most thorough knowledge of human nature, the happiest delineation of its varieties, the liveliest effusions of wit and humour are conveyed to the world in the best chosen language.

—Jane Austen, *Northanger Abbey*

. . . we live in a literary atmosphere. When we tell stories or when we write letters, we are making a form out of something which might be formless, and this is one of the deep motives for literature, or for art of any sort: that one is defeating the formlessness of the world.

—Iris Murdoch, Interview with Bryan Magee, BBC, 1978

I

On a musical analogy, what follows, the book as a whole, has a structure like that of a fugue. Different "voices" or subjects are introduced, and later themes transpose earlier ones. The subjects, countersubjects, and "answers" are in playful "flight" each before the other, leading in the end, one hopes, to harmonious resolution. As the discussion progresses, motifs appear and reappear, themes are taken up, intertwined, and developed, and modulations of key show the subjects in their varied aspects.

A central motif, as the title suggests, is that of "points of view," which surfaces throughout in connection with different themes. First, there are the points of view from which the principal subject, *fiction* or *fictionality*, is addressed: the philosopher's point of view, the aesthetician's, the literary critic's, the logician's. It will become clear that different kinds of questions arise when fiction is viewed from these perspectives and even that the subject matter itself seems to shift under these different encounters. When you think of fiction in terms of ontology, reference, existence, and possible worlds, considerations arise that are quite different from when you think of fiction in terms of narrative structure, plots, themes, and character development. Under each perspective the other seems remote, inessential. I hope to bring the interests closer together, to take the part of both philosopher and critic, but I will often question one side from the perspective of the other.

Then there are different points of view relating to the "worlds" of fiction; there is the "internal" view of participants in those worlds, where the surroundings are not fictional but real, and the "external" view of those (like us) outside looking in, where the worlds are not real but fictional. Fictional characters and events can be thought of from the point of view of their formal (linguistic) construction or from the point of view of the imaginative reality they embody. Indeed, so it seems, far from being set in opposition, these points of view represent an ineliminable double aspect of the fictional realm.

Next we have the reader's point of view in contrast to the writer's; writers invent their fictions, readers discover things about them. Furthermore, writers, as Henry James and Percy Lubbock have reminded us, present their fictional material under different narrative points of view, sometimes as omniscient observers, sometimes from within the souls of particular characters, sometimes through the eyes of unreliable storytellers. When readers imaginatively discover truths about the worlds depicted, they must recognize the narrative filters through which the worlds are set before them.

Also, works of fiction taken as a whole can project distinctive points of view on the world at large (the real world); better or worse, more or less true, visions of the world are offered by fictional representations. Can we not, by coming to share such visions, change our own outlook? Is not fiction a source of knowledge as well as inspiration? Here, perhaps the visual metaphor of "point of view" is at its least metaphorical. Imaginative seeing "with the mind's eye" can be a preliminary, even a training ground, for perception that is the real thing.

Finally, works can be read or judged from a "literary," as against, say, a historical, philosophical, or moralistic, point of view. A work might be admirable for its literary qualities but weak on historical detail, or vice versa. Yet just how are these distinctions to be drawn? What is the literary point of view? Why should it matter *how* we read?

In what follows, these different points of view will be explored and interrelated. In doing so, several more specific subjects will acquire prominence, although again in different guises. One concerns the frustratingly complex and manifold ways that fictional objects (characters, places, events) *connect* with the real world and the kinds of "reality" they themselves possess, both in ontological terms and in terms of how they are represented linguistically and psychologically. Another concerns the multitude of values ascribed to works of fiction, sometimes hesitatingly, sometimes overenthusiastically. A test case will be tragedy, where fear and pity, sympathetic imagination, and the promise of moral wisdom elicit a curious mix of disturbance and veneration. A third is the idea that fictional works of literature are unique, sui generis, "autonomous" in relation to works of other kinds, that they call for a special kind of attention and offer a special kind of reward.

II

These, then, are the "voices" of the fugue. They weave in and out of all the chapters, providing essential points of reference. But at a deeper level, a more binding theme informs the whole and provides a general motivation: what might be called a "humanistic" approach to literature and to fiction. The core idea is that works of literature, through the medium of fiction, can serve the end of advancing, helping to develop and understand, exhibiting through their themes and vision, matters of general, perhaps universal, human interest. Rather than seeing fiction as a barrier to this humanistic aim, as perhaps might Plato and others of a rationalistic persuasion, we must see fiction as an important, even indispensable, vehicle for exploring human concerns. This is not automatically to associate fictional literature with *truth*, for that, as we shall see, is deeply problematic and in some respects a distraction. But it involves showing that fiction need not be mere "play," can engage seriously with issues that matter in the real world, and, in stirring the imagination, can clarify thought and enliven perception.

For those who share this humanistic outlook, these points might seem obvious and barely in need of defense. But they have come under systematic attack by a whole generation of literary theorists, so much so that in some circles it is just taken for granted that the "old-fashioned" humanistic values of literature and art have been discredited finally and irrefutably. This antihumanist case cannot go by default. But this book is not an exercise in nostalgia; it does not scour the past for a golden age when great works of literature sat confidently on a pedestal and everyone knew what made them great. Nor is it a frontal attack on "literary theory" as such or even an attempt to offer a detailed characterization of a humanistic conception of literature.[1] For one thing it is written by a philosopher, not a literary critic (or literary theorist), and someone fully conscious, in that sense, of being an "outsider." It is not for me to try to reshape how teachers of literature either teach or conceive of their subject, and I have nothing at stake personally in how that turns out. Whether this makes the views expressed in the book any more objective or reasonable—or indeed of practical relevance in the debate—is for others to determine. I do think the points are important, however, and in a context wider than just that of pedagogy. What I hope to achieve, with regard to the defense of a New Humanism in the "humanities," is a careful examination of a cluster of terms sometimes thought to be fatally compromised by structuralist and poststructuralist theory, terms that form a core within the humanistic conception. These include fiction, fictional character, reality, author, work (as distinct from text), theme, emotion, knowledge, intention, truth, meaning, moral value, imagination, autonomy, aesthetic quality, and literary value. By applying analytical methods to an examination of these concepts, I hope to clarify presuppositions and commitments of their use; if the concepts are rejected, at the least one will know exactly what is being rejected along with them.

III

Let us look a little deeper at the sustained attack on what sometimes, disparagingly, is called the "liberal humanist" approach to literature. This attack has been a feature common to different and even incompatible schools of literary theory in the past twenty years or so. What is its basis? Certainly much has been politically or ideologically inspired, with the thought that humanism (particularly in literary studies) embodies and serves to entrench undesirable "repressive" social and political values, for

1. The humanistic view of literature has been defended in such more recent books as Stein Haugom Olsen, *The End of Literary Theory* (Cambridge, 1987); David Novitz, *Knowledge, Fiction, and Imagination* (Philadelphia, 1987); Colin Falck, *Myth, Truth, and Literature* (Cambridge, 1989); Martha Craven Nussbaum, *Love's Knowledge: Essays on Philosophy and Literature* (Oxford, 1990); Frank Palmer, *Literature and Moral Understanding* (Oxford, 1992); Richard Freadman and Seumas Millar, *Re-Thinking Theory: A Critique of Contemporary Literary Theory and an Alternative Account* (Cambridge, 1992); Peter Lamarque and Stein Haugom Olsen, *Truth, Fiction, and Literature: A Philosophical Perspective* (Oxford, 1994); and David Parker, *Ethics, Theory, and the Novel* (Cambridge, 1994).

example, an unquestioning attitude to authority, a perpetuation of complacent middle-class norms, a marginalizing of writing by minority groups, a tendency to aestheticize and thus ignore social problems, the promotion of exclusive "nationalistic" canons, and so forth. I will not take up the political challenge, for that would take me too far from my central concerns. I believe the political case against humanism is seriously misconceived, because the supposed commitments are simply not present. Although an obvious commitment to basic "humane" values is inseparable from the humanistic approach to literature, nothing *intrinsic* to that approach involves a determinate stance on any specific political issue of substance (excluding an adherence to broad procedural principles such as open debate, respect for reasoned argument, tolerance of opposing views, a presumption of the value of human life, and so forth). Indeed, it would seem strange to suppose there should be, given the almost limitless variety of moral and political attitudes that find expression in literary works themselves and the limited, subject-specific role of the literary critic acting qua critic, as conceived on the humanistic approach. In fact one might suppose the humanist critic, who takes literary works to engage with general moral and human concerns, to be potentially more receptive to dissident political attitudes than the poststructuralist critic, for example, who denies any clear distinction between fiction and fact and who sees the whole world of social reality as just a free-floating verbal construct.[2]

Of more interest to the philosopher (and literary critic) is the way that the antihumanist position characteristically focuses on a certain conception of human beings, often, wrongly, assumed to have originated in the Enlightenment. This is the conception, which the antihumanists reject in its entirety, of an autonomous, self-sufficient, rational "self," a center of consciousness and a source of meaning and value. In the literary context, this conception of a human being is associated with two views that supposedly prop up the humanistic conception of literature: first, literary works are the product of such autonomous selves, known as authors, who invest their works with meaning and value; and second, the subject matter of literary works is essentially the actions and motivations of such selves in fictional characterizations. Different schools of literary theory—from Althusserian Marxism to Lacanian psychoanalysis to deconstructionism to New Historicism—can broadly be mapped by the ways in which they attack this conception of human beings supposedly underly-

2. For a powerful critique of the moral and political commitments of postmodernist thought, see Christopher Norris, *Truth and the Ethics of Criticism* (Manchester, 1994).

ing humanistic criticism, substituting in its place their own alternative theories of authorship (or production) and their own alternative theories of narrative content.[3]

What my analyses of key concepts will show is the extent to which anti-humanist theory oversimplifies—and thus distorts—the presuppositions of humanistic criticism. Two instances of this oversimplication, relevant to the topics of the book, are the imputed claim that literary works are essentially and constitutively the products of inspired acts of the imagination (from an author, as individual "genius") and the imputed claim that fictional characters (at their best) are "fully rounded" and "living human beings." Neither claim, in an unqualified form, is integral to the position defended in the book. Indeed, it is a caricature of the humanist stance to ascribe to it an essential commitment to any particular metaphysical view of human beings or human nature.

Let us take the case of fictional characters first, as these will figure prominently in later chapters. One passage in Euripides' *Hecuba* is often extracted as a fine example of Greek ethical thought. It is a speech by Hecuba, formerly Queen of Troy but now a slave of the Greeks, her husband and sons killed and her youngest daughter, Polyxena, also a slave, snatched from her and offered as a human sacrifice by the Greeks to appease the ghost of Achilles. On hearing of the dignity and courage with which the young Polyxena met her death, Hecuba speaks of the incorruptibility of noble character:

> How strange, that bad soil, if the gods send rain and sun,
> Bears a rich crop, while good soil, starved of what it needs,
> Is barren; but *man's* nature is ingrained—the bad
> Is never anything but bad, and the good man
> Is good: misfortune cannot warp his character,
> His goodness will endure.
>   Where lies the difference?
> In heredity, or upbringing? Being nobly bred
> At least instructs a child in goodness; and this lesson,
> If well learnt, shows him by that measure, what evil is.[4]

---

3. Typical works that have articulated this attack are Catherine Belsey's *Critical Practice* (London, 1980); Terry Eagleton's *Literary Theory: An Introduction* (Oxford, 1983); and Alan Sinfield's *Faultlines: Cultural Materialism and the Politics of Dissident Reading* (Oxford, 1992).

4. Euripides, *Medea and Other Plays*, trans. Philip Vellacott (Harmondsworth, England, 1963), p. 80.

The sentiment is clear, almost Platonic, in its affirmation of the endurability of the good, the consistency of man's nature. But what is remarkable about the speech is the way it is completely undermined by subsequent actions in the play. The once noble character of Hecuba herself, whose own dignity in the face of adversity we have been led to admire, gradually disintegrates into a terrifying, savage vengefulness. On hearing of the treacherous murder of her youngest son, Polydorous, by the man to whom she had entrusted him, Polymestor, she begins to fall apart. By the end of the play, having blinded Polymestor and murdered his two children, she has literally ceased to be a human altogether; Polymestor's prophecy is fulfilled that she will end her life in the shape of a dog with fiery eyes.

Euripides' play shows the disintegration of personality under intolerable external pressure; what it does not show is a unified rational self making autonomous rational choices. Nor does it show a "rounded human being" so much as the dramatic representation of a fragment of a life being torn apart. Yet, undoubtedly, Hecuba and her tragic fate are the focus of interest in the play. We will see in the case of the Japanese Noh theater (Chapter 5) even more extreme cases where no attempt is made to depict fictional characters as autonomous selves. The theoretical point is simply this: the idea of character as applied to works of literature is far more complex than the antihumanist case implies and is not reducible to—and does not presuppose—some generalized notion of self or personal identity in the philosophy of mind. Only confusion results from thinking of fictional characters as just more "living human beings." Fictionality and the demands of fiction cannot be so easily brushed aside.

The peculiar ontological status of characters must be recognized and accommodated, that is, the groundedness of their nature and their qualities in the descriptive modes by which they are represented. Fictional characters are radically different ontologically and epistemologically from real people—their very being, their nature, and their qualities are dependent on their origins in linguistic acts conforming to artistic conventions. The ways that readers or audiences reflect on characters are tightly constrained by these modes of representation. No serious humanistic criticism can avoid this fact. Characters are constructs of a work and the appearance of being presented with a real human life—an appearance that varies enormously from one genre to another—is largely a product of an imaginative and intellectual engagement with the descriptive resources of the work. But then it is precisely in the context of such an engagement that one finds the need to speak of the events depicted *as if* they were occurring to a human being similar in certain respects to ourselves.

Fictional Points of View

I emphasize all this because so many literary theorists who strain to distance themselves from so-called "essentialist humanism" find themselves having to reinvent character to give substance to their own favored redescriptions of narrative events. One such is Alan Sinfield, in his book *Faultlines*. Consider this grandiose phrasemaking for reintroducing talk about character: "My contention is that some Shakespearean dramatis personae are written so as to suggest, not just an intermittent, gestural, and problematic subjectivity, but a continuous or developing interiority or consciousness."[5] He then goes on to talk about Olivia in *Twelfth Night* in the very terms that any humanist critic might use about the development of a character. The idea that narrative strategies, linguistic cues, allusion, cross-reference, and point of view conspire together to build illusionistically those patterns of "interiority," consciousness, motive, desire, ambition, and belief which we call "character," far from standing in opposition to humanist criticism, is in fact a necessary premise for it.

One reason for dwelling on the "humanness" of literary content (and character) is because one of the central case studies in the book, that of tragedy and appropriate responses to it, seems paradigmatically to require some reference to human values and human action. Yet the point must not be misconstrued. Certainly, to remove the idea of character altogether from a discussion of tragedy would be to remove the very element that justifies the title "tragedy," for a tragedy happens *to* someone. At the same time, we must not lose sight of the fact that characters depicted in tragic drama are also imaginative constructs fulfilling specific roles as artistic representations, the aims and achievements of which are prescribed by literary convention.

For a final word, at this stage, on fictional characters, it is worth noting a curious reversal in postmodernist thought whereby human beings and "selves" *in the real world* come to be conceived *as if they were fictional characters*. So we find the surprising view that while fictional characters should not be thought of as persons, persons should be thought of as fictions. One of the most deeply held doctrines of postmodernism is that selves are "constructs," usually of a linguistic, social, or ideological kind. There are, of course, different versions of constructivism. To the extent that it is taken (in a Humean mode) simply to be a consequence of the rejection of Cartesian mental substance, defensible versions no doubt exist. But postmodernist constructivism (often Marxist or psychoanalytic in origin) is associated with a far more radical rejection of "subjectivity" which not

5. Sinfield, *Faultlines*, p. 62.

only leaves personal identities as necessarily shifting and unstable but relativizes them, like the characters of fiction, to different modes of discourse. It is also related to a general tendency in postmodernist thought toward a constructivist (quasi-idealist or "textualist") view of the world itself. But whatever the merits (or otherwise) of such theories, they have only marginal relevance to this inquiry because, as should be emphasized, no particular *metaphysical* view of persons or the real world has any direct bearing on understanding literature or fictional characters, nor is any such view a hidden commitment in critical humanism.[6]

Similar remarks can be made about the role of authors. The charge against humanistic criticism is that it involves conceiving of literary works as springing from the inspired imaginings of an author (as individual "genius") who thereby invests the work with meaning and value. Antihumanist critics see the whole picture, particularly concerning meaning and value, as collapsing when the notion of "author" (as autonomous "self") is undermined. As we shall see in later chapters, however, not only is it absurdly simplistic to equate humanism with crude author-centered criticism but, more seriously, it is also just wrong to suppose that determinate or essentialist commitments to certain conceptions of the self are needed to sustain humanistic views about literary value and interpretation.

Although acts of creative imagination, however explained, might be necessary for making a work "literature," they are clearly not sufficient. Any adequate aesthetics of literature must acknowledge that literary works are not primarily *psychological* objects so much as *institutional* objects. Inspired imaginings on their own cannot make a text or stretch of discourse into a literary work. Without the existence of a complex social practice or institution in which texts fulfill determinate functions bound by convention, there could be no literary works. "Literature" is not a natural kind. Literary works are not part of the furniture of the world, chunks of inspired language which happen to possess independently identifiable "literary qualities"; they "emerge" from an author's inspiration only when conceived under the norms of a practice and tradition. Nor are there any linguistic properties—syntactic, semantic, or rhetorical—that are sufficient for determining literariness. It takes more than an isolated author writing inspired prose or verse to produce a work of literature. Because literature is an institutional concept, related notions such as literary interpretation and literary value are themselves explica-

---

6. For a detailed examination of constructivism with respect to fiction and literary theory, see Lamarque and Olsen, *Truth, Fiction, and Literature,* esp. pt. 2.

ble only within the conventions of the institution. All this is integral to an adequate defense of the humanistic conception, and antihumanist attacks that try to saddle this conception with naïvely psychologistic commitments are wide of the mark.

IV

In Chapter 4 a distinction is drawn between the interests of literary criticism and the interests of logic in reflecting on the nature of fictional objects. This brings us back to points of view. Does the point of view of the critic (including the philosopher interested in the aesthetics of fiction) overlap with the point of view of the formal logician? Within logic, fiction as conceived by the critic presents little more than problem cases that need to be explained; these are problems largely about reference and existence. The starting point is often the banal observation that sentences such as "Sherlock Holmes lived in Baker Street" seem to be true yet are about no existent object in the real world. Should a special realm of "fictional entities" be postulated to account for the apparent reference in these cases? For the critic and those interested in *literary* fiction, these questions are of no significance. What matters is not the ontological status of fictional entities but the ways they are represented and the insights, moral or otherwise, that their representation can afford. Do these inquiries have nothing in common?

It is worth looking a little more closely. The ontological debate about "fictional entities" traditionally divides between, as they might be called, "accommodationists" and "eliminativists," those who in different ways try to *accommodate* fictional entities—as, for example, "nonexistent objects," "possible objects," abstract entities, or kinds—and those who try, by means of various forms of paraphrase, to *eliminate* all apparent reference to "fictional entities." The issue has exercised philosophers for more than a century, indeed has been a focal point for different schools of analytic philosophy. Alexius Meinong, Terence Parsons, Nicholas Wolterstorff, Peter van Inwagen, and Charles Crittenden are a fair cross-section of the accommodationists,[7] and Bertrand Russell, W. V. O. Quine, Nelson

---

7. Alexius Meinong, "Theory of Objects," in *Realism and the Background of Phenomenology,* ed. R. M. Chisholm (Glencoe, Ill., 1960); Terence Parsons, *Nonexistent Objects* (New Haven, Conn., 1980); Nicholas Wolterstorff, *Works and Worlds of Art* (Oxford, 1980); Peter van Inwagen, "Creatures of Fiction," *American Philosophical Quarterly* 14 (1977): 299–308; Charles Crittenden, *Unreality: The Metaphysics of Fictional Objects* (Ithaca, N.Y., 1991).

Introduction

Goodman, and Kendall L. Walton, of the eliminativists.[8] But what is at stake here, and is the outcome of any relevance to literary critics?

The first thing to notice is that the ontological question arises only with respect to an "external" perspective on fictional characters, that is, a perspective from which it is asked what kind of being, if any, they possess in the real world. To the extent that critics (and "ordinary" readers) find the ontological problem remote, it is probably at least partly because an "internal" perspective, where characters are *imagined* to be actual persons in real predicaments, still predominates among readers. But, as will be emphasized in chapters to come, an awareness of the artifice involved in the presentation of characters (that is, when viewed "externally") is an essential part of an adequate humanistic criticism. Again, though, the question is not so much *what kind of entity* a character is as what aspects of its mode of representation should be recognized in reflecting on its role in a narrative. And that latter question—crucial to the literary critic—is neutral on the issue between the accommodationists and the eliminativists. Both ontological viewpoints can acknowledge the grounding of fictional characters in narrative sentences; Meinong, for example, the classic accommodationist, introduces his key idea of "objects," including "fictional objects," at least partly to explain the use of singular terms in subject position, and it is natural for eliminativists to assign the grounding narratives some role in their logical paraphrases.

There is nothing in critical discourse that imposes one kind or another of ontological commitment. Even when critics talk directly of characters—when they say, for example, "Trollope's characters are more realistic than Beckett's"—they need not be seen as incurring ontological commitments of an inflationary kind. Assuming a broadly Quinean view of ontological commitment, what commitments a critic does incur will rest not directly on what the critic says but on the ingenuity of the logician in finding a suitable (logically equivalent) paraphrase. In that sense critics themselves have nothing at stake in the ontological debate. Is ontology then completely irrelevant to literary criticism? No, because the explanations that logicians give of the nature of fictional characters can illuminate important aspects of critical practice (as shown in Chapters 2–4) such as the priority of sense over reference, human qualities over individual particulars, imagination over belief, which serve to remind

---

8. Bertrand Russell, "On Denoting" and "The Philosophy of Logical Atomism," in *Logic and Knowledge*, ed. R. C. Marsh (London, 1956); W. V. O. Quine, "On What There Is," in *From a Logical Point of View* (Cambridge, Mass., 1953); Nelson Goodman, *The Languages of Art* (New York, 1968); Kendall L. Walton, *Mimesis as Make-Believe* (Cambridge, Mass., 1990).

critics where the focus of their attention rightly lies (from the "external" perspective).

In developing their theories of fiction, logicians and aestheticians are concerned not only with ontology—that is, the nature of fictional "entities"—but also more generally with fictional representation. Wolterstorff has contrasted his own "action-theory" of representation (presented in *Works and Worlds of Art*) with Walton's "object-theory" (in *Mimesis as Make-Believe*) and has concluded: "Both Walton's theory and my theory are too constricted; we need something more general."[9] But we need not choose between fiction as act or fiction as object, for in an important sense fictions can be properly classified in terms of both acts and objects, where fictional acts are stories told, and fictional objects, the contents of those stories. The question might arise which has priority in order of explanation—it seems that Walton gives priority to objects (those having the "function" of serving as "props in games of make-believe"), whereas Wolterstorff gives priority to actions (the illocutionary action of adopting the "fictive stance" to states of affairs). But the relation between fictive acts and fictive objects seems closer than this; from a logical point of view there could be no fictive objects without fictive acts and no fictive acts without fictive objects. Why? Because the act of fictive storytelling serves to constitute and define fictional objects (that is, they are grounded in linguistic utterances), but there could be no fictional stories without a *content* that constitutes them as stories rather than statements of fact (in other words, fictional stories taken as a whole, in contrast to individual constituent sentences in works of fiction, must be about something that at some level is "made up").

V

An important distinction, which has already come up on several occasions and will play a central role in the characterization of fiction and later in the discussion of tragedy, is that between the "internal" and the "external" perspectives available in our reflections on fiction. Let me say a bit more at this preliminary stage about the motivation behind the distinction and how it relates to similar distinctions that appear in the literature. Many theorists of fiction have recognized the need for speaking in this context of what is "internal" and what is "external."

9. Nicholas Wolterstorff, "Two Approaches to Representation—and Then a Third," *Midwest Studies in Philosophy* 16 (1991): 179.

Sometimes, for example, the distinction is drawn in terms of "worlds," as does Walton: "We, as it were, see Tom Sawyer *both* from inside his world and from outside of it. And we do so simultaneously. . . . The dual standpoint which appreciators take is . . . one of the most fundamental and important features of the human institution of fiction."[10] Sometimes what looks like a related distinction is drawn between different kinds of properties that fictional characters can possess: their properties qua characters (being created by Dickens, first appearing on page twenty of such and such a novel, being abstract entities) and their properties when conceived as persons (being a detective, living in Baker Street, and so on). This distinction is integral to certain accommodationist accounts of fictional entities (for example, those of Parsons and van Inwagen). What it clearly shows is the "double aspect" nature of fictional characters: within their worlds they possess human qualities, but within the real world they have only such qualities as arise from their linguistic origins.

Another distinction, drawn by Palmer, is between two "conventions" in the way we speak about fictional characters: "According to one convention— . . . the internal convention—Hamlet not only exists, but has sword fights, falls in love, and feigns madness. According to the other convention— . . . the external convention—Hamlet neither exists nor performs deeds."[11] To the extent that talk of different "conventions" acknowledges different ways of speaking about characters—now as if they were real people ("Hamlet killed Polonius, deserted Ophelia, and said 'Alas, poor Yorick' "), now as fictions ("Hamlet never existed")—it must be right, and obviously so. But the interesting problems arise when trying to say exactly what the conventions are, particularly the "internal convention" that seems to take on ontological implications or to involve something other than literal truth.

There is yet another, fourth distinction from the context of visual art, drawn by Richard Wollheim, between an internal and external spectator:

> There is the *spectator of the picture*, and there is the *spectator in the picture*: the external spectator and the internal spectator. The two differ in where they stand and in what they see. The external spectator is located in the actual space that the painting itself occupies in the room or gallery where it hangs. . . . The internal spectator is located in the virtual space that the painting represents. . . . The external spectator can be, and normally is,

10. Kendall L. Walton, "How Remote Are Fictional Worlds from the Real World?" *Journal of Aesthetics and Art Criticism* 37 (1978/79): 21.

11. Palmer, *Literature and Moral Understanding*, p. 20.

aware of the marked surface: he will move within the actual space to ensure that this is so. For the internal spectator the marked surface does not exist: it is not visible from the virtual space.[12]

Clear analogies can be drawn with the case of a reader of narrative fiction, even though the "seeing" is here only metaphorical. To "view" the events in a fictional world as an "internal spectator" is to locate oneself, imaginatively, among the participants of the world (the clearest example of this, where the "seeing" is most nearly literal,[13] is in the cinema, where the camera offers the perspective of the internal spectator). In literary narratives the equivalent point of view of the "internal spectator" would include matters of attitude and value—for example, those projected by the implied author—as well as imagined matters of fact. To take the "external" view is to focus more on the linguistic aspects of the presentation, the literary devices, the *artifice* of the created world, and thus to "see" it *as fiction*. Because imagination is often thought to be a kind of seeing, it is not difficult to extend something like Wollheim's visual paradigm to works of literature.

All these distinctions, which are clearly not unrelated even if not identical, contribute to our understanding of fictionality. The emphasis in the book will be on the role of the imagination. The internal perspective on fiction is that of *imaginative involvement*; the external perspective, that of an *awareness of artifice*. They need not be incompatible, for there is no reason why they cannot be held simultaneously. What is of special interest, as we shall see, is the way that the external perspective can guide and constrain the internal perspective.

VI

Another topic that is treated in several of the chapters is that perennial challenge: the "cognitive value" of fiction. Following a venerable tradition, the novelist Iris Murdoch—in her novel *The Black Prince* and in her philosophical writings—argues for "truth" as the aim of art (and literature); and indeed, "truth" is the traditional focus for the discussion. But by using Iris Murdoch's influential view of "truth in art" as a case study, in Chapter 6, we find on closer inspection that the commitment to *truth* as such is not as strong as it would seem even in this paradigmatic concep-

---

12. Richard Wollheim, *Painting as an Art* (Princeton, N.J., 1987), p. 102.
13. It is questionable whether a viewer *literally* sees Citizen Kane or only Orson Welles in the role of Citizen Kane.

tion of "cognitive value." When Iris Murdoch elaborates her view, we find, over and over, that conceptions other than truth come to the fore: "Truth is not a simple or easy concept. Critical terminology imputes false-hood to an artist by using terms such as fantastic, sentimental, self-indul-gent, banal, grotesque, tendentious, unclarified, wilfully obscure and so on. The positive aspect of the avoidance of these faults is a kind of tran-scendence: the ability to see other non-self things clearly and to criticise and celebrate them freely and justly. This is a place for a definition of freedom, and for a distinction between trapped egoistic *fantasy*, and *imagination* as a faculty of transcendence."[14] This central distinction be-tween fantasy and imagination and the role of "seeing" and "vision" in art are discussed in Chapters 6, 8, and 9. One view that emerges is that a more satisfactory alternative to "truth" as an account of the cognitive value of fiction lies in the varied ways in which works of fiction can be a source of *learning* or coming to *see* things more clearly. Many of the pos-sibilities of "learning from fiction" rest on commonplace observations about the content of fiction; but what is interesting is the way that these possibilities connect with the very nature of fiction itself. Picking up in-cidental information about people, places, and things or practical skills might be a contingent by-product of reading certain kinds of fiction. But other ways of learning are more intimately connected with fiction per se.

Thus entertaining thoughts or coming to imagine states of affairs, both essential aspects of reading fiction, can obviously bring to mind things that might otherwise not have occurred to a reader through merely self-prompted imaginings. Yet it could still be asked how bringing fictive (or imaginary) states of affairs to mind could be a source of learn-ing about the real world. The first answer is simple and comes from Aris-totle, namely, that while history "describes the thing that has been," fiction describes "a kind of thing that might be." In this famous passage in the *Poetics*, he continues: "Hence poetry [that is, what is "made" or fic-tion] is something more philosophic and of graver import than history, since its statements are of the nature rather of universals, whereas those of history are singulars. By a universal statement I mean one as to what such or such a kind of man will probably or necessarily say or do."[15] In other words, fiction describes and invites readers to imagine possibili-ties—what might be the case, not just what is the case; how certain kinds of people, in certain kinds of situations, would most probably react; what

---

14. Iris Murdoch, *Metaphysics as a Guide to Morals* (Harmondsworth, 1993), p. 86.
15. Aristotle, *Poetics*, ed. Ingram Bywater (*On the Art of Poetry*) (Oxford, 1920), p. 84.

kinds of things they would say or think. Not all possibilities, of course, are of equal interest (for Aristotle, "a convincing impossibility is preferable to an unconvincing possibility"[16])—and it is rarely just a bare possibility that engages the imagination so much as the way possible states of affairs are represented, the connections proposed between them, the themes that they imply and sustain.

In Chapter 4 I argue that fictional "worlds" should not be thought of as complete, freestanding "possible worlds" but as incomplete, imaginative constructs constituted by the evaluative, perspectival aspects under which they are presented; these aspects are *linguistically determined*, grounded in fine-grained meanings. Thus another source of "learning from fiction" stems from reflection on the very meanings themselves, the propositional contents, which ultimately serve to constitute the worlds of fiction. Hilary Putnam's suggestion captures some of what is involved: "Consider the experience of reading a novel like *Don Quixote*. One thing that happens to us is that our conceptual and perceptual repertoire becomes enlarged. . . . This enlargement of our stock of predicates and of metaphors is *cognitive*; we now possess descriptive resources we did not have before."[17] But it is not just picking up a new vocabulary that gives value to fiction. It is rather the way a reader's imagination is guided by the descriptive (and structural) presentation of the fictive objects and states of affairs. Bernard Harrison, talking about what he calls "constitutive language," or the language of literary fiction, emphasizes the possibility of changes in perspective:

> The cognitive gains offered by constitutive language are of two kinds. On the first and simplest level they are gains in self-knowledge. As such they are of an essentially negative kind. They disturb the self in its natural but mistaken conviction that the terms in which it habitually construes the world are the only terms in which the world is capable of being construed, simply by displacing the language, the system of connections and differences between terms which articulates and constitutes that habitual way of looking at things. In the process of achieving this . . . shift of perspective, constitutive language necessarily . . . passes from reordering its own signs to reordering . . . our perception of the limits and scope of natural possibility.[18]

16. Ibid., p. 91.

17. Hilary Putnam, "Reflections on Goodman's *Ways of Worldmaking*," *Journal of Philosophy* 76 (1979): 614–615.

18. Bernard Harrison, *Inconvenient Fictions* (New Haven, Conn., 1991), p. 50.

Introduction

The discussion in Chapters 8 and 9 shows how such "shifts of perspective" are controlled by an author's use of language, that is, the "mode of presentation" of the fictional content.

New thoughts and ideas, new forms of expression, new applications and juxtapositions of concepts, and new perspectives on familiar themes can be brought to mind by reflecting on the propositional content of (parts of) a story. This internalization is likely to be of value not so much in the attention given to isolated propositions but in the accumulation of "thought clusters" across a whole narrative (a notion discussed in Chapter 7). Indeed, in some respects the structural organization of a narrative can, if only in limited stretches, bear an isomorphic relation to the structure of corresponding mental representations (an idea akin to that first suggested, with respect to poetry, by I. A. Richards in *Principles of Literary Criticism*).

Although readers can *learn about* a concept by entertaining propositions in which it occurs, this is more often the result of *thinking with* the concept than *thinking about* it. The learning involved in any further, active reflection on the propositional content—for example, through assessing its implications—belongs to the level of "supplementation." Before considering that level, I should note that even at the base level it is likely that emotions will be engaged, as well as intellect and imagination. A reader not only entertains propositions but also reacts to their content. Bringing to mind characters and their actions might elicit a range of responses normally accorded to real-life events: sympathy, pity, fear, dismay, outrage, envy, and so forth. One interesting feature of this relates to the idea of an "appropriate" response. The emotional response to a disturbing fictional representation, although strong and deeply felt, is likely to be more controlled than the response to any comparable event in the real world. B. J. Rosebury makes an important observation on this:

It is only when we are able to contemplate an object . . . in comparative calm—to have it as an idea rather than a raw stimulus—that we can be relied upon to respond "appropriately": perhaps because our notions of "appropriateness" in this kind of context are themselves arrived at through reflection upon ideas. In the heat of events, our petty concerns, the momentum of habit, our desires, and certain psychological safety devices against shock tend to conspire to prevent or adulterate appropriate response. . . . [T]he voluntary self-association with conceptions in the apprehension of fiction, permit, or presuppose, just the privileged calm and freedom from personal embroilment which is needed.[19]

The capacity of works of fiction to elicit and control emotional responses is undoubtedly a source of "learning from fiction" and again ties in with distinctive features of fiction itself.

One other such feature is that of the imaginative supplementation associated with reading fiction. Clearly a reader knows more about Iago, for example, than is explicitly contained in the descriptive content of Shakespeare's play. A reader will know, or at least be inclined to surmise, things like the following (taken from the introduction to the 1964 Arden edition of *Othello*): "He has a profound love of power. . . . He despises most of the rest of mankind; any man who does not keep his heart strictly attending on himself, who allows anything but reason and self-interest to guide his actions, is to Iago just a fool" (p. lxi). A reader arrives at these supplementary truths, or hypotheses, about Iago by a process of inference from what is explicit in the play. Of course, more than conceptual inference is involved. The supplementation takes place against an assumed background. The conclusion that Iago "has a profound love of power" is derivable from the play either because that predicate redescribes or epitomizes the properties attributed to Iago or because the predicate *would* be truly applicable to a person in the real world possessing just such a cluster of properties as characterize Iago. David Lewis is right that reasoning to what is true in fiction is at least sometimes like counterfactual reasoning. We ask, What other properties would a person be likely to possess who also possesses this character's properties (or a significant core of them)? But to answer that, a reader needs sufficient background knowledge about the world. We use what we know about other people to supplement what we know about characters. This process is one of active reconstruction. Its value resides in a complex imaginative operation. In reading fiction, a reader is required to summon and organize knowledge of people and the world; this will involve drawing comparisons, noting similarities and differences, reflecting on possible consequences of actions and predicaments, picturing states of affairs, imagining oneself or others acting as the characters do, and so on.

In general, at least two different kinds of judgments are involved in this reconstruction (see Chapters 4 and 6). First, a judgment is needed

---

19. B. J. Rosebury, "Fiction, Emotion, and 'Belief': A Reply to Eva Schaper," *British Journal of Aesthetics* 19 (1979): 129–130.

about the reliability of the information which is explicitly conveyed in the narrative content. Speakers, even a narrator, can be depicted as unreliable; clearly we should not accept all that Iago tells us about Othello. Second, we need to supplement the information that has been deemed reliable. Some of this will be of a quasi-factual nature—notably, to do with physical or circumstantial detail. Some will involve matters of a more theoretical or speculative kind, concerning, for example, psychological attitudes or motives. Sometimes readers are simply not provided with sufficient information to make sound judgments at this level. But sometimes (often) they are: Iago, it is clear, is not motivated by love or generosity, in spite of his protestations.

From the point of view of learning from fiction, what is most striking here is that readers will often be invited by works of fiction to make judgments of a factual, psychological, or even moral kind which in ordinary life would simply not arise for them. Readers might find themselves having to call on resources of imagination or *Verstehen*, or a sense of justice, sympathy, or impartiality concerning fictional events and characters, quite outside their normal experience. Of course, whether they rise to the test, whether what is learned in this new experience is subsequently of value, will again depend very much on the fiction and on the readers. What is clear is that reading fiction requires active involvement: readers "fill out" characters, draw implications, form hypotheses, and make judgments. Fiction can provide not only the occasion for this involvement but also a content and subject matter to which readers might otherwise have no access.

This account of "learning from fiction" is meant to focus on those features of fiction which are most distinctive. It applies to all (linguistic) fictions, ipso facto to literary fictions, yet it is not an exhaustive account of what makes works of *literature* valuable (qua literature). The cognitive value of literary works resides partly in the cognitive value arising from their fictive dimension but partly in something more, in virtue of which they are literature. This extra element draws on the thematic content of the works, the way they develop and sustain certain kinds of (more or less universal) themes. It would be misleading to regard the themes themselves as fictional, even though fiction is the vehicle through which they are expressed. Nor are themes necessarily assessable in terms of their "truth"— they are often not even propositional in form. Rather, what makes a theme important is its being embedded in a tradition (be it literary, philosophical, religious) which imputes value to it; what makes it interesting in a particular work of literature is the way it is developed and substantiated by that work. The great (canonical) works of literature are those that creatively and imaginatively explore the central themes of a culture.

VII

Earlier I suggested that three topics assume prominence in the fugue-like play of subjects running through the book: the different ways that fictional objects connect with the real world, the multiple values ascribed to fiction, and the "autonomy" attributed to literature. Let me close here by anticipating how these subjects emerge in chapters to come. First, several chapters pick up the issue of the "reality" possessed by fictional objects (characters, places, events). In Chapters 2 and 3, I lay out the basic theory of fictional objects, accounting for their ontological status and their grounding in linguistic narratives. In Chapter 3 different kinds of relations between fiction and the world are explored; verisimilitude, an inspirational source, and common properties might link fictions with real objects but should not be assimilated into the categories of "reference" or "truth." Different modes of "speaking about" fictional characters, some of which seem to acknowledge their "reality" overtly, are also examined. Chapter 5 puts the theory to work in a peculiar case study, that of fictional characters in Japanese Noh drama, showing both how these diverge from standard Western conceptions of character and how in spite of their apparent insubstantiality (the "dissolution of personality") they retain literary significance and human interest. I discuss the constraints on an audience's reconstruction of fictional worlds—what is taken to be true in those worlds—in Chapter 4, arguing that literary convention as well as background knowledge, meanings as well as facts in possible worlds, are required in the reconstruction process.

The values of fictional works and the kinds of response appropriate to them are addressed in a number of chapters: Chapter 6, on truth and art, which is an exploration of the theme of fictionality and truth in Iris Murdoch's novel *The Black Prince*; Chapter 7 on emotional response; and Chapters 8 and 9 on tragedy. The chapters on tragedy both examine the question of why the representation of human suffering and disaster should be thought to be one of the central themes of high art and the most likely to convey moral insight. An answer is developed in terms of the distinctive role of the imagination in engaging with artistic representations of tragic events. The kind of "seeing" or "vision" of which Iris Murdoch speaks is brought into the explanation, as is Stanley Cavell's not

Introduction

unrelated conception of "acknowledgment" (the latter being the topic of Chapter 9). There has been a long-standing debate in aesthetics about the very possibility of certain kinds of affective or emotional responses to works of fiction. Some philosophers, notably Kendall Walton, have argued that emotional responses such as fear and pity occur only within "games of make-believe" that audiences play with fiction and are not themselves real. This view is disputed in Chapter 7, where I propose an alternative account which accommodates the reality of such emotions and which rests on the overall theory of fiction in Chapters 2 and 3, helping vindicate Aristotle's thesis that fear and pity are fundamental responses to tragedy.

The question of the "autonomy" of works of literary fiction again concerns relations with the real world. The view I defend is that the autonomy of literature, such as it is, does not consist in literary works being "cut off" from the world (a notion that is virtually inconceivable) but in the distinctive practices that constrain the modes of reading, appreciation, and response appropriate to works of that kind. In defending autonomy, I target mainly *reductionist* views of literature, that is, views that seek to explain (in some cases eliminate) literariness and literary qualities through supposedly more fundamental (nonaesthetic, nonevaluative) concepts. One such concept is that of "text," linked with the idea of *écriture*; another is that of the work as a product of a psychological act, particularly as conceived within psychoanalysis. These two reductionist conceptions of literature are examined and criticized in Chapter 10, "The Death of the Author," Chapter 11, "Psychoanalysis and Criticism." In both I defend the idea of an autonomous practice of literary criticism and the notion that literary works are "institutional objects." I also take up the theme of fiction and reality: in the first of these chapters, I examine and reject the idea that authors must always be viewed as fictional constructs; in the second, I question the idea that literary works and their characters are suitable objects of psychoanalytic investigation.

The final chapter tackles autonomy head-on in asking what it might mean to adopt a "literary point of view" when reading or judging a work. A not untypical example of the problem is exhibited in some parenthetical remarks that John Ruskin makes, in a treatise on political economy, about Dickens's *Hard Times*: he praises Dickens for his political acumen but suggests that the literary vehicle nearly lets him down:

> Allowing for the manner of telling them, the things he tells us are always true. I wish he could think it right to limit his brilliant exaggeration to

works written only for public amusement; and when he takes up a subject of high national importance, such as that which he handled in *Hard Times*, that he would use severer and more accurate analysis. The usefulness of that work . . . is with many persons seriously diminished because Mr. Bounderby is a dramatic monster, instead of a characteristic example of a worldly master; and Stephen Blackpool a dramatic perfection, instead of a characteristic example of an honest workman. But let us not lose the use of Dickens's wit and insight, because he chooses to speak in a circle of stage fire. He is entirely right in his main drift and purpose in every book he has written.[20]

It might seem that Ruskin, in this passage, is adopting more a *political* than a *literary* point of view on Dickens's novel. After all he is critical of precisely those factors—"brilliant exaggeration," characterization—that are customarily associated with literary interests, and he praises qualities, such as "taking up a subject of high national importance," that are not obviously literary. But what makes the example interesting is that the novel, of course, has an *ethical and sociopolitical* theme even when viewed *as a work of literature*. Also, the idea of "truth" applied to literature, as here, can itself have a literary critical meaning as well as a more literal philosophical meaning. It is easy to be persuaded that boundaries between "ways of reading" become blurred in such cases (and perhaps always). Should we then abandon the very idea of adopting a distinctive "literary point of view"? I will argue not. What is important is to resist the temptation to retreat into a narrow formalism in identifying the literary domain, that is, supposing that the literary point of view rests only on matters of "coloring," stylistic features, narrative devices, rhetoric, fine writing, characterization. What needs careful examination is the idea of "literary qualities," broadening it to include matters of "content" as well as matters of "form." Fiction can be *about* matters of universal human interest without ceasing to be fiction. That was Aristotle's point, and it lies deep within what I have called the humanistic conception of literature. Just how this can be takes us to the investigation of fiction itself.

20. John Ruskin, "Unto This Last," in *The Works of John Ruskin*, vol. 17, ed. E. T. Cook and A. Wedderburn (London, 1905), p. 31. The "subject of high national importance" of which he speaks is Dickens's attack on "those who see figures and averages and nothing else—the representatives of the wickedest and most enormous vice of this time." *Hard Times* was published in 1854 and dedicated to Carlisle.

2

Fictional Characters

And as imagination bodies forth
The forms of things unknown, the poet's pen
Turns them to shapes, and gives to airy nothing
A local habitation and a name.
        —Shakespeare, *A Midsummer Night's Dream*

'Character' . . . is merely an abstraction from the total response in
the mind of the reader or spectator, brought into being by written or
spoken words.
        —L. C. Knights, "How Many Children Had Lady Macbeth?"

I

What exactly are fictional characters? We talk readily and authoritatively of Faustus and Fanny Price, Tom Sawyer and Uncle Toby, and often
delight in doing so. Furthermore, we acquire beliefs about them and
even argue about their true nature. Yet no such people exist, and we
know that perfectly well. Is all this talk, then, about *nothing at all*? What is
fictional, to be sure, cannot be *real*, but characters, it seems, cannot be
nothing. So what in the world are we talking about? That is the puzzle I
want to explore in this chapter.

The logical issue revolves round problems of reference and existence.
It is distinct from other issues that arise about the relations between fiction and reality, some of which will come up in later chapters. We often
ask what items or aspects of reality a fictional character is *based on*—what
if anything it *resembles* or is *true to* or what *gave rise* to it. But these questions about causal or accidental relations presuppose more fundamental
questions concerning what fictions are and what relations *can* obtain between them and the real world.

To say without qualification that fictional characters do not exist only
compounds the mystery of how it is we can acquire true or false beliefs
about them and how we can become so intimate with them. To say that

they "exist in fiction" is not to explain anything, for it is true only inasmuch as it repeats again that they are fictional. A more promising start is to notice, following Nelson Goodman, that while unicorns do not exist, unicorn pictures and unicorn descriptions do exist.[1] Similarly, though Faustus does not exist, Faustus characterizations certainly do; and we know where to find them. Our investigation of fictions and fictional creatures must begin with these descriptions and characterizations. The logical problems of fictional reference and existence have their origins in the peculiarities of fictional narratives and stories.

II

In virtue of what is a story or narrative *fictional* or a *work of fiction?* We will look in vain for formal or intrinsic properties of discourse which serve to identify a narrative conclusively as fictional. Two classes of such properties seem to be promising candidates: let us call them *surface* and *semantic* properties.

Surface properties would include, for example, syntactic and stylistic constructions. From a logical point of view, however, fictional discourse cannot be conclusively identified as distinct from historical or nonfictional discourse solely by reference to its surface features. This is not to deny, of course, that there are surface features characteristic of fiction; David Lodge, for example, has identified such features with some illuminating comparisons of fictional and journalistic descriptions of execution by hanging.[2] It is only to say that these characteristic features are not strictly necessary or sufficient for the writing to be fictional. After all, historical narrative can appear in many guises.

Semantic properties are those relating to reference and truth. Again, there are semantic features characteristic of fiction: the proper names typically have no denotation, and the descriptions are not true of anything in the real world. But again, perhaps surprisingly, these characteristic features in themselves seem to be neither necessary nor sufficient: not necessary, because it might just be that some of the names do denote and some of the descriptions do fit things in the world, and not sufficient because nonfictional historical discourse might just fail in its own references and descriptions.

1. Nelson Goodman, "On Likeness of Meaning," *Analysis* 10 (1949); "About," *Mind* 70 (1961); and *The Languages of Art.*
2. David Lodge, *The Modes of Modern Writing* (London, 1977).

What we must conclude is that the property "being a work of fiction" is not reducible to any set of surface or semantic properties of language but is at least partly, and essentially, to do with *intention* and *use*. Roughly speaking we can say this, contrasting fiction with history. A historical work (including biography or autobiography) is produced with the intention of describing, explaining, or reconstructing past and actual events. It is written for the most part in an assertoric mode and invites assessment by such criteria as accuracy, truth, and consistency with known fact. It is subject to verification and refutation. A fictional work, on the other hand, is produced with the intention of presenting and describing imaginary people and events. It is not written in an assertoric mode and does not invite assessment under the canons of assertion and factual truth. It is not subject to verification and refutation. The appropriate response is not belief but make-believe. Characterized in this way, the difference between the historical and fictional resides essentially in the different *purposes* for which each is produced and the different *commitments* that arise from these purposes. The conventions of storytelling release us from the commitment of truth telling and belief without incurring blame or censure. The lack of intended deceit distinguishes writing fiction from telling lies.

Let me forestall a possible confusion. I have been speaking of fiction per se, and although that includes all literary fiction, it is not so clear that it includes all literature. Not all fiction is literature, certainly, and perhaps not all literature is fiction. We sometimes apply the term *literature* to writing that was intended to take on the commitments of ordinary descriptive discourse: Gibbon's *Decline and Fall*, for example, or Boswell's *Life of Johnson*, maybe even the Bible. And some poetry, for example, Wordsworth's *Tintern Abbey*, while indisputably literature is not so obviously fiction. It has been suggested that to read discourse as literature is ipso facto to read it *as fiction*.[3] But even if this is right, it does not serve to identify literature with fiction. For the attitude that a reader takes to a work need not coincide with that of the writer, and it is the writer's intentions that determine fictionality. John Searle has suggested that "whether or not a work is literature is for the readers to decide, whether or not it is fictional is for the author to decide."[4] Although there is some truth in Searle's point, given that literature is an evaluative term, it is of more importance to note that a literary intention (that is, the intention that a work be treated as literature) is neither definitionally nor exten-

3. Cf. Jonathan Culler, *Structuralist Poetics* (London, 1975), p. 128.

4. John R. Searle, "The Logical Status of Fictional Discourse," *New Literary History* 6 (1975); reprinted in John R. Searle, *Expression and Meaning* (Cambridge, 1979), p. 59.

sionally equivalent to a fictive intention (that is, the intention that a work be treated as fiction).

Identifying fiction in terms of the intentions and purposes of a writer of fiction might not in itself take us very far toward explaining the logical connection between fiction and reality. But locating fiction within the framework of a theory of language use, rather than with reference to syntactic or semantic properties, has far-reaching consequences for most of the central problems surrounding the logic of fiction. For, most important, it provides an appropriate context for explaining the special referential function of names in fiction. And that in turn will yield explanations of what kinds of beings fictional characters are and how we can talk or hold beliefs about them.

III

Consider the following, not untypical, passage from Fielding's *Tom Jones*:

> It was now the middle of May, and the morning was remarkably serene, when Mr Allworthy walked forth on the terrace, where the dawn opened every minute that lovely prospect we have before described to his eye. And now, having sent forth streams of light, which ascended the blue firmament before him as harbingers preceding his pomp, in the full blaze of his majesty rose the sun; than which one object alone in this lower creation could be more glorious, and that Mr Allworthy himself presented: a human being replete with benevolence, meditating in what manner he might render himself most acceptable to his Creator by doing most good to his creatures.
>
> Reader, take care; I have unadvisedly led thee to the top of as high a hill as Mr Allworthy's, and how to get thee down without breaking my neck I do not well know. However, let us e'en venture to slide down together, for Miss Bridget rings her bell and Mr Allworthy is summoned to breakfast, where I must attend, and, if you please, should be glad of your company. (Bk. 1, chap. 4)

For all its ironic and metaphorical nature, nothing intrinsic to this passage determines it must be fictional. Indeed, the presence of the personal pronouns "I" and "thee" if anything increases the surface appearance of its not being fictional. But fictional it is; the sentences come from a novel, the characters are inventions of Fielding's.

Let us pursue the suggestion made earlier that the defining properties of fictional narrative are to be found in intention and use. It is helpful to distinguish the *propositional content* of a sentence from the *illocutionary intentions* or "force" with which it is presented. According to the use (or pragmatic) theory of fiction, what makes a sentence fictional is the "force" or intent behind its utterance, subject to the conventions governing utterances of that kind, not its propositional content or sense. In general an illocutionary intention is an intention to perform an "illocutionary act," for example, that of asserting, questioning, promising, or warning. The performance of illocutionary acts is governed by complex conventions that determine what is to count as an act of one kind (say, assertion) rather than of another (raising a question) and also what counts as performing it successfully. To assert is to take on a commitment to the truth of what is asserted, a sincere assertion requires the speaker's belief in what is asserted, and so on. In this sense illocutionary acts are rule-governed, which is just to say that they can be performed correctly or incorrectly, not that speakers learn them by explicit reference to the rules.

In fiction, the storyteller gives the appearance of performing nonfictional illocutionary acts (like asserting or reporting) but, because of the conventions of storytelling, in fact takes on none of the commitments associated with these illocutionary acts.[5] In the passage from *Tom Jones*, Fielding gives the appearance of performing illocutionary acts such as *stating* ("the morning was remarkably serene"), *warning* ("Reader, take care"), and *inviting* ("I . . . should be glad of your company"). But the corresponding commitments are lacking: in reality there is no such morning in the middle of May, the reader is in no danger, and there is no real breakfast that the reader could attend. Instead, the reader is invited to *imagine* these things, not take them as literal truths.

A familiar suggestion, elaborated by Searle and others, is that in fiction a writer *pretends* to perform illocutionary acts, though without intended deception.[6] That theory has been rightly criticized, however, not least for making fiction too "parasitic" on nonfiction and failing to capture its

5. R. M. Gale has described this as "illocutionary disengagement," in "The Fictive Use of Language," *Philosophy* 46 (1971): 336.
6. Searle, "Logical Status of Fictional Discourse." Related accounts in terms of speech acts can be found in Gale, "Fictive Use of Language"; Richard Ohmann, "Speech Acts and the Definition of Literature," *Philosophy and Rhetoric* 4 (1971); and Monroe Beardsley, "The Concept of Literature," in *Literary Theory and Structure*, ed. F. Brady, J. Palmer, and M. Price (New Haven, Conn., 1973).

more positive features.[7] Certainly the etymology of "fiction," from *fingere* (one of whose senses is to *feign*), suggests some connection with pretense, but it is more satisfactory to locate such pretense as is definitionally associated with fiction in the attitudes of readers rather than writers. It is readers who pretend or make believe or imagine that what they are reading is the real thing (that is, nonfictional illocutionary acts). Writers are complicit in this pretense, providing their readers with the materials for a controlled imaginative response.

An important point often overlooked in pretense theories is that not all illocutionary intentions in fiction are pretended. Take the warning in the passage quoted. The reader is apparently being warned against breaking his neck while descending a hill on Mr Allworthy's estate. Taken literally, no such warning could be heeded. But the author clearly indicates that the hill is to be taken metaphorically; the heights are of a prose style, not a landscape. We are being warned against taking too seriously the exaggerated description of Mr Allworthy in the preceding paragraph. Fielding even spells this out for us in his chapter heading: "The reader's neck brought into danger by a description." There is, then, a genuine warning here, and one that could and should be heeded. But recognition of the commitments underlying the genuine warning is triggered only by recognition that the commitments of the apparent illocutionary intentions have been suspended. Similar remarks could be made about the invitation. We cannot, indeed, join Mr Allworthy over breakfast. But, for all that, there is a genuine invitation here, namely, to get involved with the characters, to develop an intimacy with them, to think of them as our companions. Although illocutionary intentions are not always what they seem in fiction and the fictive mode invites its own response grounded in imagination, there are, nevertheless, genuine illocutionary intentions that we as readers must recognize.[8] Fielding, in this passage, is *parodying* a flowery prose style, *deflating* pompous sentiments, *warning* readers not to take everything they read too seriously, and *inviting* them to relax and feel comfortable with the characters.

---

7. Two notable critics are Kendall Walton in *Mimesis as Make-Believe* (Cambridge, Mass., 1990) and Gregory Currie in *The Nature of Fiction* (Cambridge, 1990).

8. A similar point is sometimes made as part of an argument supporting the relevance of authorial intention in literary criticism: see, for example, Quentin Skinner, "Motives, Intentions, and the Interpretations of Texts," *New Literary History* 3 (1972): 393–408; and A. J. Close, "*Don Quixote* and the 'Intentionalist Fallacy,' " *British Journal of Aesthetics* 12 (1972): 19–39.

Fictional Characters

The propositional content of a sentence is that part which stays constant through changes of illocutionary force in utterances of the sentence. We can state that the door is shut, ask whether it is shut, order that it be shut, and promise to shut it. We can think of all such contexts as possessing a common propositional content, *that the door is shut,* which could be made explicit by suitable paraphrase of the force-indicating verbs. Sentences in fictional stories also possess a propositional content that is just what it would be if the sentences appeared in other, nonfictional contexts. This is only to say that a basic semantic content of sentences is graspable independently of knowledge of truth-values or of fictional and nonfictional status. The point is of some consequence for the issue of the connection between fiction and reality. Before enlarging on this point and giving a closer characterization of propositional content, I fear it is necessary to take another detour and introduce another set of distinctions.

IV

Consider the sentence:

(1) Miss Bridget rings her bell and Mr Allworthy is summoned to breakfast.

There are at least three contexts in which this sentence might be used. The first is where it has indeed been used, namely, by Fielding in *Tom Jones.* Let us call this *the author's use.* Then there is the use by a person describing what occurs in the story, knowing that it is part of a story. Let us call this *an informed reader's use.* Finally, we can think of this sentence being used by someone who, on reading the story, believes that Miss Bridget and Mr Allworthy are real people and that these events have actually taken place. Let us call this *a misinformed reader's use.* Now these uses are distinct.

The author's use is not an assertion; it occurs within the activity of telling a story and as such the standard rules of assertion are suspended. It is an utterance conforming to the conventions of fiction, whose "point" is grasped only when it is registered as "made up," a piece of fictional storytelling. Here we can see the difference between history and fiction at its most stark. The historian makes assertions and thereby describes, truly or falsely, accurately or inaccurately, independently existing states of affairs. A writer of fiction, in an author's use of a sentence, makes no asser-

Fictional Points of View

tion and in using the sentence *stipulates* fictional states of affairs. There is no question of correspondence with the facts and thus no truth-value can be appropriately assigned to a sentence like (1) in an author's use.[9]

An informed reader's use is different from an author's use, even when the same sentence is involved. An informed reader, knowingly talking of a fiction, can use sentence (1) to make an assertion, assessable as true or false. Of course, a reader could be merely quoting or reading the sentence or using it to *retell* (part of) the story, in which case, as with an author's use, no assertion would be intended.[10] But where an assertion is intended, it is about the story. In such a use, (1) can be thought of as elliptical for some such sentence as "In Fielding's *Tom Jones*, Miss Bridget rings her bell." In this case the assertion would be true, and its truth derives directly from the author's use of (1). The references are not being made up but refer to actual components of the story, that is, to characters (what that means we will come to later). Here some similarities are evident between history and fiction. The reader of fiction, like the reader of history, acquires beliefs, true or false; the former acquires beliefs about *what occurs in the story*, whereas the latter acquires beliefs about *what occurs in the world*. These beliefs can be the basis for true or false assertions, be they about a story or about the world. Further, the acquisition of beliefs in both cases can call for investigation, the collection of evidence, and the assessment of data. In the case of fiction, readers are called on to *supplement* what appears explicitly in the sentences of the fiction, usually by reference to shared background knowledge, and even to *reject* or *modify* what appears explicitly. We will be pursuing this further in

9. Not all sentences in fiction are of the same kind as sentence (1), containing names of fictional characters and overtly describing (stipulating) fictional states of affairs. Some sentences seem more amenable to truth assessment even in an author's use. Two kinds of examples come to mind. First, there are sentences that coincidently might turn out to be true: "There was once an old lady who lived in a forest." Then there are those which express a general proposition, for example, "It is a truth universally acknowledged, that a single man in possession of a good fortune, must be in want of a wife," which again seem to admit of truth-valuation. The latter cases are discussed in Chapter 6. The former cases must still be judged to be fictive utterances (in an author's use) so any independent (coincidental) truth-value will not be relevant under an appropriate fictional construal. For a full discussion of these issues, see Peter Lamarque and Stein Haugom Olsen, *Truth, Fiction, and Literature: A Philosophical Perspective* (Oxford, 1994), chaps. 2–3.

10. Kendall Walton has suggested that in much of our ordinary discourse about fictional characters we are not making assertions but only *make-believedly* doing so, in effect continuing the make-believe of an author's use (e.g., Walton, "How Remote Are Fictional Worlds from the Real World?" *Journal of Aesthetics and Art Criticism* 37 [1978]: 20–21). My concern here is with those cases where a speaker offers the sentence *as a truth*.

Chapters 4 and 6. Is Mr Allworthy truly "a human being replete with benevolence"? From this passage alone it would be rash to draw such a conclusion; after all, the reader is warned to "take care." The "true" Mr Allworthy has to be constructed from all the information supplied, carefully filtered through the layers of irony, hyperbole, and fictional speaker's prejudice.

Finally, the misinformed reader's use is made under the mistaken belief that the proper names refer to real people. Here, unlike the informed reader's use, there is no implicit fictional operator. We can say that an *attempted* assertion is made, about actual events, but because of a radical failure of reference in this use of the proper names, the assertion is defective. Nothing true or false has been said about real people because no real people are denoted. Of our three uses, only the misinformed reader's use can be described as a reference failure.

V

We can now return to the question of the propositional content of sentences in and about fiction. It is instructive to recall certain suggestions made by Gottlob Frege. According to Frege, when we read fiction, or indeed poetry, our interest is concentrated on the *thoughts* or propositions expressed rather than on the *reference* or *truth-value* of what is expressed: "In hearing an epic poem, . . . apart from the euphony of the language we are interested only in the sense of the sentences and the images and feelings thereby aroused. The question of truth would cause us to abandon aesthetic delight for an attitude of scientific investigation."[11] This redirection of attention from reference to sense is one consequence of the fact that the sense of a sentence, in an author's use, is not asserted, and the apparent references are not intended to pick out anything in the actual world.

Those sentences in fiction that do not contain names of fictional characters, for example, sentences of the kind "The morning was remarkably serene," present no special problem when it comes to identifying propositional content. The content or sense of such sentences in either an author's or an informed reader's use is just what it would be in nonfictional contexts, as determined by conventional truth conditions. The sense is

---

11. Gottlob Frege, "On Sense and Reference," *Philosophical Writings of Gottlob Frege*, trans. and ed. P. Geach and M. Black, 2d ed. (Oxford, 1970), p. 63.

not affected by the fictional context. What happens in the author's use is that the fictional or storytelling context suspends the normal conditions governing an assertive force of the sentence. In an informed reader's use, the assertive force is again suspended from the sentence itself, though it reappears governing the wider, more explicit sentence with the prefix "In the novel." This wider sentence, as we have seen, can be used to make an assertion about the novel. In effect it says that the novel expresses (or implies) the sense of the component sentence.

Identifying the propositional content of sentences in fiction which contain the names of fictional characters is a little more complex. But the principles are the same. Again the distinction is needed between the sense of the sentences and the standard illocutionary force or intentions with which they are used. How do these proper names operate in sentences in fiction? Although, in sentences like (1), they have the appearance of being ordinary names of people and as such might take in the misinformed reader, this is, of course, not the referential function they have in either the author's use or an informed reader's use. The standard referential intentions associated with names of that kind are suspended. For in these uses the names denote not people but fictional characters. But what does that mean? Here we must tread carefully.

The danger in talk about fictional characters is to confuse what I have called an *internal perspective*, that from within stories, with an *external perspective*, that from the real world. Within stories, fictional characters are indeed ordinary people, at least those of the Miss Bridget and Mr Allworthy kind. Furthermore, within the story of *Tom Jones*, Mr Allworthy can refer to Miss Bridget and say true or false things about her, just as he can have breakfast with her. Within the story, that is, from an internal perspective, the names "Miss Bridget" and "Mr Allworthy" function as ordinary proper names denoting ordinary people. Let us call this *internal* reference. Now, internal reference is possible, strictly speaking, only for a speaker within a story. Those of us not in the fictional world can merely *imagine* referring to Mr Allworthy *as an actual person*. To the extent that we can adopt the same internal perspective as those within the fiction, we do so by *imaginative involvement*. In contrast, the appearance of these same names in an author's or informed reader's use, say, of sentence (1), must fall under the external perspective. This will be *external* reference. To understand what it means to *refer to a fictional character*, we must explore the logic of such external reference.

It is again to Frege that we owe the insight that in certain contexts names lose what he called their "customary reference" and take on an "indirect reference," which he identified as their "customary sense." These contexts, according to Frege, including, for example, reports of people's beliefs, bring about a shift from reference to sense. A name appearing in such a context comes to refer only to its sense rather than to the object of its customary reference. Both an author's use and an informed reader's use of sentences containing names of fictional characters can be thought of as just such contexts. The clue here is to observe certain similarities between sentences under the scope of prefixes like "A believes that" and sentences following the prefix "In such and such a novel." Both contexts, for example, block existential generalization. From "John believes that he saw the Loch Ness monster" we cannot infer that the Loch Ness monster exists, just as we cannot infer that Mr Allworthy exists from the true claim that "In the novel, Mr Allworthy is summoned to breakfast." Pursuing the parallel with names in belief contexts, we can think of the internal reference of names of fictional characters as something like their customary reference, and the external reference of such names, like indirect reference.

My suggestion, then, is this: when names of fictional characters appear in the context of either an author's use or an informed reader's use, that is, when they are used from an external perspective, *the internal references of the names (to the ordinary people in the world of the fiction) get transformed into indirect references (to the senses of the names themselves)*. In short, proper names of fictional characters, as used by an author or an informed reader, refer only to senses, not to persons or particulars of any kind. The names lose the internal references they have when used by other fictional characters. What that means is that we, as readers, cannot refer to fictional characters in the way that other characters can, even though we can imagine or pretend that we are doing so. From our perspective, *we* can refer only to the *senses* of the names *they* use to refer to *persons*.

What is the sense of a proper name? Since John Stuart Mill pronounced that proper names have denotation but no connotation, the question of whether proper names can be said to possess a sense as well as a denotation has been a matter of perennial philosophical controversy. Rather than debate that issue here I will simply propose that names at least of fictional characters should be thought of as having a sense. This does not commit me to the view that all names have senses. I take the sense of a name, where there is one, to be, roughly, what Frege called the "mode of presentation" of the reference of the name or, as characterized by Michael Dummett (in *Frege: Philosophy of Language*), *the means by which a name identifies its reference*. In connection with the names of fictional characters, the reference here will, of course, be internal reference, that is, the reference to persons within stories. The sense of a fictional name is the means by which a person in a fictional world is presented and identified in a story. It can be specified by descriptions and predicates that serve to identify the internal reference. So, for example, the sense of the name "Mr Allworthy" will be given by those descriptions in, or derivable from, the novel *Tom Jones* which identify the fictional Mr Allworthy: the person called "Mr Allworthy," who found the infant Tom Jones lying in his bed, who banished him from his home after being deceived by Master Blifil, who in the end reached a warm-hearted reconciliation with Tom Jones, and so on. These descriptions can be said both to *identify the person* Mr Allworthy, from the internal perspective, and to *define the character* Mr Allworthy, from the external perspective. They give the sense of the name which becomes the object of reference in an external use. This sense identifies for us a set of properties which constitutes a fictional character. And, finally, it is this sense that becomes a constituent of the propositional content of sentences in which the name appears in either an author's or an informed reader's use.

VI

For all the apparently convoluted detail concerning different ways of talking about fictional characters, the basic proposals here for understanding what characters are and what access we have to them are fairly simple. We need to capture the intuition that in some respects fictional characters (of the Mr Allworthy/Tom Jones variety) are just like you and me—they are *persons*—while in other respects they are radically unlike you and me—they are mere *fictions*. What the theory emphasizes is the groundedness of fictional characters in the descriptions that characterize them in the first place. It is these descriptions, not the proper names, that give the clue to their nature. It is the descriptions, in and implied by a fictional narrative, that yield such knowledge as we have of the characters. We use the descriptions to imagine people of a certain kind. Characters are made up of intricate webs of properties and relations, and readers come to imagine that these are instantiated in particular individuals. To say that characters are (merely) sets of properties is not to diminish them or reduce them to mere formulas, for the properties involved, as we know from reading complex novels, are enormously varied: they include a vast array of human qualities, attitudes, values, actions, and relations, indeed everything that descriptive predicates can represent.

Although this theoretical framework needs to be supplemented and refined, as will be done in the following chapters, it offers some immediate benefits toward explaining many remaining puzzles concerning relations between fiction and reality. To begin with, we can now explain our initial intuition about fictional characters that as fictions they cannot be real but as characters they cannot be nothing. Fictional characters, like Mr Allworthy or Miss Bridget, do not exist in the real world *as persons*. They are fictional persons or persons-in-a-story, to be contrasted perhaps with fictional robots or fictional elephants, but that, of course, does not entail that they are, in fact, persons. As characters, though, they can be said to exist, but only as *abstract* entities, as conceptions, kinds, or sets of properties.[12] What in a fictional world are persons are merely characters or abstract entities in the real world. The Fregean shift from internal to external reference is precisely the shift from internal reference to persons to external reference to characters. The persons do not exist, but the characters do.[13]

Identifying characters as abstract entities from the external perspective accords with the etymology of the word *character*. The word belongs with other abstract nouns such as *characterization* or *personality*. There is even a conventional device in English for referring to the *character* of an actual person without referring to the *person* as an individual: we speak of so-and-so being a Napoleon or an Einstein or of someone's being the Genghis Khan of the philosophy department or the Bill Clinton of British politics. This is a rhetorically powerful way of identifying and ascribing properties, namely, those commonly attributed to the person whose name is used. Furthermore, it is easy enough, storytelling apart, to describe a character not exemplified by, or drawn from, any (one) actual person; a criminologist or psychologist, for example, might do so in constructing a "profile" or "type." In describing a character, a novelist does much the same, though probably in more detail and no doubt for different ends. The labeling of a fictional personality or character with a proper name is of no logical significance and does not affect its abstract nature. It simply aids the effectiveness of the storyteller's pretense.

---

12. For an argument that fictional names are *concept* words, see R. Martin and P. Schotch, "The Meaning of Fictional Names," *Philosophical Studies* 26 (1974): 377–388; for an argument that characters are *kinds*, see Nicholas Wolterstorff, *Works and Worlds of Art* (Oxford, 1980), pt. 3, § vi.

13. See Peter van Inwagen, "Creatures of Fiction," *American Philosophical Quarterly* 14 (1977): 302, for further reasons for the conclusion that characters exist.

It might be objected that a novelist, in presenting a "rounded" character, is not presenting a *type*, as a psychologist or criminologist might be, but rather something unique and individual. But the claim that fictional characters are individuals, at least from the external perspective, is simply false; it involves a category mistake. What we correctly call the uniqueness, even individuality, of some fictional characters is rather a feature of the combination and perhaps complexity of the properties that constitute them (one such property is likely to be "being a unique individual"). Even if, by coincidence, all the properties making up a fictional character were found to be instantiated in one individual in the real world, it would still be wrong to identify that individual with that character. No individual can be a character, again precisely because a character belongs essentially in the category of abstract entities.[14] Of course, when readers imagine or bring to mind a fictional character they imagine something individual.

Another advantage of the theory is that it explains how it is that readers have no difficulty understanding fictional stories, at least with respect to their being fictional. Once the conventional practice of storytelling has been grasped, allowing for the suspension of normal illocutionary (and referential) intentions, and the focus of interest turns to the senses or propositional contents of the story's sentences, there is no further barrier to understanding. Grasping the senses of sentences in fiction is no different from grasping the senses of nonfictional sentences. Readers of fiction use the propositional content as the basis for imagining fictional states of affairs. When they reflect on this content, including the descriptive senses of the fictional proper names, they are bringing to mind kinds and qualities that are likely to be familiar through exemplification in the real world.

Although we would not expect to find in the world exactly the combination of properties that constitute the character of Mr Allworthy, we

---

14. Jeanette Emt, in a perceptive discussion, has argued that fictional characters cannot literally be thought of as *characters* in the sense in which we speak of a person's character because fictional characters themselves can be said to have characters in that sense (and even characters that change in the course of a story). The character of a fictional character would then be a further abstraction in the defining set of properties. Also, more and different kinds of properties constitute fictional characters than would normally be thought of as character properties. This seems right, but the point of introducing the broader conception of character is simply to exemplify the ontological category into which fictional characters fall: they are abstract entities in much the way that a real person's character is an abstraction. Emt herself endorses the view that fictional characters are abstract entities. See Jeanette Emt, "On the Nature of Fictional Entities," in *Understanding the Arts: Contemporary Scandinavian Aesthetics*, ed. Jeanette Emt and Göran Hermerén (Lund, 1992).

nevertheless will recognize in people of our acquaintance many of these properties or significant combinations of them. We can take up Fielding's invitation to *get to know* the characters better by using our imagination to call to mind their constitutive properties as we entertain and reflect on the descriptive content presented by the author. As we have seen, we also need to supplement the author's descriptions by pursuing imaginatively certain of their implications against an assumed background. We draw on what we know about actual people—those, for example, similar in significant respects—to "round out" the characters with supplementary properties. Here, disputes between readers are likely to be at their most acute. All in all, this imaginative exercise goes a long way, I think, toward explaining the pleasure or even instruction associated with fictional works of literature.

Corresponding to the imaginative exercise of readers in understanding fiction is the imaginative effort of writers in creating fiction. The theory accords well with the practice of writing fiction in stressing the idea of the construction of characters, through language, by formulating descriptions that pick out defining clusters of characteristics. From a logical point of view, a writer is able to draw on any properties at will in constructing a character, although in practice there will be constraints of plausibility, verisimilitude, and aesthetic coherence.

The theory has the further benefit of providing a straightforward explanation for the notorious problem of the "incompleteness" of fictional characters. Characters are radically unlike actual individuals in that for a great number of properties it seems to be neither true that they have that property nor true that they do not have that property: hence the much discussed case of the mole on Sherlock Holmes's back.[15] Nothing in the Holmes canon indicates whether Holmes does or does not have a mole on his back, and no form of inference will allow us to determine the matter one way or the other. Accounts of fictional characters as possible individuals (or individuals in possible worlds) will have difficulty accommodating facts such as this. For every property, it seems that individuals must either possess or lack that property. But if characters are no more than sets of properties, then there is no requirement that every property or its negation be a member of the set. The set, after all, is made up of just those properties designated or implied by the author. However, even though the constitutive set does not contain property P or property not-

15. The example is discussed in Wolterstorff, *Works and Worlds of Art*, and Terence Parsons, *Nonexistent Objects* (New Haven, Conn., 1980).

P, that is not to say that it might not contain the disjunctive property *either P or not-P*. Sherlock Holmes, being a fictional person and not a logical freak, no doubt possesses the disjunctive property of either having a mole on his back or not;[16] but it does not follow that the property of having a mole is in the Holmes constitutive set or the property of not having a mole is in the set.[17]

Another advantage of the theory is that it accounts for how fiction can be realistic. A fiction is realistic if it describes characters with combinations of properties that would not be strange or out of place if exemplified in individuals in the real world. More interesting, it affords an explanation of our response to certain forms of allegorical, fantasy, or science fiction writing. How is it, for example, that a novel such as George Orwell's *Animal Farm* can strike us as "realistic" or "true to life," when ostensibly it describes a world radically different from our own, one in which farmyard animals speak, think, and reason exactly like human beings? Many children's stories present the same problem. An account of fiction in terms of possible worlds would require us to conceive the world of *Animal Farm* as radically different from our own world. Yet this runs counter to our intuition that the power of the novel resides precisely in its striking similarity to the real world. What is needed here is an appeal to levels of interpretation or understanding. On one level, we say, the story is about farmyard animals; on another, easily recognizable level, it is about people and political ideologies. Our theory of fictional characters can help to explicate the metaphor of "levels," for we can think of these as different stages in the abstraction of properties. On the literal and surface level, the characters are identified with all the properties attributed directly, or implicitly, to them in the novel. At another level, we can abstract and then set aside those properties that belong specifically to farmyard animals, being left as a result with only those properties attributable to familiar humans, notably (though not exclusively) psychological properties. It is these, forming a major component of the characters, that come to the fore when we react to the book as being

16. If this were not the case, Holmes would be an example of what Howell has called a "radically incomplete object." This notion is in contrast to that of a "nonradically incomplete object" where the matter is simply indeterminate: see Robert Howell, "Fictional Objects: How They Are and How They Aren't," *Poetics* 8 (1979): 134. See also Parsons, *Nonexistent Objects*, pp. 183–184.

17. Although I follow the general line of argument here from Parsons, *Nonexistent Objects*, pp. 56 and 183–184, and Wolterstorff, *Works and Worlds of Art*, p. 147, the present theory does not imply that characters are either "incomplete" (Parsons) or "nondeterminate" (Wolterstorff).

"true to life." The ease with which we can move between these different levels is straightforwardly explicable on the view that fictional characters are sets of properties. For what is happening is that we direct our attention to particular elements within the total set of constituent properties; and that presents no special imaginative or intellectual difficulty. It is just this possibility of selective attention that explains how we can recognize ordinary human qualities in the most bizarre or outrageous fictional creations.

Finally, the theory can be used to explain the possibility of emotional response to fictional characters. The emotions can be seen as directed to mental representations characterized by just those descriptions that identify the characters and fictional events. We will explore this in detail in Chapter 7.

3

Fiction and Reality

"You know very well you're not real." [said Tweedledum.]

"I *am* real!" said Alice, and began to cry.

"You won't make yourself a bit realer by crying," Tweedledee remarked: "there's nothing to cry about."

"If I wasn't real," Alice said—half laughing through her tears, it all seemed so ridiculous—"I shouldn't be able to cry."

"I hope you don't suppose those are *real* tears?" Tweedledum interrupted in a tone of great contempt.

"I know they're talking nonsense," Alice thought to herself.

—Lewis Carroll, *Through the Looking Glass*

. . . there had been a brief exchange of letters inquiring whether the character of Anstey, the librarian [in Philip Larkin's novel *A Girl in Winter*], was based on any real person and therefore libellous. "The answer to your question," Larkin had said, "is as usual, yes and no. Anstey was based as far as personal manner goes on a real person. . . . The circumstances I placed him in were imaginary and invented to fit the book itself."

—Andrew Motion, *Philip Larkin: A Writer's Life*

I

The componental nature of fictional characters, as outlined in the previous chapter, suggests different ways in which characters might relate to people and facts in the real world. Consider this not untypical disclaimer at the beginning of Saul Bellow's novel *The Dean's December*: "Although portions of this novel are derived from real events, each character in it is fictional, a composite drawn from several individuals and from imagination." In just such a way are most fictional characters created. Many of the properties of which they are constituted are shared, of course, by real people. Bellow continues, though, using a phrase all too familiar in such disclaimers: "No reference to any living person is intended or should be inferred." Being acknowledged are different connections between the novel and reality, in this case what it *derives from* and what it *refers to*. It would be wrong to think that works of fiction denote or make reference to or are about whatever it is they derive from. Reference—and by implication truth—is sometimes thought to be the key relation that anchors fiction to reality, but on closer inspection it turns out to be just one of several such relations and not necessarily of central importance.[1]

In general it is helpful to keep apart different questions about the relation of fictions to the world; for example: (1) Where did the idea for such and such a fiction *come from?* (2) What people or things in the real world are the fictional characters *similar to?* (3) What properties are *attributed to* the characters in the fiction? (4) Who or what specifically does the author intend to *refer to?* These questions are significantly different; the method of investigation in each case is different, and each has a different bearing on the relation of fiction and reality.

Question 1 is about the genesis of a fictional creation. In the case of ordinary characters in novels, the question is biographical. We need to know something about Bellow to know which of his acquaintances gave rise to the Dean. But those we find are not, Bellow assures us, intended as objects of reference, and the properties of the fictional Dean might be quite unlike the properties of any one of the people who gave rise to the original inspiration. As a piece of a priori psychology, reminiscent of Hume, it is no doubt right that in creating fictions, writers draw on reality. But what they draw on in this way they do not necessarily write about. The genetic ancestry of a fiction stands to referential relations, such as denotation, extension, or author's reference, rather as the etymology of a word stands to its present meaning. When I say I will meet you on Monday, I have not, of course, referred to the moon.

Question 2, about similarities between fictions and actual things, likewise has little to do with reference. The trouble with similarities is that they can be found anywhere. Mr Allworthy, no doubt, is a bit like the chairman of the school board and similar in some respects to the ticket collector at the local station. But Fielding, *Tom Jones*, and the name "Mr Allworthy" cannot be said to refer to these people, nor are these people, or others like them, in any sense *components* of the character Mr Allworthy. Similarity does not imply denotation or reference. To establish a similarity we need only to find covering predicates or class terms, applicable

---

1. Graham Dunstan Martin, in "A New Look at Fictional Reference," *Philosophy* 57 (1982), is one who argues for the special prominence of reference.

to fictional and nonfictional entities. That is easy enough: Lear is an old man, a king, an infatuated father, and much else besides. But it would be absurd to suppose that the name "Lear" as used by Shakespeare refers to or identifies—or even has as its extension—members of all these classes.

Question 3 concerns the properties attributed to a character, as determined by the descriptions that appear in the relevant work of fiction. These properties, as we have seen, constitute the character. Bellow's Corde is a college dean, married to an astronomer, trying to bring to justice the murderer of one of his students, and so on. Many of the properties will also be possessed by real people. But although these real people might figure in an answer to question 1, they bear only indirectly on question 3. The hoary example of unicorns nicely illustrates the difference between questions 1, 2, and 3. Perhaps the imagined combination of horses and horns gave rise to the concept of a unicorn (question 1). But *being a horse* is not a property of unicorns or part of that concept (question 3), even though *being horselike* is (question 2).

Question 4 is the only question that directly involves reference per se, in this case an author's intended reference, but it does not rely on the componential analysis. Bellow denies any intended references in his novel, but other writers, especially satirists, do aim their descriptions at particular people. But this referential connection, though it might be facilitated by drawing on shared properties, is not defined by that. In other words, a writer who wants to make a specific reference is likely to draw a character with the appropriate corresponding properties, but doing so is neither necessary nor sufficient for the reference to occur. It is not necessary because the writer might disguise the reference completely, perhaps through allusion or analogy, and not sufficient because the similarities might be coincidental or fortuitous. The investigation here is again a matter of biography; we need to know about the context of the writing and the author's intentions. This type of reference is a rather special case in fiction.

The term fictional reference is itself multiply ambiguous, covering at least the following:

Case A: One character referring to another, as when Lear say, "We two alone will sing like birds," referring to himself and Cordelia, an example of what we have called "internal reference"

Case B: A critic or reader referring to a character, as when Johnson says "Cassio is . . . ruined only by his want of stubbornness to resist an insidious invitation," referring, from the external perspective, to one of the characters in *Othello*

Fiction and Reality

Case C: A writer of fiction referring to particular places and events

Case D: A writer of fiction referring to general characteristics or universals

What becomes of the links between fictional characters and real-world counterparts under these different aspects of fictional reference? With case A it is clear that whatever correlates (that is, actual exemplifications) the character Cordelia has in the real world, it is not to them that Lear is referring. For one thing he is referring to a person, not an abstracted set of properties, and he has no contact with those people in the world who might share Cordelia's properties. Case B seems surprisingly similar to A. Literary critics, at least when describing what goes on in a work of fiction, are not referring to corresponding items in the real world (except perhaps to words and descriptions). The truth conditions of their propositions, such as Dr. Johnson's in B, rest not on how things are *in the world* but on how things are portrayed *in the fiction*.

We have already looked at the special case of C where a writer intentionally refers to particular things. It is only in that case that the links with real things become denotative. It remains to consider case D, in which a writer might be said to refer to general characteristics. This notion is important, for it raises interesting questions concerning what fictions are "about" and ultimately how they might be bearers of "truth." It would be absurd to deny that fictions can be about anything just because they are fictions.

If we want to identify what a fiction is about with respect to general characteristics—a type of person, a type of love, the workings of bureaucracy, and so forth—we must look to the descriptive predicates in the fiction, not to its proper names. It is for this reason that "reference" is somewhat misleading here, given its association with singular rather than general terms. There will be a connection between the real world and the general predicates in a novel (including the *fictional* proper names), but this, we have seen, is more a connection of sense than of reference. Readers can reflect on propositional content without being concerned whether it represents ("corresponds" to) actual states of affairs in the world. Attention is directed to *universals*, not to individuals that instantiate them, which ultimately becomes a defining feature of fiction and a source of its most enduring values. Of course, readers can note parallels and similarities between the content of fictional propositions and events that are actual and known to them just as in attending to universals they can bring to mind instances in reality. But it would be wrong to say that these actual events or instances are the *referents* of the propositions in the fiction. The connection is rather that the very same predicates that feature in fictional descriptions could be applied to real-world events and probably are, in fact, true of many such events. Works of fiction depict universals: that is what they are "about." This notion of "aboutness" will come up again in Chapters 4 and 6.

II

In the meantime, still further difficulties confront the theory of fiction sketched in Chapter 2, calling for further refinements. A logical account of the relation of fiction to reality must explain how we can say true or false things about the contents of fictional works. The complication is that we can say, truly or falsely, different kinds of things about them; there are different kinds of predication.[2] Concentrating again on fictional characters, let us consider, for example, the following:

(A1) Fielding created Mr Allworthy.
(A2) Mr Allworthy is a fictional character.
(B3) Mr Allworthy grew fond of Tom Jones.
(B4) Mr Allworthy is an honest and forgiving man.
(C5) Tom Jones would have been a hippy in the 1960s.
(C6) Tom Jones would never have married Fanny Price.

The sentences (A1) and (A2) contain the fictional name "Mr Allworthy" but do not seem to be amenable to analysis in terms of either an author's use or an informed reader's use. That is, the sentences are not presented as part of a story under the conventions of fictive utterance, nor do they seem to be paraphrasable into sentences containing the intensional operator, "In the fiction (novel)." Both, however, seem to be true and able to be asserted. I suggest that the best way to understand the use of the name "Mr Allworthy" in such sentences is as a truncated form of the description "the Mr Allworthy character." This usage is made possible by prior occurrences of the name in an author's use. Here the reference to the character is direct and explicit. The original Fregean analysis, however, can still be applied. For we can think of the context "the ____ char-

2. R. Howell, "Fictional Objects: How They Are and How They Aren't," *Poetics* 8 (1979), uses as a test for the adequacy of a theory of fiction how it deals with such different predications.

acter," filling the space with a proper name, as an intensional context in which the name has only its indirect reference. In definite descriptions of the kind "the X character," the character is identified through the sense of the name.

To say that the Mr Allworthy character is fictional, as in (A2), is to say that the name and constituent properties are introduced in a fiction under the conventions of storytelling. It is not to say that no individual in the world possesses the properties, even though that is probably the case. To say that Mr Allworthy *does not exist* is ambiguous between saying that the character is fictional, a claim about its presentation, and saying that no individual realizes the constituent properties, a claim about its instantiation. The truth conditions under these two readings are different.

There is a further problem about sentence (A1). Strictly speaking, if a character is a set of properties, a writer cannot truly be said to *create* a character. Fielding did not create the properties constituent of Mr Allworthy, so correspondingly he did not create the set of those properties. It might be thought a weakness of the theory that it should have such a seemingly paradoxical consequence. I think, however, that everything we want from sentence (A1), insofar as it expresses a truth, can be captured in some, albeit prosaic, paraphrase of the form "In the novel *Tom Jones*, Fielding presented for our imaginative attention, through his creative choice of descriptions, the Mr Allworthy character." Fielding's, and any author's, creativity and imaginative skill reside in the careful use of descriptive language to identify and juxtapose complex combinations of human qualities and attributes.

Sentences (B1) and (B2) offer a kind of predication different from (A1) and (A2).[3] We have seen how sentences of the (B) kind can be analyzed in an author's or informed reader's use such that the name "Mr Allworthy" comes to make an indirect reference to the sense of the name. This sense—and thus new reference—can be thought of as identifying a set of properties as determined by descriptions elsewhere in the fiction. It would be a mistake, though, to suppose that the predicates

3. Parsons, *Nonexistent Objects* (New Haven, Conn., 1980) p. 23, marks this difference by distinguishing "nuclear" predicates, as in (B1) and (B2), from "extranuclear" predicates, as in (A1) and (A2). The difference seems to have been overlooked by Frank Palmer, in *Literature and Moral Understanding* (Oxford, 1992), p. 23, in that he fails to distinguish the properties that *constitute* (but are not *possessed* by) a fictional character (i.e., from the external perspective) and the properties *attributed* to a character qua person in a fictional world (i.e., from the internal perspective).

"grew fond of Tom Jones" and "is an honest and forgiving man" are being attributed in (B3) and (B4) directly to *sets of properties*. This would make the sentences categorially absurd. (B4) does not assert that a *set* is honest and forgiving. What we must say, strictly speaking, is that the predicates are not so much *true* of the character (though from an internal perspective they are true of a person within the novel) but rather identify properties that are *included* in the set of properties which constitutes the character. In an author's use, this membership is being *stipulated*; in a reader's use, it is being *reported*.

Sentence (B3) suggests a difficulty for the identification of characters. A full specification of the constituent properties of Mr Allworthy will require reference to Tom Jones and other characters, but likewise, a full specification of the constituent properties of Tom Jones will require reference to Mr Allworthy. Does this involve a vicious circularity? I think not. If the problem is one of assigning a truth-value to sentences like (B3) in an informed reader's use, then we can do so simply on the basis of an identifying core of nonrelational properties associated with each character. If the problem is one of the independent identity of characters, then either we must ground this (from a practical standpoint) on the nonrelational core or, more interesting, we must recognize a holistic element in fictional stories in accordance with which characters and states of affairs can be fully conceived only within the context of complex indissoluble unities.[4] The point serves to remind us that fictional characters acquire what identity they have from their embeddedness in complete narratives.

The third category of predications concerns counterfactual attributions: in the case of (C5), regarding a fictional character vis-à-vis the real world, and in the case of (C6), regarding characters from different fictions. Although we might have difficulty assigning a definite truth-value in such examples, we do at least feel that the sentences make sense. What, then, are their truth conditions? We should remember that it is only from the perspective of the real world that characters are sets of properties; from the internal perspective of the story, they are persons. So from the perspective of some possible world other than the real world, we can also think of them as persons, exemplifying in that world those properties which identify a person in the original fiction and constitute a character in the real world. Roughly speaking, the truth conditions of (C5) rest on the relation between the Tom Jones

---

4. The latter is the line taken by Gregory Currie in *The Nature of Fiction* (Cambridge, 1990).

characteristics as described in *Tom Jones* and the hippy characteristics as perceived in the 1960s. More specifically, I suggest that we are being asked to conceive of a world in which the maximum number of (important) properties of the Tom Jones character are realized in some individual and which also conforms to the background of the 1960s and to compare it with other similar worlds in which a like individual does or does not possess the properties associated with being a hippy. What is important is not what result would be obtained from this investigation but rather the underlying principle of counterfactual reasoning about characters. This principle, which involves the maximal realization of properties in individuals across worlds (other than the real world, where the character is simply an abstract entity), applies as well to cases such as (C6). In this example, again under an informal characterization, we must consider worlds where the Tom Jones set of properties is maximally realized in some individual and the Fanny Price set is maximally realized and then ask of these worlds whether it is those in which the individuals get married or those in which they do not that preserve the best balance between an assumed background and the (important) properties of the two characters. The rationale for this account is that if we want to inquire what fictional characters would be like under different conditions, our speculations can best proceed by conceiving the exemplification of the characters in individuals in different worlds. In effect we are comparing alternative fictions, preserving as much as possible of the original.

My appeal to the modal logician's notion of possible worlds is strictly limited to explaining a certain type of reasoning about fictional characters. The view I have developed overall, which sees characters as abstract entities in the real world, is distinct from those views that see them only as individuals in possible worlds. One merit of this account is that it allows in principle for characters to possess logically incompatible or contradictory properties. If a character is constituted by a set of properties, there is no reason why that set should not contain contradictory properties identified perhaps explicitly by predicates F and not-F in a fictional narrative. There might not be much aesthetic merit in such a character, but a theory of fiction should be able to accommodate the unrestricted freedom of a writer to stipulate whatever properties he or she likes for a fictional construct. Writers are not confined to describing possible worlds. Of course, no character that does have contradictory properties could be the subject of counterfactual reasoning that involves the realization of the character in individuals across worlds, at least not until the contradiction has been eliminated in some way. Also, no such character, with the contradiction intact, could be pictured or imagined by readers, except under selected aspects.

If a fictional character is constituted by a set of properties, then any change in the membership of the set will produce a different character. A character possesses its constituent properties essentially. It might seem that this inflexibility produces undesirable consequences for the theory. For example, don't our intuitions suggest that Tom Jones *might have been different?* Was it *necessary* that he did everything just so? Here, though, we are trading on a recurrent ambivalence about characters, arising from their likeness to real persons. It is certainly true that within the fictional world of *Tom Jones,* Tom, as a person, might have acted differently (unless, that is, we take the world to be bound by hard determinism). But from the external perspective, Tom Jones is a character, and now what might have been different is not Tom Jones but *Tom Jones.* Fielding might have written a different novel under the title "Tom Jones." In this different novel a central character named "Tom Jones" might have been portrayed with properties different from those possessed by Tom Jones. But this alternative Tom Jones would, strictly speaking, be a character different from the one that we have, however similar their constituent properties. A character is what it is stipulated to be by an author, though an author might have stipulated differently.

One might object that this reply discounts the possibility that the same character might appear in different novels, being ascribed different properties. Three cases come to mind here. Certain characters—such as Sherlock Holmes, Plantagenet Palliser, and George Smiley—appear in a series of stories. Is it the same character in each member of the series? Surely it is. Here we can think of each series as making up a single fiction. The properties that constitute the characters are those ascribed to them in all the novels in the series; until the series is complete, the character itself, strictly speaking, is not complete, though we might possess a great deal of information about it.[5]

---

5. Perhaps we need to distinguish between those series of novels which are conceived as a whole (and are thus not different in principle from a Victorian "triple-decker" published in three volumes), where the complete character does not emerge until the end, and those series which seem more open-ended, added to seemingly haphazardly by the author (the Sherlock Holmes stories might be an example), where, as Jeanette Emt puts it, it is "more reasonable to stipulate that a fictional character at *t* is determined by the set of properties the *existent* works of a series at *t* ascribe to it" (Emt, "On the Nature of Fictional Entities," in *Understanding the Arts: Contemporary Scandinavian Aesthetics,* ed. Jeanette Emt and Göran Hermerén [Lund, 1992], p. 170).

Fiction and Reality

A second case concerns a novel that is rewritten. John Fowles, for example, has produced a second and altered version of *The Magus.* Do the same characters appear in the rewritten novel? I think that the correct answer here is similar to the answer to the third kind of case. These are cases in which a writer takes over, as we might say, characters from the fictions of other writers and, in a new story or a new version of an old story, gives them different and even incompatible properties. Faust, for example, is described by Goethe and Marlowe (among others), Rosencrantz by Shakespeare and Tom Stoppard. Is it the same character in the different stories? The best approach here, following a suggestion by Nicholas Wolterstorff, is to distinguish, as he describes it, the Faust character *simpliciter* from the Faust-in-Goethe's-*Faust* character and the Faustus-in-Marlowe's-*Dr Faustus* character.[6] The set of properties constituting the Faust character *simpliciter* consists only of certain core properties, essential to something's earning the title "Faust" in any version. The Goethe and Marlowe characters contain this core, and as such qualify for the name "Faust," but also contain more properties as well. With respect to the core, they are the same; with respect to the further characterizations, they are different. I suggest, then, that what we normally mean by saying that the same character appears in different fictions, including the characters in the two versions of *The Magus,* is that the same significant *core* of properties is identified as constitutive of some (fictional) individual in the different stories. Where our concern is with fine details beyond this core—and where these differ—we must say that the characters, too, differ in that respect. In practice, character identity is interest-relative; what counts as the same character for a literary historian might count as different characters for a literary critic concerned with finer nuances.

III

Appeal to a core of properties is important to explain our epistemic relations with fictional characters. For with respect to complex characters, we rarely know and indeed are rarely interested in all the properties that constitute a character. This, however, leads to a difficulty given our association of the sets of properties constituting a character and the sense of fictional names. For if we do not know all the properties that constitute a character, can we truly be said to understand sentences containing the

---

6. Nicholas Wolterstorff, *Works and Worlds of Art* (Oxford, 1980), pp. 148–149.

name of that character? There are two distinct issues here. The first concerns what it is to *know or identify* a character, and the second, what it is to understand sentences about characters.

It would seem that to know a character is to know what properties belong in the set constitutive of that character. But, as I say, complete knowledge of that kind is rare. We need some notion of the *partial* knowledge of a character, or knowledge *sufficient for identification*. There seem to be at least two components of such partial knowledge: one is the requirement that we know some central core of properties belonging to the character set; and the other is that we are able to give a general characterization of the set itself, for example, through specifying a *route* by which the remaining members could be identified. So *partial* knowledge of Tom Jones (that is, sufficient for identification) requires not only a knowledge of salient properties that make up the character but also knowledge that this is a character whose constitutive properties can be discovered in a certain way, for example, directly through reading Fielding's novel or indirectly through summaries or descriptions of the novel. We do not have adequate knowledge for identifying Tom Jones if we think that he is a real person, even if we do know a large number of his central attributes.

It is partial knowledge of this kind to which we can appeal in answer to our second question concerning what it is to understand sentences about characters. As long as we know a core of properties picked out by a fictional name and some route by which the remaining properties can be identified, we have sufficient knowledge to understand a sentence containing the fictional name.

There remains a further and related difficulty, that of accounting for our psychological attitudes to fictional characters. When can we be said to be *thinking about* a particular fictional character? Or liking, admiring, despising, or fearing that character? And when can two people be said to be thinking about, admiring, and so on, the *same* character? The conditions we have discussed for *identifying* characters or *understanding* sentences containing fictional names are not, I think, sufficient for capturing the appropriate objects of our psychological attitudes toward characters.

Suppose we reflect on the properties: being a kindly squire who brings up a foundling, falls out with him through various misunderstandings but later reaches a happy reconciliation. This reflection is not yet sufficient to qualify as thinking about Fielding's Mr Allworthy, even though the content of the reflection captures certain core properties of that character. Not even if one of the properties in our reflection is "being a man named 'Mr Allworthy' " will we have a sufficient condition; indeed that property is not even necessary for reflection on Mr Allworthy. Now suppose that we have the additional belief that the properties in question are attributed to a character in a novel by Fielding. Will that make our original reflection a thought about Fielding's Mr Allworthy? It does establish a connection between the properties and the novel. But this epistemic connection is still not enough to secure the identification we require of the appropriate psychological attitude. After all, our psychological attitude—in this case reflection or thought, but the same goes for admiration or fear—might have quite the wrong *genesis*. We might have been brought to think about a kindly squire, a foundling, and so forth from a source quite independent of Fielding's novel, and even though we have certain additional beliefs about that novel and the characters in it, we nevertheless could not under those conditions be said to be thinking about Mr Allworthy. In fact, we might be thinking about some actual person. Our attitudes *to Mr Allworthy* must he anchored to Fielding's novel, not merely epistemically, but *causally*.

Remember that what makes a character *fictional* is precisely that it is presented in a *fiction* by an author under the conventions of storytelling. The author's original use of names and descriptions in a fiction must play some explanatory role in accounting for the attitudes that readers subsequently acquire about the characters so presented. If we are correctly to be said to be thinking about Mr Allworthy, there must be a causal route connecting our thoughts with Fielding's use of names and descriptions. As with the epistemic route we discussed earlier, this causal route will either be direct when our reflections or attitudes derive from our reading of the novel or indirect when we come to think about a character not through our own reading of the novel but through someone else's report of it.

In general we can say this: our psychological attitudes toward a fictional character must be anchored through some causal chain to an original *presentation* of that character. This is not surprising when we recall that it is only through an author's use of a fictional name, leading to subsequent uses by informed readers, that references to a character by means of a name are possible. A fictional character is presented by an author in a fiction, and that initial presentation must figure in any explanation of subsequent attitudes that readers form toward that character. Suppose, though, that two writers, quite independently, produce two type-identical fictions, perhaps in the manner of Jorge Luis Borges's *Pierre Menard, Author of the Quixote*. What can we say about the identity of the characters portrayed? The internal properties attributed to the characters in the two stories seem to be the same, yet they are the products of two separate and independent acts of presentation. To the extent that the constitutive properties are identical we must surely insist that the *same character* is presented, even though the presentations are distinct in origin. Any subsequent attitudes toward that charcter will have alternative routes back to one or other of the authors. However, it might be that the different acts of presentation themselves generate differences between the characters by determining (with the aid of contextual features) connoted or implied properties that do not show up in the explicit content. It is conceivable that the character-as-presented-by-A and the character-as-presented-by-B, even where the originating texts are type-identical, might be distinct characters and might be the cause of different attitudes in readers. Perhaps this is just the point that Borges is making.

Finally, I do not pretend that it is always a straightforward matter to determine exactly what properties do constitute any given fictional character. Nor am I certain, in the case of even moderately complex novels, that some determinate set of properties is associated with each fictional name. As it is, recalling a point emphasized earlier, when reading fiction we are rarely concerned with identifying more than a central core of properties, though a concern with peripheral, as well as central, properties can generate acute critical disagreement. One of the tasks of the literary critic is to weigh the evidence in favor of this property or that. What implications can be drawn from such and such a description? How reliable is the testimony of such and such a speaker? Beyond this quasi-factual investigation is the further task of *literary interpretation*, which involves assigning significance to descriptions within some overall pattern of thematic development. It might be that a character under different interpretations is assigned radically different, even incompatible, properties. If the fiction can support both interpretations, we might have to conclude that it projects two different characters under a single proper name. In such cases a character will acquire an identity only *relative to an interpretation*, a point I explore further in the next chapter.

IV

Let me summarize some of the main conclusions and implications of the analytical inquiry of the last two chapters. First, I hope to have vindicated the commonsense view that when critics—or anyone else—talk about fictional characters, they are not talking nonsense or speaking, by virtue of their subject matter, either vacuously, metaphorically, or falsely. Their talk can be meaningful, literal, and true. It can also be subject to reasoning and based on evidence. I have stressed the importance in discussions of "the language of fiction" of distinguishing *an author's use, an informed reader's use,* and *a misinformed reader's use* of sentences and descriptions, even though what is uttered might be the same in each case. Questions of truth and falsity bear differently on these different uses. To speak, as philosophers sometimes do, of fictional names as "vacuous" or "empty" or to assimilate them to cases of "referential failure" is to ignore these important distinctions. To characterize an author's use of language in storytelling, one must distinguish the *identification* of properties through predication or propositional content and any *assertion* that those properties are instantiated or exemplified in individuals. Only in special circumstances does an author of fiction make assertions.

To determine what a fictional character is, I have drawn on a clue from the etymology of the word *character,* which suggests that a person's character is something *abstract* and concerns the person's salient and distinguishing qualities. In general, to speak of a character is to speak of something abstract constituted by properties; we can specify and describe a character whether or not it is exemplified by some real person. A fictional character is a set of properties identified by descriptions under the conventions of storytelling (that is, in an author's use). This definition derives from an *external* perspective—from our point of view in the real world. From an *internal* perspective, within the world of the fiction, what we call "characters" exist as ordinary people.

It is sometimes said that when critics discuss fictional characters, they are *really* talking about either words on a page or ideas in someone's mind. Although neither suggestion corresponds to the view advanced here, the motivating thoughts behind both can be accommodated on this view. A writer will no doubt start with at least a partial idea of a character in the mind identified through reflection on human qualities; the writer will then present and refine the character through descriptions in a story. Creativity and skill reside in both the imaginative and descriptive exercises. It might be that the descriptions themselves help to determine what the character is like even for the writer. In this sense, the identity of a fictional character is rooted in the descriptions in a fictional narrative, and those descriptions, often if not invariably, are products of the imagination. When readers attribute a property to a fictional character, which strictly speaking is to say that the property is *included* in the constitutive set, they speak truly only if the property is either identified in relevant descriptions presented by the author or derivable from those descriptions in suitable ways.

Apart from any *causal* relations between fictional characters and reality to do with their genesis or their effects, perhaps the most significant relation is something like the traditional *mimesis*. Again, on the account given, the commonsense view is vindicated that fictional characters can be *similar* to real people. The explanation is simple: we will often have observed in real people properties or combinations of properties that we find attributed to characters in a fiction. In this way we *recognize reality* in fiction. We "see" ourselves and others in fictional characters when we recognize properties identified in fictional descriptions as those exemplified by people we know.

It might be objected that an emphasis on the *abstract* nature of fictional characters is at odds with the *human* interest we take in novels. I think the specificity of "rounded" characters, as distinct from mere stereotypes, goes a long way toward answering the objection. But also worth noting is that our interest in humans often itself takes an abstract form. We have a natural curiosity for ideas, attitudes, dilemmas, predicaments, feelings, and emotions *in themselves*, apart from any particular people who exemplify them. Perhaps this partly explains why our interest in newspaper stories about people unknown to us seems comparable to our interest in fiction. It also explains why fiction can play a serious and instructive part in our lives.

4

Logic and Criticism

We may classify a sentence containing empty singular terms as bet-sensitive if a bet, that so-and-so did such-and-such, can be won or lost according as the sentence "so-and-so did such and such" or a contrary of it is rightly assented to, yet not lost even given that "So-and-so does not exist" is rightly assented to. "Sherlock Holmes lived in Baker Street" is bet-sensitive; "The present King of France is bald" is not.

—John Woods, *The Logic of Fiction*

The relation of Elizabeth Bennet to Darcy [in Jane Austen's *Pride and Prejudice*] . . . expresses itself as a conflict and reconciliation of styles: a formal rhetoric, traditional and rigorous, must find a way to accommodate a female vivacity, which in turn must recognize the principled demands of the strict male syntax. The high moral import of the novel lies in the fact that the union of styles is accomplished without injury to either lover.

—Lionel Trilling, *The Opposing Self*

I

It is not always easy to reconcile the requirements of a logic of fiction with the requirements of an aesthetics of fiction. What a logician has to say about fiction per se is often remote from what a literary critic has to say about particular works of fiction. A logician, for example, will inquire about the reference of names in a fictional context or the truth-value of fictional propositions or the ontology of fictional objects. This logical inquiry is indifferent to literary or aesthetic value. A critic, on the other hand, will inquire about the meaning and value of particular works or their themes and characterizations or their truth from the point of view of perceptiveness or verisimilitude.

It might be argued that the difference is simply one of *level* or of *generality*, such that the relation between logic and aesthetics (or literary criticism) is something like the relation between philosophy of science and science itself. But this cannot be right. The difference is more complex and more interesting, for in certain respects the inquiries are incommensurable. When a logician, for example, speaks of a fictional object simply as the referent of a fictional name, virtually no common ground exists with a critic who speaks of a fictional character as performing a certain function in a literary narrative. Or when a logician, in the context of semantic theory, assesses the truth conditions of fictive sentences and a critic, in the context of literary interpretation, assesses the thematic contribution of fictive descriptions, the judgments barely share even a common subject matter.

In this chapter I will explore one instance of this tension between logic and literary criticism: the idea of *reasoning to what is true in fiction*. Ostensibly, this topic is one in which logicians and literary critics have a common interest. Both can agree on one sense of "true in fiction" where it means simply truth about a fictional world. In this chapter that sense will be the focus of attention; its connection with other senses of "true in fiction" will be examined in Chapter 6. Every reader of fiction is concerned with what happens in a fictional narrative, what the "facts" are, as it were, about the fictional world. Of course, we must not assume that this concern will always be uppermost. Whether it is will depend to a large extent on the type of fiction. The assumption that all fictional narrative depicts a coherent, ordered, "realistic" world is not acceptable to the literary critic, even though it often seems to underlie discussions of the logic of fiction. Some modern theories of narrative even encourage the working assumption that narrative is not descriptive of a "world" except in particular, clearly defined genres. Nevertheless, we should not be deflected from the obvious truth that all narratives to some degree invite readers to form beliefs about their content. Questions about the principles governing this grasp of content exercise both logicians and critics. These principles we can think of as relating to *reasoning to what is true in fiction*.

II

Nowhere does the tension between logic and criticism emerge more strikingly than in the well-known and subtle analysis of "truth in fiction" offered by the philosopher David Lewis.[1] Lewis bases his analysis on the identification of *fictional worlds* with the *possible worlds* of modal logic. But for all its ingenuity, even plausibility, from a logical point of view, it fails

---

1. David Lewis, "Truth in Fiction," *American Philosophical Quarterly* 15 (1978): 37–46. Page references are given in the text.

radically, as I will argue, to address the concerns of literary critics even though, so it seems, common issues are at stake. Exploring exactly why that is so will yield important lessons for the very enterprise of applying analytical (logical) methods to theoretical problems of literary criticism.

Lewis takes us through a progression of three analyses which are increasingly sensitive to intuitions based on the common experience of reading fiction. The analyses are follows:

> ANALYSIS 0: A sentence of the form "In fiction f, ϕ" is true iff ϕ is true at every world where f is told as known fact rather than fiction. (P. 41)

> ANALYSIS 1: A sentence of the form "In fiction f, ϕ" is non-vacuously true iff some world where f is told as known fact and ϕ is true differs less from our actual world, on balance, than does any world where f is told as known fact and ϕ is not true. It is vacuously true iff there are no possible worlds where f is told as known fact. (P. 42)

> ANALYSIS 2: A sentence of the form "In fiction f, ϕ" is non-vacuously true iff, whenever w is one of the collective belief worlds of the community of origin of f, then some world where f is told as known fact and ϕ is true differs less from the world w, on balance, than does any world where f is told as known fact and ϕ is not true. It is vacuously true if there are no possible worlds where f is told as known fact. (P. 45)

Analysis 0 rules out any reasoning to what is true in a work of fiction beyond what is explicitly given in the content of the sentences in the work. Lewis is right to reject this analysis as too restricted. Both literary critics and ordinary readers take it for granted that inferences beyond what is explicit are not just permissible but indispensable in understanding fiction. Analyses 1 and 2 are offered as genuine alternatives, though the latter, Lewis thinks, conforms better to intuitions arising from literary criticism. What they have in common is the idea that truth in fiction is a product of two sources: the explicit content of sentences in the relevant text and a background against which we reason beyond that content. In Analysis 1 this background consists of facts about the actual world. In Analysis 2 it consists of beliefs overt in the community of origin of the fiction. Analysis 2 is offered as a way of eliminating the use of esoteric facts about the actual world (unknown perhaps to the author and readers of the text) to reason to what is true in the fiction.

Lewis's counterfactual basis for explaining our reasoning about fiction is in many ways highly attractive. It is easy to think of fictional narratives as describing what *would be the case if*. They speak, for the most part, of the possible, not the actual. They describe worlds, often similar, but not identical to, our own world. We can reason about what we are to take as true in a fiction beyond its explicit content, because we read fiction against a presupposed background. All this is nicely captured by Lewis's account.

Yet I see a fundamental flaw in the account (in any version), which makes it unacceptable as a contribution to the aesthetics of fiction (and also to literary criticism). The flaw is that it excludes entirely the *intentionality* of fictional content and the *interpretive* nature of our reasoning about that content. It fails as an account of *literary* reasoning. By referring only to what is *true at such and such a world*, Lewis introduces a realist assumption into the reasoning—that is, an assumption that there are "facts" about the fictional worlds waiting to be discovered—and thus a certain kind of determinacy, which is not warranted in literary criticism. Ultimately, the critic is not so much exploring *facts* as uncovering *meanings*: not chronicling a *world* so much as constructing an *interpretation*. Nowhere is the critic more at odds with the logician. Let us pursue these objections.

III

Lewis explains our reasoning to what is true in fiction in terms of a balance between the world (or worlds) explicitly presented in the text of a fiction and some background world. I will look in more detail at what he says about both components, for his characterization of both, I suggest, is unacceptable to the demands of the literary critic.

Let us begin with his basic conception of the world(s) of a fiction. Lewis argues that the worlds explicitly presented are those where the fictional story is "told as known fact." This eliminates the actual world, because in the actual world, the story is told *as fiction*. So even if, by massive coincidence, all the events and characters depicted in a fiction turn out to have exact counterparts in the real world, the fictional world would still not be identical with the real world, as the acts of storytelling in the two worlds would be different. Lewis's condition, quite rightly, gives precedence in determining fictionality to what a storyteller intends rather than to how things are in the world. In other words it is not literal truth or falsity that makes a narrative factual or fictional but only the mode under which the narrative is presented, how it is told. This is the view I defend in Chapter 2.

But there are problems with the requirement that in the fictional world the story is "told as known fact." First, by covertly introducing the notion of truth via that of knowledge, it threatens the account with circularity. The worlds that we are invited to consider when assessing what is true in a particular fiction are those which contain only what is known to be true by the storyteller. Therefore, to discover what the storyteller knows to be true, we need to know what is true ourselves. Second, this becomes a difficulty in precisely those stories in which the storyteller is depicted as unreliable or in which occur narrative strategies, shifting points of view, a preponderance of dialogue, and so forth. Lewis's account requires that the narrator tells the truth in a pretty straightforward way, recounting only what he knows and doing most of the talking himself. But this is an unwarranted assumption, at least as far as literary criticism is concerned. For one thing the device of the unreliable narrator is common enough in fiction: in Agatha Christie's *The Murder of Roger Ackroyd*, for example, the narrator conceals until the very end the fact that he himself is the murderer, and in three of Iris Murdoch's first-person novels, *Under the Net, The Black Prince*, and *The Sea, The Sea*, the narrators are depicted as self-deceived in varying degrees (the cases are discussed in Chapter 6). Lewis recognizes such cases in which "the storyteller purports to be uttering a mixture of truth and lies" and suggests that the way to deal with them is to "consider those worlds where the act of storytelling really is whatever it purports to be . . . here at our world" (p. 40). This suggestion merely highlights the general problem of determining what those worlds are: specifically, which are the truths and which are the lies.[2]

Other features of narrative content, such as irony, hyperbole, metaphoric or symbolic construction, or changing points of view, also threaten Lewis's requirement that a narrator tell only what he *knows*. At the root of the problem is an underlying assumption throughout Lewis's analyses that, as far as truth in fiction is concerned, a sharp distinction is to be made between what is presented explicitly and thus can be accepted as true and what is not explicitly presented and thus requires some construction by the reader against an assumed background. But discovering what is true in a fictional world is not characteristically as clearcut as that. An adequate account of reasoning to what is true in fiction needs to capture the fact that at nearly every level, the reconstruction of fictional worlds needs to invoke a variety of background data,

2. For a discussion of some of the issues, see Peter Lamarque, "The Puzzle of the Flash Stockman: A Reply to David Lewis," *Analysis* 47 (1987): 93–95.

including recognition of genre, ironical or satirical intent, symbolic or allusive frame, narrative mode, historical context, and implicit or connotative meanings.

It is a peculiarity of fictional narrative that it depicts not merely a world but a world-under-a-description. Acts of storytelling generate intentionality in fictional content; there are not just facts reported but facts-as-told as well. Lewis rightly emphasizes the importance of the act of storytelling in identifying fictions: "Different acts of storytelling, different fictions. When Pierre Menard retells *Don Quixote*, that is not the same fiction as Cervantes' *Don Quixote*—even if they are in the same language and match word for word" (p. 39). But this does not go far enough. Acts of storytelling are individuated by storytellers and by the very mode of telling. As I argued in Chapter 3, if Cervantes had retold his story with slight variations, he would have generated a different fiction (and world). The predicates in fictive sentences are not externally but internally related to the situations they characterize in the sense that the particular aspects, attitudes, and values embodied in the predicates help to constitute the situations (events, characters, and so on) depicted. In Borges's story, what makes Menard's *Quixote* a different fiction from Cervantes's is not merely that they are told by different people but also that the implied meanings and attitudes conveyed *by the very same words* differ in the two tellings.

What we discover about a fictional world derives from both *what is said*, where truth conditions alone are at issue, and *how it is said*, where fine-grained meaning, nuance, tone, and point of view must also be taken into account. In short, a fictional world itself is, as I will put it, constitutively aspectual; the complex network of aspects and values characterized by the precise narrative mode of presentation in a work of fiction constitutes the world of the work.[3]

A reader's task is to reconstruct this world by identifying and weighing the aspectual (connotative, evaluative, and so on) qualities in the fictive descriptions. This involves much more than simply accepting as true, or as known fact, what is explicitly reported. Information about fictional worlds is presented through a series of narrative filters. Even at the level of explicit content, readers must determine not only what sentences to accept at face value (recognizing unreliable narration, irony, hyperbole, speaker's point of view) but also what paraphrases of the content of those sentences are licensed (recognizing connotative features, tone, figurative

---

3. For a detailed account of the "aspectual" nature of fiction, see Peter Lamarque and Stein Haugom Olsen, *Truth, Fiction, and Literature: A Philosophical Perspective* (Oxford, 1994), chap. 5.

usage, satire, allusion). Fictional worlds given under a description place severe constraints on which *redescriptions* of fictional content accurately record the "facts." We can only discover what is true in a fictional world through a clear grasp of the manner in which the world is presented. One cannot escape the introduction of an interpretive element right at the start of our reasoning about fiction.

It might be possible to accommodate this complexity within the terms of Lewis's analysis by broadening the initial characterization of the worlds of a fiction. What is explicitly presented, the narrative content, might be thought of not just as "known fact" but as *linguistic data* out of which the facts must be *(re)constructed.* Readers, somewhat like scientists or historians, frame and modify hypotheses about fictional content, assessing the quality and connectedness of the data, attempting to construct (fictional) states of affairs such that they render maximally coherent the evidence available.[4] The transparency of fictive descriptions should never be taken for granted.

One problem with this proposed revision of Lewis's analysis is that it introduces an element of indeterminacy even in the overt descriptive content of a fiction. If all the "facts" about a fictional world are subject to a particular way of construing a fictional text, then we might seem to have lost the idea of "facts" altogether and thus a "world." But bearing in mind that fictional worlds (like characters) are constituted by the (senses of) descriptions in a fictional narrative and accepting that the construal of such descriptions need not itself be indeterminate, we have still retained a recognizable conception of "truth in fiction." Of course we do need constraints on the interpretations we place on the textual data. Familiar literary critical constraints—which we might call *principles for the evaluation of content*—operate at the finer level of judgments about tone, irony, point of view, and narratorial reliability. At the broader level at which we judge global features of the fictional world, more general principles seem to apply: a *presumption of verisimilitude*, for example, which assumes the fictional world to be similar to the real world in the absence of clear indications of respects in which they differ, and a *presumption of truthfulness*, which enjoins us to accept as true what we are directly told about the fictional world unless there is specific evidence to doubt this. In the end it is probable that these constraints will yield much the same set of truths as Lewis recognizes at the basic level. But the principles of

4. For a discussion of the phenomenology of reading, involving "an active interweaving of anticipation and retrospection," see Wolfgang Iser, *The Implied Reader: Patterns in Communication in Prose Fiction from Bunyan to Beckett* (Baltimore, 1974), pp. 274–294.

reasoning are fundamentally different moving from the concept of a storyteller reporting "known facts" to the concept of a reader constructing a world by construing (the meaning of) a text.

IV

Let us move to a consideration of the background world that, according to Lewis's analysis, will serve as a basis for our reasoning to what is true beyond what is explicit in a narrative. For Lewis, this background is either the actual world itself (Analysis 1) or "one of the collective belief worlds of the community of origin" (Analysis 2).

It is helpful to draw a rough distinction between, on the one hand, facts about the physical setting in which a fiction takes place and, on the other hand, more "theory-laden" facts about the actions, motives, intentions, and attitudes of the characters in the fiction (narrator included). More often than not the focus of our interest—and disagreements—in reading a novel will be on the latter, whereas we take the former for granted.

Lewis's account of the background world is more readily applicable to the physical than the psychological inferences we are inclined to draw in reading fiction. It would be natural to appeal to generally prevalent beliefs about the physical world at the time the fiction was created as a source for factual information of a physical kind not made explicit in narrative content. Thus, for example, current skepticism about the influence of the supernatural should not lead us to reason that the witches in *Macbeth* could not have been witches after all. And in Lewis's example, we should not conclude from our knowledge that Russell's vipers cannot climb ropes that in the Sherlock Holmes story "The Adventure of the Speckled Band," either the snake reached its victim in some way other than climbing the rope or Holmes bungled the case.[5]

The psychological inferences we make over and above what is explicit in a narrative are more complicated than the physical inferences. But they do not differ in principle from the point of view of relying on some construal of textual data. I suggest that two different kinds of indeterminacy affect our reasoning about characters, neither of which can be accommodated on Lewis's account but both of which are of significance to

---

5. It seems unlikely that there were any generally prevalent beliefs in England at the end of the last century about the rope-climbing capacities of the Russell's viper. Perhaps, with the story, Conan Doyle created such beliefs.

the literary critic. One is a general indeterminacy in characterizing human action, and the other, an indeterminacy in literary interpretation. Neither indeterminacy can be explained in terms of possible worlds.

First, Lewis's appeal to the "collective belief worlds of the community of origin" of a fiction to guide us in our inferences to what is true in the fiction puts undue restrictions on our understanding of fictional characters or the appropriate (invited) responses to them. One obvious difficulty is that of determining the relevant community. Those beliefs common to an entire society will be so few or so general as to license only the most mundane inferences. But how could the community be narrowed except in an ad hoc way? Lewis might simply concede these points and conclude that the only supplementation that is licensed on human or psychological assessments in a fiction will necessarily be of a low-level kind; after all, he proposes his analysis precisely to rule out psychoanalytic speculation. But this runs counter to our intuitions. The inferences we draw in a fiction are not limited to physical descriptions and very general psychological facts. Nor are they limited only to beliefs common to the majority in a community. We feel this especially when we consider innovative works of literature. We want to acknowledge at least the possibility that an author might transcend commonly accepted attitudes and invite us to perceive human characteristics in a way not embodied in the collective beliefs. A simple example might be Thomas Hardy's *Jude the Obscure*. An ordinary reader of the time who shared the collective beliefs about how young ladies should behave and what attitudes were appropriate to marriage might well have attributed selfish and unreasonable motives to Sue Bridehead. We are not explicitly told that she was selfish or inconsiderate or that she deserved her fate (in fact, the opposite is strongly implied), but it seems that whether or not she was or did should not be decided merely by appeal to a general moral consensus in Hardy's Britain. It also seems clear that what we say about her intentions and motives is going to be determined, in part at least, by some overall perspective we as readers take on the novel.

It might be objected that the kinds of detailed inferences we are inclined to draw about the psychological attitudes of fictional characters should not be counted among the *truths* in a fiction but at best considered only as *hypotheses*. Lewis's criterion is strictly for what is true in fiction. My reply is twofold. First, a great deal of our reasoning to what is true in fiction is hypothetical in nature. This is partly a consequence of the idea developed earlier that we should treat a given text not as a report of known facts about a (fictional) world but as a set of linguistically-based data awaiting construal according to general interpretive principles. In that sense hypothesizing (about meaning) occurs at the most fundamental level. Second, the hypotheses we advance about fictional characters and actions often share just the kind of indeterminacy or relativity that we find in our judgments about the actual world (or actual people). They cannot be dismissed simply as "truth-value gaps." There is a difference between the kind of indeterminacy that afflicts fiction qua fiction, like the unspecified number of Lady Macbeth's children, and the kind of indeterminacy that directly reflects an indeterminacy in the actual world, for example concerning attitudes, beliefs, desires, and values, as expressed in a fiction. Lewis's account has to run these together.

Let me develop this last difficulty in more detail. According to Lewis we have a truth-value gap wherever some proposition is true in some worlds of a fiction and false in others, given that these worlds all differ least from the background world. While I would agree that propositions for which we have no evidence at all, either from the text or from the background, might best be considered as lacking a truth-value, I do not think we should automatically dismiss in the same way all propositions about a character's (or narrator's) attitudes and beliefs over which there is some indeterminacy. I am inclined to say, at least of some propositions of this kind, that they are true on some readings of the text and false on others or that they are true *relative to an interpretation.*

To say that a proposition is true relative to an interpretation is to say something more than just that it is true in some worlds and false in others. The former might entail the latter, but it is not equivalent to it. An interpretation is not a world, though it might help determine a world. This is again where the interests of the literary critic diverge from those of the logician. We form hypotheses about characters from the evidence before us, and we take the hypotheses as true in relation to the fictional world (or worlds) determined by them. But many such hypotheses—for example, about the reliability or point of view of a narrator—will determine in an all-embracing way what we take the specified truths to be. Here we find something like a hermeneutic circle. A general interpretive scheme will determine many of the truths within a fictional world, but these truths will in turn give support to the interpretation. There is no neutral ground from which to judge the truth of such propositions.

The hypothetical nature of some of our inferences about fictional characters reflects an indeterminacy in the explanation of action. To explain a person's actions is at least partly to show them to be consistent with propositional attitudes held by the agent. We say that agents have acted rationally precisely in case their beliefs and desires provide them with a reason for doing as they did. Unfortunately, we can discover their propositional attitudes only by observing their actions (including what they say); having beliefs and desires is (at least partly) being disposed to act in certain ways. But, in turn, to understand actions, to call them intentional or rational, we need to know something about propositional attitudes. We can break into this hermeneutic-like circle only by making some initial suppositions about agents, for example, that they act consistently for the most part.

On one level, rational action is not something we discover but something we assume. The concept of a person is conceptually linked with that of rationality. Here I follow Donald Davidson: "Crediting people with a large degree of consistency cannot be counted mere charity. . . . To the extent that we fail to discover a coherent and plausible pattern in the attitudes and actions of others we simply forego the chance of treating them as persons."[6] But there need not be any one coherent pattern, any single or correct theory or explanation, that alone captures and makes sense of the evidence available.

Exactly parallel observations, I believe, apply also to the interpretation of fiction. We need to make initial assumptions about the coherence of a work of fiction before we are able to reason to what is true in that work. And we would not expect any one interpretation to accommodate uniquely the evidence that the text provides for our reasoning. How far can we press the parallel between our reasoning about human motivation and our reasoning to what is true in fiction? At one level, of course, the parallel is close because much of our interest in fiction—at least literary fiction—will precisely involve issues about human moral and psychological motivation. Making sense of a fictional character calls for many of the same kinds of judgments as are required in explaining any (real) human action.

But a further, more interesting parallel sheds light on the literary critical nature of some of our reasoning about fiction. It also highlights the second source of indeterminacy in that reasoning, as mentioned earlier. The parallel is between making sense of human action and offering a literary interpretation. Literary interpretation applied to fiction is quite unlike the kind of reasoning described by Lewis. It is not a matter of discovering truths about a world so much as assigning thematic significance to component parts of a work. It is a search for coherence and sense. It involves mak-

6. Donald Davidson, "Mental Events," in *Essays on Actions and Events* (Oxford, 1980), pp. 221–222.

Fictional Points of View

ing connections by subsuming more and more elements in a work under a network of thematic concepts.[7] Part of this literary interpretation will involve making sense of the actions and thoughts of characters. But interpretation goes well beyond that. It is also concerned with general themes or symbolic structures that bind together all the elements in a work, not just psychological factors. Again there is no a priori reason why any one interpretation should capture all the possible or interesting connections.

Peter Jones has suggested various respects in which "understanding a novel" is comparable to "understanding a person." "To understand a person," he writes, "involves not only judging his behaviour to consist of actions that are purposeful and pointful, but grasping their point, and perhaps seeing grounds for their appropriateness in the context."[8] Similarly, to understand a novel we must assume that "the work is purposive," though "this does not commit us to search for the actual purposes that informed the work."[9] Jones's account of what he calls "creative interpretation" allows for the possibility that different readers will postulate different purposes for different elements in a work; they might "take" the text in different ways, find different significance in it. We could say that on this view literary interpretation is radically underdetermined by the evidence supplied by the text of a literary work.

A similar view has been developed, in a different context, by Ronald Dworkin, who compares literary interpretation and interpretation in law. Dworkin characterizes interpretation as follows:

> Interpretation of works of art and social practices . . . is indeed essentially concerned with purpose not cause. But the purposes in play are not (fundamentally) those of some author but of the interpreter. Roughly, constructive interpretation is a matter of imposing purpose on an object or practice in order to make of it the best possible example of the form or genre to which it is taken to belong. It does not follow, even from that rough account, that an interpreter can make of a practice or work of art anything he would have wanted it to be. . . . For the history or shape of a practice or object constrains the available interpretations of it. . . . Creative interpretation, on the constructive view, is a matter of interaction between purpose and object.[10]

---

7. For a clear account of the principles of literary interpretation, see Stein Haugom Olsen, *The Structure of Literary Understanding* (Cambridge, 1978).

8. Peter Jones, *Philosophy and the Novel* (Oxford, 1975), p. 196.

9. Ibid., p. 197.

10. Ronald Dworkin, *Law's Empire* (London, 1986), p. 52.

According to this view, common to Jones and Dworkin, interpretation by its very nature is "constructive" or "creative" in that it involves the postulation of purpose or significance. It is concerned with projected meanings rather than given facts. Lewis's model of fictions as possible worlds makes radically different assumptions about what it is to understand fictional content. Although Lewis sees reasoning to what is true in fiction as a quasi-factual investigation about objectively given worlds, the Jones/Dworkin view emphasizes the interpreter and the search for sense and connectedness. Truth is relativized to interpretation. This hermeneutic view introduces an indeterminacy quite different from that of the "truth-value gap."

Interpretation in the Jones/Dworkin sense provides a framework within which we can reason to particular fictional truths. A good example of this "creative interpretation" and the truths it generates can be found in Jones's reading of *Middlemarch*. Jones sees George Eliot's novel as presenting a complex theory of the imagination. Here is one part of his argument:

> The third role of imagination is in the sympathetic understanding of other men; such understanding cannot be reached by those exclusively concerned with themselves, but it rests upon the use of imagination to interpret the outward signs of men's inner lives. Lydgate and Casaubon differed entirely on the uses to which they put their constructive imagination in their professional work; but they both failed to see that such imagination is also essential in their social lives. The mental world of the imagination is quite separate from the actual world in which we live; to connect the two demands a disciplined exercise of will-power.[11]

In this and in the rest of his discussion, Jones offers a number of philosophical concepts and hypotheses as a framework for finding significance and connectedness in the novel: concepts such as "constructive imagination," "sympathetic understanding," "disciplined exercise of will-power," and so on. Within this framework, judgments can be made about what is "true in the fiction," for example, about the characters and their attitudes: hence Jones's judgment that "Lydgate and Casaubon . . . failed to see that such imagination is . . . essential in their social lives." This judgment is made possible only by the interpretive framework within which it is set.

11. Jones, *Philosophy and the Novel*, p. 48.

It is hard to see what status such a judgment could be given on Lewis's account. Because it might be true in some possible worlds derived from the novel and false in others, Lewis would have to categorize it as "neither true nor false." But that does no justice to its peculiar status as part of a literary (and philosophical) interpretation. The kind of reasoning that Jones undertakes to arrive at such a judgment is not a reasoning about "facts" in a possible world. It makes no appeal to "collective belief worlds." Rather it involves its own imaginative reconstruction of the text; it proposes a new "way of looking" at the textual data, a new conception of the novel's thematic coherence. A large number of critical judgments are of this kind and are familiar to literary critics. We must, I suggest, assess these judgments as *truths relative to an interpretation.* Needless to say, we must not suppose that any judgment whatsoever can acquire the title of truth in this way. The judgments correctly deemed to be truths will need to be well supported by a plausible and consistent interpretation, subject at least to the constraining principles mentioned earlier for evaluating narrative content.

I have suggested a parallel between literary interpretation and Davidson's view of human action, conceived as a search for coherence on the assumption of rationality. The parallel is supported by the view of "creative interpretation" developed by Jones and Dworkin. But it would be a mistake to suppose that literary interpretation is entirely assimilable to the ways we make sense of human action (Jones) or social practices (Dworkin). There is much that is sui generis in literary interpretation. The conventions for making sense of a literary work and for exploring connections within a work, as well as the concepts we apply in interpretation, are all rooted in a distinctive practice of literary criticism. Critical reasoning in support of hypotheses such as Jones's on *Middlemarch* is subject to specific principles of evidence and argument. Although I have not looked in detail at these principles, it should at least be clear from the conclusions we have drawn, and the examples themselves, that the principles go well beyond those embodied in Lewis's Analyses 1 and 2. The possible-world model is not adequate to explain the kind of reasoning that is an indispensable part of literary interpretation.

V

We have come a long way from Lewis's original analyses. It has certainly not been my intention to reject the entire enterprise in which Lewis is engaged. My concern has been to identify points of tension between the logician's approach to "truth in fiction" and the requirements of the literary critic. According to Lewis, our reasoning to what is true in fiction is counterfactual; we make inferences about what would be the case in worlds where the story is told as known fact, setting the data directly presented in the narrative against a wider background world. There is no objection to the idea that at a basic level we sometimes reason counterfactually about fiction in order to fill out a fictional world. But from the point of view of the literary critic, this can at best be only part of the procedure for determining what is true of such a world.

The details that Lewis provides, both about the direct data in a narrative and the background world by which we generate inferences, are not adequate to the complexities recognized by literary critics. First, treating explicit narrative content as constituting worlds in which the story is "told as known fact" fails to take into account the many different kinds of narrative strategy familiar in literary fictions, such as unreliable narration, shifting points of view, and ironic or symbolic representation. I have proposed instead that we treat narrative sentences not as reporting facts but as embodying meanings that require the reader not just to accept what is given but to construe what is given. This is still within the spirit of Lewis's account. I suggested that certain principles (or working assumptions) operate in our initial sorting of fictional truths: principles of coherence, verisimilitude, and trustworthiness, as well as specific critical principles about textual meaning.

Second, Lewis's account of the background world as "the collective belief worlds of the community of origin" of the fiction, to which we appeal in making inferences beyond what is explicitly presented, is also inadequate for literary criticism. The account might be sufficient for reasoning about facts in the physical world, but it is too limited to do justice to literary critical hypotheses about character and theme. On such matters we need some concept of *interpretation*. At one level we have the kind of interpretation that Davidson introduces in understanding human action. At another level we have more distinctively literary interpretation that identifies thematic development in a fictional narrative. With the concept of interpretation comes the idea of indeterminacy. Rather than supposing there are determinate *facts* to be discovered about the worlds of a literary fiction, we must work with the idea of *truths relative to interpretive frameworks*. But this indeterminacy or relativity is not reducible to "truth-value gaps."

In effect I have introduced, on behalf of the literary critic, complexities at every stage of Lewis's analysis. It might be that a separate formal analysis could be offered for the revised conception of "truth relative to an interpretation." But it is far from clear that any simple formalized principle could capture the kind of reasoning that a critic undertakes to arrive at—and support—an interpretation. The value of any very general principle would be questionable. It might be argued that my objections to Lewis apply only to *literary* fictions and that his aim is to produce a principle applicable to *all* fiction, or fiction per se. Certainly not all fiction is literature, and maybe not all literature is fiction. But I think that our response to literary fiction is on a continuum with our response to any fiction. Rudimentary interpretive procedures apply at the most basic level of reading, certainly at the level Lewis is concerned with, where we make reasoned inferences about narrative content. The imposition of meaning in a fictional narrative, over and above the discovery of facts in a possible world, is an indispensable part of our reasoning to what is true in fiction.

5

Expression and the Mask

'I would but find what's there to find,
Love or deceit.'
'It was the mask engaged your mind,
And after set your heart to beat,
Not what's behind.'

—W. B. Yeats, "The Mask"

The plots of Noh plays are so simple that we can hardly call them stories: it would be more correct to call them a series of hints that guide the audience in a dramatic way. . . . The acting, singing, and timing in Noh . . . are simply media that evoke and glorify what we really seek in a play: the common human themes and sentiments embodied by the hero. A Noh play, in other words, is not the telling of a series of events but an exploration, an evocation, and indeed a song of praise.

—Kunio Komparu, *The Noh Theater: Principles and Perspectives*

I

A familiar objection to character or story-based criticism is that it fits only a narrowly circumscribed class of literary works, notably realistic narrative-centered fiction, typified by the nineteenth-century realist novel. Character is altogether irrelevant, so the argument goes, to modernist or postmodernist fiction. As there are no characters in the *nouveau roman*, so character must be inessential to the fundamentals of fiction.

It is certainly not my aim to resurrect character-centered criticism, in the style, say, of A. C. Bradley, but I do think that the concept of character is more resilient and more flexible than its detractors suggest. Rather than illustrating its flexibility by looking at characterization in postmodernist literature, I will examine a potentially more difficult, but in some ways not dissimilar, case, that of the Japanese Noh theater.

The problem, expressed in a Kantian formulation, is just this: How is the portrayal of character possible in a dramatic form as stylized and aus-

Fictional Points of View

tere as Noh? The question presupposes, of course, that the portrayal of character is possible in Noh and also, I suppose, that a significant feature of Noh is that it aims to portray character. These presuppositions will need to be supported. In fact, we will see that role playing, in a special sense, stands at the very heart of the aesthetics of Noh. I believe that the discussion is of intrinsic interest, but I also hope it will help bring out the practical application of the abstract conception of character which I developed earlier.

Let me begin by refining, but also compounding, the problem by introducing another factor. On the face of it there are two irreconcilable requirements of a Noh actor (in the central, or *shite*, role). One is that he[1] should bring alive the character he is portraying, breathing into the part both spirit and expression. The other is that he should conform unwaveringly to the strict conventions of the role, under which every gesture and intonation are prescribed: his own facial expressions are concealed behind a mask; the words he chants and intones are passages of dense, allusive poetry; his dance movements are symbolic and ritualistic; virtually no props appear on the bare stage; and the character he portrays—an old woman, a warrior, a god—seems insubstantial, even stereotypical. What room is there for expressiveness behind this mask of formality?

A crucial element in the puzzle, though it cannot yet furnish a solution, is the injunction to the *shite* actor to identify himself totally with the character he is representing. The spirit of the role is his own spirit transformed. During the solemn ritual of donning the mask, before entering the stage, the actor must somehow transform his inner being into that of the character. How this might be done and what difference it could make in the face of the conventionality of performance will need further explanation. We are soon immersed in complex aesthetic issues: the nature of character portrayal, the relation between inner state and outward appearance, the function of formal conventions in expressing emotion and atmosphere, and, of course, the very conception of Noh as a form of theater.

Before we set out along this path, we should note the extent to which the problem as stated rests on deeply ingrained presuppositions from the Western theatrical tradition (at least the premodernist tradition). The injunction that an actor give life and spirit to a role, that he think himself

---

1. Noh actors are traditionally all males. Although some women do now belong to Noh troupes, it would be rare for them to perform major roles.

Expression and the Mask

into a part, is a commonplace in the Western tradition.[2] But it goes hand in hand with other assumptions: for example, that the character being portrayed has a suitable degree of complexity and interest (close involvement with a merely stock character would seem absurd, if not impossible); that there is scope in the performance for realistic or lifelike representation; that the personality of the actor plays a crucial role in the effectiveness of the portrayal; that the particularity of character is matched by a particularity of gesture, movement, facial expression, and dramatic interaction; and, finally, that the liveliness of the characterization is in good measure a function of the vitality and realism of the spoken text. As we will see, none of these assumptions applies to the Noh plays.

II

Having set up the problem, I now offer some methodological remarks. The first is an acknowledgment of the fact that in discussions of drama, many different points of view can be adopted. Most obvious are the points of view of performer and spectator. Interests here do not necessarily coincide. The skill required to project a dramatic effect is not the same as that required to appreciate it. There are also the points of view of the writer and reader of a work of drama, which might, but need not, coincide with those of performer and spectator. Finally, there is the point of view of the aesthetician or theorist attempting to generalize about a whole dramatic genre.

In my account of the portrayal of character in Noh, I will concentrate on character portrayed in performance, from the point of view of both actor and audience, not the portrayal merely in the texts of the plays, as might concern a reader whose interest is in critical or historical scholarship. This reflects another important difference between Noh and the conventional Western theater. The character of King Lear can be studied and understood through a careful reading of Shakespeare's play. But the text of a Noh play provides only one element in the development of the play's characters. So integrated is a Noh performance between music, dance, poetry, mask, costume, and, above all, mood and atmosphere that

2. There has been, however, a recurring debate in the Western tradition about the desired extent of "empathy" in acting: see Toby Cole and Helen K. Chinoy, eds., *Actors on Acting* (New York, 1972), pp. 350–352, 356–360.

characterization cannot be understood through any single element in abstraction.

This emphasis on performance, however, should not be taken to imply that characterization in Noh is relative to a performance in the sense in which we speak of Olivier's Hamlet or Scofield's Lear. It is not that each performance affords a new interpretation of a character; rather, each performance strives for an ideal that itself uniquely expresses the essence of a character. Noh performance does not aim to reinterpret characters in novel ways but to portray, through the prescribed conventions, what is taken to be the purest form of the ideal.

It is common for theoretical discussions of Noh, within literary aesthetics, to draw on two particular relations with Western theater: the influence of Noh on twentieth-century modernist drama and the analogy with classical Greek drama (notably tragedy). I will say a word about each of these, but I will also give reasons why our philosophical inquiry must go beyond such comparisons.

It is clear that the influences on twentieth-century European drama are real enough.[3] W. B. Yeats, for example, wrote several dance dramas between 1915 and 1921 closely modeled on Noh. In his essay "Certain Noble Plays of Japan," Yeats reveals what attracted him most about Noh: its "distance from life," its "aristocratic form," its indirectness and symbolism, and its dignified treatment of ancient myths and legends.[4]

For our purposes, though, there remains a crucial difference between Noh and its modernist imitators. The modernists adopted the dramatic techniques of Noh as an intellectual curiosity, an experiment, a self-conscious reaction against realism; their use of these techniques can be understood only against this background. Noh itself, on the other hand, arose as an artistic expression of certain inherent cultural dispositions. There was no realist (dramatic) tradition in Japan to react against, only a deep aestheticism to refine. It is these original principles rooted in the culture that I will seek to identify. We must not be seduced by the appearance of the avant-garde in Noh.

3. The influence arose from the dissemination of the work of Ernest Fenollosa, the first Western scholar to make a systematic study of Noh. Ezra Pound's enthusiastic editing of Fenollosa's papers and the subsequent publication, under their joint names, of *Noh, or Accomplishment* (London, 1916), containing translations and commentaries, sent a ripple through literary circles. T. S. Eliot, for example, reviewed the book favorably in "Noh and the Image," *Egoist* 4 (1917): 102–103.

4. W. B. Yeats, "Certain Noble Plays of Japan," in *Essays and Introductions* (London, 1961), p. 221.

Expression and the Mask

To understand the aesthetic principles underlying Noh, we must turn not to Western imitations but to the early articulation of those principles by one of the founders of Noh, Zeami Motokiyo (1363–1443). Zeami and his father, Kannami (1333–84), crystallized Noh into its canonical form out of disparate contemporary traditions.[5] Both were actors as well as playwrights; the plays they wrote and performed remain the core of the Noh repertoire. But Zeami also wrote about Noh in some twenty treatises, the primary purpose of which was the private initiation of his sons and successors into the secrets of Noh performance. The treatises are, though, much more than just actors' manuals. Drawing on a deep knowledge of Japanese aesthetics, the poetic tradition, and Buddhist teachings, Zeami developed a subtle theoretical framework for Noh, supported by a number of key aesthetic concepts. Much of the discussion that follows is drawn from these writings.[6]

As for the frequently noted parallels with classical Greek drama, superficial similarities abound: the use of masks; the integration of dance, music and poetry; the presence of a chorus; the all-male cast.[7] Furthermore, both Aristotle and Zeami employ the conception of "imitation" in their accounts of drama; make prescriptions for the organic unity and development of a plot; and emphasize the value of using familiar, and epic, stories. The devices of "reversal" and "recognition" are common to both Noh and Greek tragedy, and in both, the main events tend to take place offstage. There is evidence, too, of similar styles and structures, for example, in the plays of Aeschylus and Zeami.[8]

The similarities, however, are not always sustained under more detailed examination. In Noh, unlike in Greek drama, not all the players wear masks; the chorus in Noh has no distinctive point of view and describes rather than comments on the action; Greek mimesis and Japanese *monomane* (imitation) differ in ways that will emerge later; Zeami's description of plot structure, the *jo-ha-kyu* pattern—introduction, devel-

5. See P. G. O'Neill, *Early No Drama: Its Background, Character, and Development, 1300–1450* (1958; rpt., Westport, Conn., 1974).

6. I will refer to the following edition: Zeami Motokiyo, *On the Art of the Nō Drama: The Major Treatises of Zeami*, trans. J. Thomas Rimer and Yamazaki Masakazu (Princeton, N.J., 1984).

7. Many writers have catalogued the similarities, for example, Ernest Fenollosa, "Fenollosa on the Noh," in *The Translations of Ezra Pound*, ed. Hugh Kenner (London, 1953), pp. 269–270; Arthur Waley, *The No Plays of Japan* (London, 1950), pp. 51–52; and Yamazaki Masakazu, "The Aesthetics of Transformation: Zeami's Dramatic Theories," *Journal of Japanese Studies* 7 (1981): 234.

8. For a detailed and illuminating account, see Mae J. Smethurst, *The Artistry of Aeschylus and Zeami: A Comparative Study of Greek Tragedy and Nō* (Princeton, N.J., 1989).

opment, climax—is more dynamic than Aristotle's beginning, middle, and end, involving, for example, increase in pace through a performance.[9] There are also more profound differences. The elevation in Greek tragedy of plot and action over character; the moral and psychological elements of hamartia, miasma, destiny, even catharsis; Aristotle's idea that "the power of tragedy is independent both of performance and of actors"[10]—all are at odds with the unique dramatic principles underlying Noh, to which we now turn.

III

My general thesis is this: although characters in Noh seem almost unrecognizable as such in familiar Western terms, they do nevertheless embody a coherent and distinctive conception, which has its place in a fully developed aesthetic system. And this conception quite nicely draws out some of the logical features of fictional representation. The crucial element in this conception is what I will call *the dissolution of personality*. Characterization in Noh, as exhibited in performance, exemplifies individuality without personality. I will develop this idea in detail, aiming, above all, to stress the positive features of the notion "dissolution of personality." It is important, for example, that it does not collapse merely into that of "stereotype" or "stock character" as used in the Western literary tradition. It couldn't be more different.

Although more metaphysical considerations are undoubtedly also involved in the conception of character in Noh, I will do little other than gesture toward these. Character in Noh is closely related to a conception of human nature stemming from the religious mystical tradition, partly, though not exclusively, that of Zen Buddhism. The dramatic form in which the characters are portrayed instantiates a kind of perception that, according to the mystical view, can give access to otherwise inaccessible spiritual truths. By pointing beyond the merely contingent deliverances of sensory perception and intellect, the austere performances seek to convey and symbolize something deeper about the human spirit—about personal identity, the restlessness of the soul, ultimate redemption—with both an intensity of focus and a universality of application.

9. See Donald Keene, *Nō: The Classical Theatre of Japan* (Tokyo, 1973), p. 21; *The Noh Drama: Ten Plays from the Japanese*, selected by and trans. the Special Noh committee, Japanese Classics Translation Committee, Nippon Gakujutsu Shinkokai (Tokyo, 1955), pp. xi–xii.

10. Aristotle *Poetics* 1450b.vi, 28.

A prerequisite for understanding this metaphysical context is a clear grasp of the conception of character itself. My limited aim is to try to substantiate this conception in relation to certain defining features.

The first cluster of features helps identify the status or nature of character portrayal in Noh, epitomized in the concept dissolution of personality. The characters are *abstract* to a high degree; their constitutive attributes are *impersonal*, albeit retaining some individuality; and they seek to embody *universal*, rather than historical or contingent, significance.

The second cluster of features offers something of a rationale for this abstracted, depersonalized, and universal nature. The portrayal emphasizes emotion rather than motivation; inner spirit rather than action; mood rather than factual detail; and suggestion rather than realistic representation. Such a conception of character, far from being constrained by the formality of the drama—the mask, the austere stage setting, the condensed poetry—both requires and is strengthened by it.

IV

I will begin my development of this conception with the first cluster of features: abstractness, impersonality, and universality. Donald Keene has suggested that "the creation of character, in the sense that the term is used in other forms of drama, is meaningless in No[h]."[11] He has in mind here the apparent lack of autonomous identity in the characters. And Ernest Fenollosa speaks of the emotion embodied in the drama as "always fixed upon idea, not upon personality." He goes on: "The solo parts express great types of human character, derived from Japanese history. Now it is brotherly love, now love to a parent, now loyalty to a master, love of husband and wife, of mother for a dead child, or of jealousy or anger, of self-mastery in battle, of the battle passion itself, of the clinging of a ghost to the scene of its sin, of the infinite compassion of a Buddha, of the sorrow of unrequited love. Some one of these intense emotions is chosen for a piece, and, in it, elevated to the plain of universality by the intensity and purity of treatment."[12] The first thing to note is the special sense of "character" in Fenollosa's phrase "great types of human character." He clearly means human character traits, as exemplified

11. Keene, *Nō*, p. 18.
12. Fenollosa, "Fenollosa on the Noh," pp. 279–280.

by "brotherly love," "love to a parent," and so on. He does not mean character in the sense that Lear and Othello are characters. But I suggest that the appropriate sense of character in Noh lies somewhere between the universal characteristics in Fenollosa's list and the particularity of well-developed characters like Lear or Othello. There is not, in fact, a difference in kind between these two extremes. That has been the thesis of earlier chapters. The concept of character in both senses belongs in the ontological category of abstract entities or universals. When we speak of an individual's characteristics, such as generosity or brotherly love, we are referring to qualities abstracted from that individual. When we speak of a fictional character portrayed in a drama, part of what we mean, from a logical point of view, is a complex imaginative concatenation of many such abstracted qualities.

What makes a fictional character "individual" or "particular" is a function of the specificity of its portrayal, not its ontological type (that is, being a particular rather than a universal). Some dramatic characters are finely developed, others only lightly sketched. Noh characters can retain an individuality as characters, without lapsing into stereotypes, even though they lack specificity with regard to personal or psychological detail. The focus in the characterization is on some specific emotion or predicament, not on the development of a "rounded" personality. The individuality of the character resides in the precise form in which the abstracted emotional qualities are symbolized and, as we will see, with the mood and suggestiveness thereby created. This lack of personal detail, combined with a concentration on specific abstracted qualities, is part of what I call the dissolution of personality. How is it manifested?

Among the small number of parts in any Noh play, the *shite* role is nearly always the center of interest. The subsidiary role, the *waki* (literally, "at the side"), at least in its customary form, barely qualifies as a character, normally having no name and an identity only as a messenger, a priest, a traveler, and so on, whose function is to engage the *shite* in conversation. Both *shite* and *waki* might have attendants (*tsure*), but these, too, normally have no significant character identity. The abstractness of the *waki* or *tsure* parts, to the extent that they are mere dramatic intermediaries, is not of much philosophical interest; they are like minor parts in any tradition.

The *shite* role, in contrast, has altogether more substantiality. There are five classes of Noh plays, which are distinguished by the character type of the *shite* role. In a complete program of five Noh plays (which would be alternated with *kyogen*, or "comic interludes") each class would be represented. The cycle of five plays follows the overall rhythmic pattern of *jo-ha-kyu* as exemplified in the individual plays. This cycle, which is now almost never performed in its entirety, is intended to represent a full spectrum of human emotion and experience. Each class of play has a characteristic mood or emotion associated with it.

The five classes are as follows.[13] First, there are the god plays (*kami-no*), dignified and celebratory, where the primary emotions are joy and affirmation. Next come warrior plays (*shura-mono*), which usually recount tragic events, defeat, or death in the epic period of Japanese history, evoking a mood of poignancy and regret. The third category, woman plays (*kazura-mono*, or "wig" plays), are thought to be the quintessence of Noh, signifying love, always intense, sometimes tragic, and often recollected from old age. The fourth group, intended as a miscellaneous category, in fact gives prominence to madness (*kurui-mono*): the emotions of sadness and lament predominate, often arising from the loss of a child or a lover; as with the woman plays, an atmosphere of longing or yearning and ghosts or possession by spirits are characteristic. Finally, the lively demon plays (*kiri-mono*) complete the program; the dancing is energetic, the mood triumphant, informed with the mystery of the supernatural.

A good deal more particularity is found in the *shite* characters than indicated merely by the very general types: god, warrior, woman, mad person, and demon. Within each group one finds a considerable variety of character and incident. The warriors in warrior plays or the women in women plays retain a significant amount of individuality; the characters are by no means interchangeable. Yet an intensity of focus in the character portrayal leads away from realistic representation.

Keene gives a good example of this dramatic refinement in his account of Zeami's treatment (in one of his plays) of the death of Atsumori, derived from *The Tale of the Heike.* In the original, as Keene points out, much subtle psychological detail is presented to explain the circumstances under which the warrior Kumagai killed the youthful Atsumori on the battlefield.

> Comparing the two stories we see that almost every element of pathos or drama in *The Tale of the Heike* has been deleted from the play. Atsumori's youth, his resemblance to Kumagai's son, his insolence in response to Kumagai's solicitude, Kumagai's regret when forced to kill Atsumori—all

13. I have drawn here from the useful schematic account of the classification of plays in the appendix of Richard Taylor, *The Drama of W. B. Yeats: Irish Myth and the Japanese No* (New Haven, Conn., 1976).

are eliminated, leaving only the story of a man unable to forget his defeat at an enemy's hands. Of course, the audience was familiar with the story as told in *The Tale of the Heike*, but Zeami's play does not depend on this knowledge; instead, he chose to delete everything particular about the two men in the interests of achieving a stylized, universal tragedy. One man kills another; by this act he brings salvation to both. Kumagai's remorse over killing Atsumori leads to his taking Buddhist orders, and this act in turn ultimately brings Atsumori salvation.[14]

The example brings out well both the lack of personality in the characterization and the attempt to universalize the story. But Keene's comments underplay, I believe, the residual specificity in the treatment which affords a far more distinctive character portrayal (through the overall performance) than implied by "only the story of a man unable to forget his defeat." Three important features emerge.

First, in the play *Atsumori*, as in nearly all the classical repertoire of Noh plays, the *shite* role is based on a well-known figure in Japanese history or legend. The individuality of the character is grounded in the familiar name and the core of associations that go with it. Zeami insists that a writer of Noh plays take special care in selecting subjects for portrayal. Mere fame or notoriety in the subject is not sufficient. The chosen figure must have appropriate qualities. Somewhat blandly, Zeami says only that these should be amenable to the Two Basic Arts of Noh, namely, dance and music (which includes poetry).[15] But from his examples, it is clear he has in mind aesthetic qualities such as artistic or aristocratic elegance. Dramatic characterization in Noh begins with a figure well-known from history or legend, whose life is already associated with some abstract quality such as grace, poignancy, or forbearance. It is that abstract quality which finds aesthetic expression in the dramatic representation.

The second feature is the stripping away of descriptive content. A Noh play will invoke very little factual detail about its protagonists. The detail is left either to the imagination or to the vague associations that the audience might have with the named character. To compound the matter, many of the *shite* roles, as we will see, involve radical transformations during a play, often having their true identities concealed or disturbed at crucial points.

Then, third, there is the abstraction from personality. Distinctive personal characteristics are refined or dissolved into a core of essential emo-

14. Keene, *Nō*, pp. 50–51.
15. Zeami, *Art of the Nō Drama*, p. 148.

tional qualities, leaving, often literally, only the shadow or ghost of the original subject. But this core of qualities is highly specific and focused in the central character. Attention is directed to a purified and intensified emotion, unmediated by mere contingencies of personality. We are not invited to explore the complexities of motivation, reason and cause, or background circumstance. The appropriate response is not reason but experience. We are led experientially, through dramatic spectacle, not by psychological or intellectual inference, to see the emotional significance of some basic human predicament as exemplified in a historical or legendary figure. It is not fortuitous that the personality of the actor must be extinguished in the performance. Following a hint from T. S. Eliot, we can say that the emotion is "symbolized," rather than "expressed," in the actor's formal movements.[16]

A significant feature of the play *Atsumori* is that in the first act the hero appears in disguise, as a humble reaper playing a flute, and in the second, as a ghost of his true self, recalling his previous life. The two devices of disguised identity and ghostly recollection are utterly characteristic of Noh. When Arthur Waley illustrated the essence of Noh by suggesting how the theme of *The Duchess of Malfi* might be handled by a Noh writer, he used both devices. He suggested that the first act might see the ghost of the Duchess visiting a shrine in the anonymous guise of a young woman, whereas the second act might show the ghost, whose identity is now revealed, reliving her final hours.[17] In Noh, ghosts seem to have more reality than living persons, and the remote recollected past, more immediacy than the present.[18] Personality is dissolved into ghostliness, disguise, and the remoteness of distant memory.

The use of the mask and the formal motions of the dance accentuate this remoteness yet at the same time help to refine and symbolize the abstracted emotion at the core of the play. The mask depersonalizes and universalizes. From the audience's point of view, it promotes a double distancing: it distances actor from character and character from reality. Yet it heightens rather than diminishes emotion. The considerable variety of masks in the Noh repertoire allows some singular aspect of a char-

---

16. The thought comes from a discussion by T. S. Eliot in which he praised the "abstract gestures" of a contemporary actor, Massine. See T. S. Eliot, "Dramatis Personae," *Criterion* 1 (1923): 305.

17. Waley, *No Plays*, pp. 53–54.

18. T. S. Eliot makes the point, perceptively: "It is only ghosts that are actual; the world of active passions is observed through the veil of another world." See "Noh and the Image," p. 103.

acter—wistful old age, youthful beauty, divine grace, wrathful spirit—to be frozen into a universal type. Once selected, that aspect or that type becomes inescapably present; the hypnotic stare of the mask, albeit susceptible to fine shades of variation, forces an unrelenting concentration of image.

Another, more complex example of the dissolution of personality is the classic play *Sotoba Komachi*, by Kannami. The central character is based on the renowned and glamorous poetess of the Heian Period, Ono no Komachi. Here, dissolution of personality occurs at two levels: at the level of performance common to all Noh plays, through mask and formality, and at the more specific level at which the Komachi character herself suffers a disintegration of personal identity. The character undergoes radical transformations in the course of the one-act play, from "a highly intellectual poetess, to a decrepit old beggar, and finally to a volatile madwoman."[19] In this final state, the character even assumes the spirit of her angry rejected suitor, Fukakusa. The play coheres partly through the well-known legendary associations with the name Komachi but more significantly through the sustained mood of nostalgia and remorse. The predicament of Komachi, driven to exile and abject poverty, haunted by her mistakes in the past, at the same time both proud and tormented, gives substance and interest to the universal themes of worldliness and transience, redemption and the hope of enlightenment. Nevertheless, the transformations of the central role, the shifting allusions across Japanese poetry and Buddhist teaching, and the fact that it is left to the chorus to recall the historical Komachi—all reinforce a distance from the more personal characteristics of the subject.

V

The second cluster of features I identified in Noh character portrayal—the emphasis on mood, inner spirit, and suggestion—I described as offering a rationale for the first cluster of features, involving the dissolution of personality. Zeami developed three key aesthetic concepts, applied to performance, which substantiate the conception of character as based on inner spirit and mood rather than outward action: *hana* (liter-

---

19. See Etsuko Terasaki, "Images and Symbols in *Sotoba Komachi*: A Critical Analysis of a No Play," *Harvard Journal of Asiatic Studies* 44 (1984): 176.

ally, "flower"), a special quality in an actor's performance making it effective and appealing to an audience; *jugen*, a kind of "grace" or "elegance"; and *monomane*, meaning "imitation," "mimicry," or "role playing." The concepts, at least in Zeami's treatment, are closely related and serve to highlight the blend of mysticism and aestheticism underlying his conception of Noh.

As an actor develops in his career, beginning at the age of seven, he advances through different levels of *hana*.[20] Zeami identifies nine such levels from "the way of crudeness and leadenness" up to the rarely attainable "flower of peerless charm."[21] The influence of Zen Buddhism is manifest in his description of the upper levels; the highest level gives rise, as he says, to an ineffable "Feeling that Transcends Cognition." The route to *hana* is *monomane*; the upper levels can be reached only by attaining a certain kind of elegance (*yugen*) in role playing (*monomane*). The requirements of *yugen* and *monomane* give a clear indication of the spiritual and emotional nature of character portrayal.

The concept of *yugen* has a long history in Japanese aesthetics and was used in the Heian Period as a criterion for poetry contests, denoting profundity and subtlety.[22] By Zeami's time it had entered common parlance, with little more than the meaning of graceful elegance. In Zeami's own work, however, the term gradually acquired more mystical connotations, again under the influence of Zen Buddhism.[23] In subsequent treatments, it has come to epitomize a distinctly Japanese sensibility, an appreciation of subtle, understated beauty or elegance, tinged with the sadness of mutability.[24] The concept has been discussed extensively in Japanese aesthetic and Buddhist commentaries.

For our purposes, as the highest ideal of a Noh performance, *yugen* becomes a determining factor in the portrayal of character. The gracefulness of a highly stylized gesture or a dance movement or an intoned verse is more likely to express *yugen* than the naturalistic bustle and display familiar in the Western theater. This reflects the acute aestheticism of Noh, so typical of medieval Japan. Keene gives an example: "The thought of a

20. Zeami, *Art of the Nō Drama*, p. 4.

21. Ibid., pp. 120–122.

22. See Hisamatsu Sen'ichi, *The Vocabulary of Japanese Literary Aesthetics* (Tokyo: Centre for East Asian Cultural Studies, 1963), p. 33.

23. See Andrew T. Tsubaki, "Zeami and the Transition of the Concept of Yūgen: A Note on Japanese Aesthetics," *Journal of Aesthetics and Art Criticism* 30 (1971): 55–67.

24. See Makoto Ueda, "Zeami on Art: A Chapter for the History of Japanese Aesthetics," *Journal of Aesthetics and Art Criticism* 20 (1961): 75–76. See also, Toshihiko and Toyo Izutsu, *The Theory of Beauty in the Classical Aesthetics of Japan* (The Hague, 1981), pp. 26–28.

woman performing the role of, say, the courtesan Eguchi is repugnant to lovers of No[h] who insist that a man in his sixties with a cracked bass voice and large ugly hands has more *yugen.*"[25]

The mystical element of *yugen* implies a kind of perception beyond the surface of things to a hidden essence.[26] And it is here the concept of *monomane* is involved. An actor can express *yugen* and thus attain the upper levels of *hana* only by adopting and projecting some essential spiritual quality of the character he is portraying. Although *monomane* literally means "imitation," in Zeami's use it crucially involves the imitation of inner spirit, that is, a hidden essence, not (or not merely) outward mannerism or appearance. Already we have a connection between *monomane* and our discussion of characters as abstract types. The true object of an actor's imitation—what the actor must symbolize in his performance—is an abstracted quality, such as an emotion, a mood, or a state of mind, rather than something particular or overt, such as an action or incident. The translation of *monomane* as role playing makes sense only when the true nature of the roles is understood.[27]

Of course, there must be some outward manifestation of inner spirit, even though in this context a crudely realistic representation is irrelevant. Zeami, speaking as the practical actor-director, offers some tips on how to play, for example, the role of an old man: "It is important, first of all, to make no attempt merely to imitate the external attributes of old persons."[28] To capture the fact that the old man's "limbs are heavy and he is hard of hearing," the gestures and movements in the dance should be fractionally behind the beat. But to capture the inner longing of the old to be young again, "one should basically play the role in a youthful manner such as that which an old person would wish to assume. In this way the actor can show through his performance the envy the old feel for the young."[29] Another example is the portrayal of a madman. What is important here, according to Zeami, is to represent the inner *cause* of the madness, the obsession—perhaps a parting, a loss, or death—rather than the outer symptoms.[30]

25. Keene, *Nō*, p. 23.

26. For an emphasis on the mystical nature of *yugen*, see Izutsu, *Theory of Beauty*, pp. 26–44.

27. This translation appears throughout Zeami, *Art of the Nō Drama.*

28. Ibid., p. 55.

29. Ibid., p. 56.

30. This example is discussed in Ueda, "Zeami on Art," p. 74.

Zeami sees an intimate connection between the essential defining qualities of a character and the inner mental state of the actor portraying the character. I mentioned earlier the injunction that an actor nullify his own personality and identify totally with the role he is playing. Zeami returns to this again and again: "For any part involving Role Playing [*monomane*] an actor must learn to truly 'become' the object of his performance."[31] Indeed, there comes a level of identification with the role beyond which imitation ceases altogether: "When every technique of Role Playing is mastered and the actor has truly become the subject of his impersonation, then the reason for the desire to imitate can no longer exist."[32] This he elsewhere calls "Internalization."[33] It is also the "artless art," the loss of self-consciousness, the loss even of personality, which is required at the highest levels of *hana*.[34]

How literally are we to take this identification? In portraying a madman, must the actor become mad, or in portraying a demon, become a demon, and so on? Clearly not. In fact, at times Zeami seems directly to contradict his often-stated injunction. Thus, "when an actor plans to express the emotion of anger, he must not fail to retain a tender heart."[35] Perhaps the best explanation is to appeal again to the mystical, Zen Buddhist element in Zeami's teaching whereby the identification of actor and character should be perceived not on a literal or psychological level but only on the level where a distinctive mood is conveyed in the actor's bearing.

In discussing what he calls the Three Basic Roles—an old man, a woman, and a warrior (these are roles that every Noh actor must perfect before hoping to master the substantial parts)—Zeami distills the requisite inner state into Zen-like aphorisms: for example, an old man becomes "Relaxed Heart Looking Afar," a woman becomes "Concentration of Mind and Relinquishing of Strength," and a warrior becomes "Physical Strength, Splintered Heart."[36] These slight, suggestive images are meant to conjure a mood fitting to each portrayal. By adopting the appropriate state of mind, the actor will project that mood through his smallest gestures.

31. Zeami, *Art of the Nō Drama*, p. 77.
32. Ibid., p. 55.
33. Ibid., p. 143.
34. See Michiko Yusa, "*Riken no Ken*: Zeami's Theory of Acting and Theatrical Appreciation," *Monumenta Nipponica* 42 (1987): 337.
35. Zeami, *Art of the Nō Drama*, p. 58.
36. Ibid., p. 141.

VI

Most of the features that make up the conception of character in Noh—the abstractness, the emphasis on emotion and mood and inner spirit—are epitomized in the final ingredient, that of suggestiveness. The suggestion of character in performance acquires a much greater importance than does overt representation.

The preference for what is hidden and suggested rather than what is manifest and explicit runs deep in Japanese aesthetics. In medieval Japan, particularly the fifteenth and sixteenth centuries, the curious union of aestheticism and Zen mysticism brought to their fullest expression a number of unique art forms—flower arrangement, the tea ceremony, haiku poetry, *sumi-e* (ink painting), and the rock gardens of Zen monasteries—all of which rested crucially on the aesthetics of suggestion. Noh too belongs in this category. The underlying attitude is well indicated by, for example, the Zen monk and poet Shinkei (1406–75), who advised giving attention to "inconspicuous objects such as white, single-petalled plum blossoms blooming among bamboos, or the moon revealed through the gaps in the clouds."[37] The twentieth-century Japanese novelist Tanizaki in his classic essay "In Praise of Shadows" (1933), reveres this same aesthetic principle: "Such is our way of thinking—we find beauty not in the thing itself but in the patterns of shadows, the light and the darkness, that one thing against another creates."[38]

This veneration of the suggestive, the evocative, and the simple is a key element in the aesthetics of Noh.[39] It can explain the stylization of the acting, the austerity of the drama, and the spareness of the characterization. The much praised moments of "nonaction" in Noh are comparable to the empty spaces in a *sumi-e* line drawing. The aesthetics of suggestion combined with the principle of *monomane* (the imitation of essence) leads to the paring down of gesture and movement into highly symbolic forms. Keene provides another example: "When the blind Yoroboshi appears on the stage the angle of his head at a certain moment (certainly not any gesture of sniffing) exactly suggests that he has caught the scent

37. Quoted in Tsubaki, "Concept of Yugen," p. 60.

38. Jun'ichiro Tanizaki, *In Praise of Shadows*, trans. Thomas J. Harper and Edward G. Seidensticker (New Haven, Conn., 1977), p. 30.

39. The point is emphasized in Hung-ting Ku, "The Influence of Zen on Noh Plays in Japan," Occasional Paper Series, no. 38, Institute of Humanities and Social Sciences, College of Graduate Studies, Nanyang University, 1976.

of plum blossoms, telling him as he wanders in the dark of his blindness that he has reached his destination, the Tennoji Temple."[40]

Many formal dance movements have symbolic meanings: a single sweep of a fan with the left hand indicates shooting an arrow; if repeated twice it denotes fluttering wings or the wind.[41] A slight lowering of the mask casts a shadow and is suggestive of grief; a raising of the mask, which lightens it, expresses happiness.[42] The stage props, when there are such, are also symbolic and simple: a boat is a bare frame, a well the outlines of a cube.[43] The texts of Noh plays themselves employ numerous literary devices of suggestiveness: word-plays; detailed allusions to Japanese and Chinese classical poetry, as well as to religious works and the famous "tales" (*monogatari*); and, above all, a refined use of imagery for evoking place and feeling.[44]

What is the effect of this suggestiveness in Noh? One external effect, of course, actively encouraged in the Tokugawa shogunate, is to make Noh highly esoteric.[45] The density of symbolism and allusion promotes a special "cultivation of intimacy" among the cognoscenti, serving no doubt social and cultural, as well as aesthetic, ends.[46] The primary dramatic intention, though, is to make possible the evocation of those specific but subtly changing moods that are deemed the best, perhaps the only, route to the inner state portrayed.

All characterization by its very nature involves an imaginative "filling in." On the basis of what is presented—in play, novel, or poem—the observer constructs an imaginative reality. In the Western tradition, this undertaking is often as much intellectual or cognitive as purely imaginative. We think, as well as feel, our way into the characterization. Such characters as Raskolnikov, say, or Dorothea Brooke are presented with a sufficient complexity of moral and psychological detail as to permit reasoned reflection on such matters as motivation and psychological attitude.

40. Keene, *Nō*, p. 25.
41. Taylor, *Drama of W. B. Yeats*, p. 216.
42. Keene, *Nō*, p. 62.
43. Hung-ting Ku, "Influence of Zen," p. 4.
44. Keene, *Nō*, pp. 46–56.
45. The remote, ritualistic style of Noh in fact developed after Zeami's time. Under the Tokugawa shogunate, Noh acquired the status of a court ceremonial from which the public were excluded. Zeami himself put the highest emphasis on entertaining a general audience. See Jacob Raz, "The Actor and His Audience: Zeami's Views on the Audience of the Noh," *Monumenta Nipponica* 21 (1976): 251–274.
46. I borrow the phrase, with a similar application, from Ted Cohen, "Metaphor and the Cultivation of Intimacy," in *On Metaphor*, ed. Sheldon Sacks (Chicago, 1978).

In the case of Noh, the imaginative "filling in" invited of an observer is of a quite different kind. In place of physical, moral, and psychological detail, we are offered only a suggestive mood heightened by the full visual and auditory spectacle. The concentration of focus in a performance on the abstracted inner spirit of a character, centered on one poignant incident (itself often recollected from a ghostly distance), encourages not a cognitive but an affective response. The *shite*'s use of mask and stylized gesture keeps the audience from being distracted by a realistic surface and guides the imagination away from mere factual reconstruction. The personality of actor and character must be invisible. In this way, human interest and attention are channeled directly into the emotional core that is the play's meaning.

VII

I started with the question, How is the portrayal of character in Noh possible? My answer has been to develop the underlying conception of character and to defend its coherence within a framework of aesthetic principles. Let me end with a few brief remarks about the ramifications of this conception in the wider context of aesthetics and philosophy.

First, there is much of interest here for the theory of fiction. The very idea that fictional characters can exhibit *dissolution* of personality seems paradoxical in the light of the conventional (Western) view that literary characterization must involve the imaginative *construction* of personality. But the conception in Noh cannot be simply dismissed as impoverished characterization or "character without detail." What I have stressed throughout is the different kind of detail—and specificity—in Noh characters. The symbolization of emotion and the refinement of mood in performance yield an individuality of character quite as rich, in its own way, as in character studies that draw on more intellectual resources.

Another important lesson from Noh is that fictional characters, to retain our interest, need not always be manifest and realistic representations of human beings. We are reminded of the original etymological basis of "character" meaning abstracted quality. A human predicament can be imaginatively conveyed in dramatic form without merely, in the Aristotelian sense, *imitating* that predicament.

Philosophical interest exists, too, beyond aesthetics. The concept dissolution of personality, as expounded, invites reflection within the philosophy of mind, particularly on personal identity and the nature of emotion.

There is a broad consensus—though probably not unanimity—in the Western philosophical tradition that (1) in addition to the flux of experience, there are subjects of experience—persons, selves, souls—that persist through time (I can speak of being the same person today as I was yesterday), and (2) a necessary condition for personal identity across time is some kind of coherence or connectedness in a person's life. Broadly speaking, Western philosophers have employed what might be called a "biographer's conception" of a person, requiring for identity that some coherent story can be told linking episodes in a person's life.[47] Debate has centered not on the need for coherence but on the form it should take (physical continuity, memory, mental connectedness, and so on). The biographer's conception constrains not only the abstract conditions for personal identity but also our idea of what it is to know or understand a person. We feel that understanding is limited if we have access only to discrete fragments of a person's history, however well-described the fragments might be. We have the biographer's urge to make connections, to find some informing principle ("character" or "personality") that unites the fragments into a coherent whole.

In contrast to both aspects of this Western perspective stands a widely held view in Buddhism, the *Anatta* doctrine, which rejects any enduring "self" over and above the flow of consciousness, and, more radical, a view in Zen Buddhism which seems even to reject the condition of coherence.[48] The aim of Zen is to attain a state of awareness, Satori (or Enlightenment), where the need for connectedness in life is perceived as superfluous[49] and the most fundamental distinctions relating to personality—self and other, subject and object, inner and outer—are abandoned.[50]

Inevitably, Noh drama shows more affinity to Buddhist doctrine than to Western philosophy of mind. Noh is disconcerting from the Western philosophical perspective precisely because it appears to reject the biographer's conception of a person; it deliberately isolates fragments of a life, it expunges biographical detail, and it seeks individuality in the presentation of character without the coherence of personality. We are prompted to reflect on a radically different, though by no means unin-

47. Individual identity is sometimes seen explicitly in terms of narrative. For example, see David Novitz, *Knowledge, Fiction, and Imagination* (Philadelphia, 1987), pp. 227–231.

48. See, for example, Christmas Humphreys, *Buddhism* (Harmondsworth, England, 1967), pp. 20–21.

49. See D. T. Suzuki, *Essays in Zen Buddhism*, 2d ser. (London, 1970), p. 36.

50. See Toshihiko Izutsu, *Toward a Philosophy of Zen Buddhism* (Tehran: Imperial Iranian Academy of Philosophy, 1977), essay 1.

telligible, conception of individual identity that rests not, as it were, on "horizontal" connectedness across time but on "vertical" intensity at a time. Although there are temporal connections in the narrative structure of many Noh plays, with earlier and later stages of a life drawn together through recollection, just as often time itself is fragmented and the sense of coherence is threatened by the juxtaposition of dreams, distant memories, and ghostly apparitions. The invocation of the past serves not so much to explain the present as to heighten its dramatic intensity. The striking suggestion seems to be that personal identity is encapsulated in some vivid and momentary fragment of a life.

When we turn to the nature of emotion, we find a further challenge to assumptions of connectedness and causation. In Noh the dramatic aim is to present emotion, as far as possible, in a pure, abstracted form: abstracted both from the personality of its subject (character or actor) and also from its conventional behavioral manifestations (that is, it is not portrayed realistically). From the point of view of standard theories in philosophy and psychology, this should make identification of the emotion (by an audience) difficult if not impossible.

In philosophical orthodoxy, an emotion is not just an isolated solipsistic state; rather, the identity of an emotion is determined partly by the logical and causal relations in which it stands both to other mental states and to nonmental events.[51] To identify an emotion is to locate it within such a context; identification is closely tied to explanation. The Western literary tradition commonly exploits these familiar assumptions by taking care to delineate the circumstances in which emotions and their consequences arise.

Here, then, is another contrast with Noh. Although the performance of Noh affords some outer manifestation of emotion and also some causal connectedness, recognition of emotion, as we have seen earlier, relies far less on the assessment of external circumstance than on the evocation of a mood through dramatic spectacle. The aim is to offer, or attempt to offer, direct access to the inner phenomenology of an emotion by somehow embodying it in the actor's performance. The portrayal of emotion can be made compatible with the dissolution of personality only if its symbolization is "pure" in this sense.

Many philosophical problems confront the idea of an abstracted or "pure" emotion. Is what is left, when personality is removed, genuinely

51. For an account that ascribes to emotion a very strong relation with other psychological and social facts, see Ronald de Sousa, *The Rationality of Emotion* (Boston, 1987).

an emotion? Is it possible to represent the specificity of any experience without a corresponding specificity in the context surrounding that experience? In trying to understand Noh, however, we would be wrong to become too distracted by these philosophical questions. In the end, judgment must rest with dramatic effectiveness. It is not the purpose of Noh to offer an intellectual challenge to philosophical theses or to advance any itself. The dissolution of personality is a dramatic, not a philosophical, aim. By expounding this conception I have hoped, at least, to counter the negative opinion about Noh, which might be based on misguided philosophical or aesthetic speculation, that only limited human interest can arise in so austere a theatrical form.[52]

52. My interest in Noh was kindled by the performances of the Ryokusenkai, Kanze Noh Troupe, in Tokyo in 1983–84, when I was a visiting professor at the University of Tsukuba. I am particularly grateful to Dr. Nicholas Teele, Doshisha Women's College in Kyoto, for introducing me to the troupe and for detailed comments on an earlier draft of this chapter. I am also grateful to Dr. Akiko Tsukamoto, University of Tokyo, for many stimulating discussions on Japanese aesthetics; to Dr. Etsuko Terasaki, Ithaca, New York, for her helpful advice on Noh and her recommendations for readings; and to Keiji Hoshikawa for help with translations.

6

Truth and Art

Art is informative and entertaining, it condenses and clarifies the world, directing attention upon particular things. . . . Art illuminates accident and contingency and the general muddle of life, the limitations of time and the discursive intellect, so as to enable us to survey complex or horrible things which would otherwise appal us. . . . Its condensed, clarified presentation enables us to look without sin upon a sinful world.

—Iris Murdoch, *Metaphysics as a Guide to Morals*

The most important thing in acting is honesty; once you learn to fake that, you're in.

—Sam Goldwyn

The issue of how literature relates to truth is ancient and complex. That truth has *something* to do with literature is neither surprising nor controversial; where there are propositions and meanings, the possibility of truth-valuation is never far behind. But just how literature intersects with truth, what relevance truth has to literary value, whether literature is essentially to be conceived as a vehicle for truth, even what "truth" might mean when applied to works of fiction: these questions go to the very heart of literary studies. Rather than address these questions directly, I will examine the views of one specific author, Iris Murdoch, who in her roles as novelist and philosopher has made a singular and influential contribution to the debate and who locates her discussion firmly in the philosophical humanistic tradition. Of particular interest is the way she seemingly harmonizes the two opposing classical schools, deploying her essentially Platonist instincts in defending a position more recognizably Aristotelian.

My detailed case study will be her novel *The Black Prince* (1973), which raises the key issues in a striking novelistic form. At the end, though, I will look beyond this novel to other (including philosophical) writings of Iris Murdoch and ask just what concept of truth she is working with in her passionate, if at times equivocal, defense of the truth-telling capacities of art.

Truth and Art

I

"Art," writes Bradley Pearson, protagonist and narrator in *The Black Prince*, "is concerned not just primarily but absolutely with truth."[1] Bradley Pearson is also concerned with truth. And understandably so, as he has just taken the rap and been imprisoned for a murder he claims he never committed. We have here two rather different concerns with truth: the high-minded concern of the artist, and the more pragmatic concern of the despised and falsely convicted man writing his "apologia." The careful juxtaposition of these two appeals to truth is a central theme in *The Black Prince.*

The bulk of the novel purports to be a first-person narration of events in the later life of Bradley Pearson. Bradley is a writer who has been waiting patiently and silently for the inspiration, "the dark blaze," to produce a great work of art. This "dark blaze" eventually shows itself as the "black Eros," in a passionate but short-lived love affair with the young Julian Baffin. Bradley is reflecting on these events from his prison cell, guided by his mentor and fellow prisoner, the "editor" P. Loxias (a witty reference to Apollo, god of truth). He sees his art and his love as stemming "from the same source" (p. 172), and although sensitive to his shortcomings as an artist, he believes that through divine inspiration he has attained a kind of Platonic tranquility in the presence of truth and self-knowledge. But through the device of "postscripts," purportedly written by other characters, we are presented with another picture of him rather different from his own. His former friends, more down to earth, though variously self-interested, depict him as a pitiful, even contemptible, charlatan lost in fantasy and delusion and a suitable case for psychoanalysis. What, then, is the real Bradley Pearson? Is he the pathetic, fantasy-ridden creature of the "postscripts"? Or is he, as he thinks, the great artist inspired by the gods and by Eros who has seen the revelation of truth?

By forcing us to raise these questions about the novel, Iris Murdoch, I suggest, is inviting us to reflect on and to relate two concerns we might have with truth in works of fiction. The first is with truth internal to the novel, truth-within-fiction, which informs us about the fictional characters and events. In *The Black Prince*, our attention is focused on unraveling and assessing the "truth" of Bradley's account. The second is with truth proper, as it might be revealed *through* fiction. This truth is not

---

1. Iris Murdoch, *The Black Prince* (London, 1973), p. 40 (hereafter cited as *BP*, with page references in parentheses in the text).

about the fictional world but about the nonfictional real world. It is often maintained that novels can instruct us in acquiring knowledge of the world. This, I suggest, is the type of truth that Bradley, so grandly and solemnly—and frequently—identifies with art. The nature of such truth is the main topic of this chapter.

II

What sense can we make of Bradley's repeated claims to the effect that "good art speaks truth" (p. xi)? One answer, reflecting an obvious feature of literary works, is that propositions about the world are often expressed, explicitly, within a fictional context; they might be uttered by one of the characters or in passing commentary by the author. *The Black Prince* offers many such propositions, some of which, on the nature of art, I shall be considering in detail. Examples are plentiful. Thus, Bradley remarks on marriage: "People who boast of happy marriages are, I submit, usually self-deceivers, if not actually liars. The human soul is not framed for continued proximity" (p. 64). He meditates on love, "The foreverness of real love is one of the reasons why even unrequited love is a source of joy" (pp. 173–174), and discusses jealousy (p. 207). He also reflects on human consciousness and responsibility (p. 155) and on selfishness and goodness: "The burden of genuine goodness is instinctively appreciated as intolerable, and a desire for it would put out of focus the other and ordinary wishes by which one lives" (p. 149).

Such explicit propositions seem to carry us beyond the confines of the fictional world and invite our consideration as reflections on our own world. But is any special significance attached to them by virtue of their appearance in a work of fiction? Does it matter if we, the readers, *believe* them or not? Or are they to be taken only as thematic guides or clues to understanding the characters? Clearly an author's own commitment to their truth will vary from case to case. A reader is not always—or automatically—invited to accept them as true, so much as to entertain them or reflect on them. But even where an author is offering them as truths (to be believed), does the fictional context afford opportunities for truth telling that nonfictional contexts might not? It does seem that fiction is able to provide a peculiar and possibly unique context. As Bradley suggests, "Art . . . is the only available method for the telling of certain truths" (p. 55), and "the artist is learning a special language in which to reveal truth" (p. 40). For it might even be that precisely what is expressed can be conveyed and understood only in some particular fictional context. How is this so?

At least two ways exist of accounting for the special significance that fiction has as a vehicle for nonfictional assertion. The first involves irony. As Bradley himself says, "We may attempt to attain truth through irony. Irony is a form of 'tact' " (p. 55). Being tactful, like being ironic, is a matter of dressing up what is said, of conveying a thought indirectly or by implication, not bluntly and explicitly. In general, ironic utterance forces a gap between the standard meaning of the words used and the particular sense and purpose of their use in context. In a work of fiction, we cannot always identify what is meant by some worldly observation without concern for the precise context in which it occurs, the character who utters it, and the circumstances surrounding the utterance. And in this contextualization can lie the uniqueness of fiction as a mode of expression. At its simplest, the author can manipulate the meaning of what is said by selecting a specific speaker to say it. Only fiction affords this possibility.

Consider, as an example, Bradley's remark that "the foreverness of real love is one of the reasons why even unrequited love is a source of joy" (pp. 173–174). It would be absurdly simplistic to take this as a bald assertion about love by Iris Murdoch, even though it comes ultimately from her pen. In giving the remark to Bradley, who we later discover has suffered badly from the lack of "foreverness" in love but who nonetheless claims that love has been a source of inspiration, even of joy, Iris Murdoch has invested it with a rich ironic force. Against the whole background of the novel, which explores the relation between "real love," as a form of perception, and the failings and transience of an ordinary "love affair," this otherwise unremarkable and unconvincing generalization acquires a new interest and significance. This is the working of irony.

There is a second way in which fiction can provide a special and perhaps unique context for its explicit propositions seemingly about the world at large. This arises from the peculiar means afforded to fiction of supporting the general observations it proposes. Although it is not uncommon to find argument, reasoning, and evidence used in fiction to support general propositions, this logical or scientific method is not an essential or even important characteristic of fiction. Fiction is unique in being able to provide not only argument but a special kind of *illustrative support* for the generalizations it contains. These in themselves might even be trite or jejune, as are many of Bradley's: life is horrible, the world is a place of suffering, and so on. But their carefully placed appearance in a novel can give them new authority, added conviction. By acquiring in the first instance the status of thematic statements, fleshing out characterization, and binding together elements in the work, they allow for more considered reflection on the underlying rationale behind such pronouncements. Thus, reading the novel might provide further reasons for accepting them as true, under their new nuanced interpretation. Perhaps the views come to seem so completely justified in the context of events in the novel that the reader's imaginative involvement in these events makes the justification seem even more irresistible. Or perhaps by noting parallels between their own lives and those of the fictional characters readers come to see added force in the pronouncements by those characters. Of course, it was just such manipulation of beliefs by the poets that appalled Plato, but it does seem beyond doubt that readers' attitudes can be affected in this way.

A good example of the way a novel can provide illustrative support for such explicit propositions is the relation in *The Black Prince* between the substance of the novel, particularly the complex character of Bradley, and the views it implies on truth and art. This takes us into altogether more difficult and controversial issues concerning the cognitive status of fiction, to which I now turn.

III

The main idea I want to consider is the possibility of a writer's conveying truth through fiction other than directly through explicit statement. For when Bradley says that "good art speaks truth, indeed is truth," it seems clear that something rather more complex than explicit propositional content is meant. What emerges is the suggestion that art is able to *show* as well as to *state*, that not all we learn from a literary work is explicitly stated in it, or indeed could be so stated.

It is a compelling feature of the complexly ironic and self-reflective structure of *The Black Prince* that through the use of explicit comment, irony, and illustration, a clear and finely worked thesis emerges about the very possibility and limits of using art to express any thesis at all, either explicitly or implicitly. Many of the claims about truth and art which I shall be discussing are asserted by characters in the novel. I will attempt to be sensitive to their ironic force, though in a novel such as *The Black Prince*, it is never absolutely clear which claims to take at face value. For this reason, where necessary, I shall seek support for my reading of the novel from views expressed elsewhere by Iris Murdoch.

Iris Murdoch has claimed that an artist, through the medium of fiction, is able to provide a *view* of the world. She lays much stress on the visual metaphor; the artist offers us a *vision* or *picture* of the world and invites us to *see* the world in new ways. In *The Sovereignty of Good*, she says that the "study of literature . . . is an education in how to picture and understand human situations."[2] And in other passages in that book, the same idea is emphasized: "What we learn from contemplating the characters of Shakespeare or Tolstoy or the paintings of Velasquez or Titian . . . is something about the real quality of human nature, when it is envisaged, in the artist's just and compassionate vision, with a clarity which does not belong to the self-centred rush of ordinary life. . . . The greatest art . . . shows us the world . . . with a clarity which startles and delights us simply because we are not used to looking at the real world at all" (*SG*, p. 65). Furthermore, the artist's "just and compassionate vision" is precisely analogous to, if not identical with, the "just and loving gaze" of the "active moral agent" (*SG*, p. 34).[3] "A great artist," she writes, "is, in respect of his work, a good man" (p. 64). And, "Virtue is *au fond* the same in the artist as in the good man in that it is a selfless attention to nature" (p. 41).[4] On this, Bradley speaks for Iris Murdoch when he says, "I have always felt that art is an aspect of the good life" (*BP*, p. 152). One way, then, in which art "speaks truth" might be by giving us a picture of the world as it appears in the vision of the "good man." How is this possible?

In *The Black Prince* two criteria seem to be implied and illustrated whereby the artist can attain truth, through nonexplicit means, by revealing a "just and compassionate vision" of the world. What the novel also illustrates, in the character of Bradley, is how difficult it is to reach such a vision. The criteria are *objectivity* and *particularity*. The artist should attempt a *selfless* and *particular* vision of the world. In good art, these are brought together, "fused," by imagination, for "without imagination you have stupid details on one side and empty dreams on the other" (p. 26). I shall examine each in turn.

2. Iris Murdoch, *The Sovereignty of Good* (London, 1970), p. 34 (hereafter cited as *SG*).

3. Iris Murdoch has argued elsewhere for the importance of vision in morality, for example, in "Vision and Choice in Morality," *Proceedings of the Aristotelian Society* 30, suppl. vol., *Dreams and Self-Knowledge* (1956).

4. The identification of art with morality, which I shall not directly discuss in this chapter, is suggested elsewhere in her writings, for example, in "The Sublime and the Good," *Chicago Review* 13 (1959).

IV

Bradley's early advice to Julian is, "If you write, write from the heart, yet carefully, objectively" (p. 40). The problem of achieving objectivity, or selflessness, is one on which Bradley often reflects. He has two worries that gain particular significance in the circumstances of his writing: What sort of picture has he presented of himself, and has he given a fair and just account of the others? "How can one describe a human being 'justly'? How can one describe oneself?" (p. 55).

In his metaphysical moments, he feels that a just and true description of a human being is impossible, save for some "ineffable understanding"; indeed, "almost all speech," he writes cryptically, "which is not so illumined is a deformation of the truth" (p. 337). This fear of deforming the truth underlies his creed of silence for the artist: "Art has its martyrs, not least those who have preserved their silence. There are, I hazard, saints of art who have simply waited mutely all their lives rather than profane the purity of a single page with anything less than . . . what is true" (p. xii).

His more immediate concern, though, is with the impression his readers have acquired of him. He is aware of the different images he projects. Thus, he twice speculates that his readers will dismiss him as merely sexually frustrated (pp. 113, 173). Of his "Foreword," he says, "how meagrely it conveys" him (p. xviii), and he admits in his "postscript" that he was "heartily hated" (p. 334) during his court case and that "the court saw [him] as a callous fantasy-ridden man" (p. 335). Perhaps in the context of *The Black Prince* we should see this concern of Bradley's primarily as an ironic confirmation of the egoism and *lack* of selflessness that we are clearly invited to attribute to him. But his views about the intrusion of self and the striving for objectivity take us farther than that. The device of first-person narration in the novel highlights the problem of acquiring an objective point of view, particularly of oneself. In the end it comes down to a problem of self-knowledge: "There is . . . an eternal discrepancy between the self-knowledge which we gain by observing ourselves objectively and the self-awareness which we have of ourselves subjectively: a discrepancy which probably makes it impossible for us ever to arrive at the truth. Our self-knowledge is too abstract, our self-awareness is too intimate and swoony and dazed" (p. 155). Here we have an explicit generalization that is carefully illustrated in the substance of the novel. It brings into focus a prominent theme; we come to *see* in the character of Bradley just what the discrepancy is of which he speaks.

Truth and Art

What emerges of especial interest from Iris Murdoch's complex use of point of view in the novel is an interplay between our two types of truth in fiction. On the one side, we find ourselves closely involved in trying to reach a fair assessment of Bradley and the other characters. That is, we try to construct some sort of "truth" about the fictional characters from the shifting and distorted points of view we are given. Our concern for fairness reflects and parallels Bradley's own concern. On the other side, we find that this exercise in perception and understanding takes us beyond the confines of the fictional world. The mark of a good novel, on Murdoch's view, is that it shows us how to *see*—and thus understand—other human beings. The good novelist, with the use of fictional invention and literary form, can instruct us by guiding and clarifying our perceptions and judgments. As a result, we might come to view the real world, and people in it, in a different way, perhaps more fairly and justly.

Certainly *The Black Prince*, with its devices of "editor," "forewords," and "postscripts" and its first-person narration, makes us acutely aware of point of view. By way of prompting us even further to raise questions of objectivity, Bradley's account is filled with warnings of his own shortcomings: "How prejudiced is this image of Arnold, how superficial this picture of Priscilla! . . . When I write of Arnold my pen shakes with resentment, love, remorse, and fear. . . . When I think of my sister I feel pity, annoyance, guilt, disgust and it is in the 'light' of these that I present her, crippled and diminished by my perception itself" (p. 56). He offers detailed descriptions of both Arnold (pp. 8–10, 151–153) and Priscilla (pp. 43–46, 153–154), the two who die during the events of the narration and are thus unable to speak for themselves in the "postscripts." But the descriptions, particularly of Arnold, cause him concern: "I am anxious . . . about the clarity and justice of my presentation of Arnold" (p. 8). One curious effect of these disclaimers is that they tend to increase, rather than diminish, our confidence in Bradley as a speaker of the truth. We give him credit for at least being aware of the difficulties. His self-conscious efforts to attain an objective vision give to his point of view an authority lacking in that of the "postscript" writers precisely because the latter are so unashamedly self-centered and self-justifying.

Furthermore, Bradley's consciousness of the dangers of prejudice and self-centeredness serves to emphasize what a complex process it is for a reader to acquire knowledge of fictional characters. A novel like *The Black Prince* reminds us that what we are entitled to take as true within fiction is not automatically coextensive with the explicit descriptive content of the sentences in the fiction. This explicit sentential content, as I have suggested in Chapter 4, might best be thought of as the *data* that, if scientific language is appropriate here, provide something like the *evidence* from which we form *hypotheses* about the characters. The accumulation and assessment of this evidence and the drawing of conclusions from it call for an effort of both investigation and imagination. It will involve, for example, identifying points of view, unraveling ironies, and filtering the narration through what we know of the narrator. We require and use for this process a great deal of our knowledge of the nonfictional world as an assumed background for drawing what inferences we may about the fictional characters.

What precisely are the dangers that Bradley faces in his striving for objectivity? Iris Murdoch often contrasts objectivity in art and morality with fantasy. Fantasy, she has written, is the "proliferation of blinding self-centred aims and images" (*SG*, p. 67), and, "We can see in mediocre art, where perhaps it is even more clearly seen than in mediocre conduct, the intrusion of fantasy, the assertion of self" (*SG*, p. 59). Indeed, she believes the escape into fantasy is deeply rooted in our perception of the world: "We are . . . benighted creatures sunk in a reality whose nature we are constantly and overwhelmingly tempted to deform by fantasy."[5] Bradley seems to be just such a benighted creature. To what extent is his quest for objectivity hampered by fantasy?

The court, we remember, thought of Bradley as "fantasy-ridden" (*BP*, p. 335), and the burden of Rachel's "postscript" is to condemn his account as a "mad adolescent dream": "Perhaps the kindest thing to say is that he wanted to write a novel but found himself incapable of producing anything except his own immediate fantasies" (p. 351). In the circumstances, such judgments are hardly reliable, but there seems little doubt that we are invited to see the "intrusion of fantasy" into Bradley's story. He admits to being prone to fantasy. In his "Foreword," talking of earlier love affairs, he writes, "The majority of my conquests belonged to the world of fantasy" (p. xv).

Perhaps the surest indication of fantasy, of "blinding self-centred aims and images," is the emphasis on the "grip of destiny" (p. 113) which Bradley sees as impelling him toward "great art" and "intense love" (p. 155). This is where his histrionic nature is most in evidence. He admits that he "nourished . . . the notion that before [he] could achieve greatness as a writer [he] would have to pass through some *ordeal*" (p. xvii). His self-confidence is at times self-indulgent: "I had within me at last a

5. Iris Murdoch, "Against Dryness," *Encounter* 16 (1961): 20.

great book. There was a fearful urgency about it. I needed darkness, purity, solitude" (p. 97). Shortly before his Shakespearean discussion with Julian, he feels "an increasingly powerful sense of the imminence . . . of a great work of art" (p. 155), with "the hand of destiny heavy upon" him (p. 158).

It is not so much the "grip of destiny" that holds him but the grip of a self-image, of fantasy: perhaps the two are not ultimately distinct. In a telling passage, he admits to himself that "a 'feeling of destiny' can lead . . . into the most idiotic of servitudes. A dramatic sense of oneself is probably something one ought never to have and which saints are entirely without" (p. 114). Inevitably, in the circumstances, Bradley possesses just such a "dramatic sense" of himself, and it is a nice irony of the novel that this fact alone is sufficient, on his own criterion, to prevent his work (though not, of course, Iris Murdoch's) from being a great work of art. At one point he even condemns the "thought of anything so vulgar as writing 'about' Julian" (p. 176), and by way of final irony, he asserts that "life and art must be kept strictly separate if one is aiming at excellence" (p. 176).

If the artist and the "good man" must strive for objectivity or selflessness, their surest way, according to Iris Murdoch, is through love. For her, "It is in the capacity to love, that is to *see*, that the liberation of the soul from fantasy consists" (*SG*, p. 66), and "Love, and so art and morals, is the discovery of reality" ("The Sublime and the Good," p. 51). Echoing this, Bradley says, "Love brings with it also a vision of selflessness" (p. 174). There are powerful descriptions and evocations of love in *The Black Prince* (for example, on pp. 169–171 and 204–205). For Bradley, love of Julian brings about a "transformation of the world" (p. 171): he looked younger (p. 178), he became open and friendly with other people, and, most important, he felt a "release from self" (p. 174). Only then, he claims, did he come to *see* Julian (his earlier failure to *see* her is emphasized quite literally, on their first encounter in the novel, when he thinks she is a man [p. 30]). "Now," he says, "I could see. Can any lover doubt that now he sees truly? And is the possessor of this enlivened vision not really more like God than like a madman?" (p. 171). He dismisses as "false" the view that "love is blind" (p. 171).

Soon, though, after the initial intensity of his love, when he was "simply a saint" (p. 204), practical realities reassert themselves: physical desire (p. 206) and jealousy (p. 207) become manifest, "self was reviving" (p. 205). He talks of the "false loss of self" involved in the "early phase of this madness" (p. 204). With this revival of self and self-consciousness and a sense of the impossibility of the situation, a harshness comes over Bradley, which shows itself in a brutal confrontation with Julian outside the opera (pp. 221–230). When Julian tries to talk about Bradley's love, he rebuts her: "I endlessly *imagined* talking to you about it, but that just belonged to the fantasy world. I can't talk love to you in the real world. The real world rejects it" (p. 222). Finally, at the violent consummation of their love, as it exists in the real world, "the black Eros" (p. 283) takes over. The "dark" and hidden powers of the ego, so familiar in Iris Murdoch's novels, had won the day. Bradley had failed in love just as he had failed in art—and for the same reasons.

The Black Prince proposes objectivity as the first and crucial condition for truth in art and, indeed, for moral goodness. Bradley's account expresses and illustrates the difficulties of attaining the required objective vision. What is never clear, though, is how this objective vision could be attained or how is it recognizable. The negative marks manifested in Bradley are reasonably clear, namely, self-centeredness and fantasy, but the positive features are not so easy to identify. Love, which is offered as one such feature, is idealized, possessed only by saints and mystics. What we are shown in Bradley are the failures of ordinary mortals, "benighted creatures," to attain such love. Iris Murdoch's view of morality and art as transcendent makes this recognition all the more difficult, for by its very nature, the objective vision of the artist and the good man eludes both the analysis of concepts and empirical test. A mystic element in it sometimes suggests that only by *experiencing* the vision can we come to know it. This strain is present in *The Black Prince*, in the thought that "all great truths are mysteries, all morality is ultimately mysticism" (p. 337) and in the hints of "ineffable understanding" and the not wholly ironic endorsement of the merits of silence in art. The trouble is, at a more prosaic level, if recognition of objective vision and therefore truth in art becomes too elusive, the criterion must inevitably lose some of its bite in application to particular cases.

V

Nevertheless, the novel does offer a further condition for determining truth in art: good art reveals the *particular*. Here, particularity is not contrasted with universality but rather with generality or theory. The view is, therefore, not necessarily in opposition to the Aristotelian doctrine that art yields universal truth in contrast to the particularity of history. There is no reason why such universal truth should not be attained through attending to the particular in fiction.

The artist's objective vision focuses our attention on the particular with an aim to "contemplate nature with a clear eye" (*SG*, p. 64). But, as Bradley notes, where fantasy and self intrude, "emotions cloud the view, and so far from isolating the particular, draw generality and . . . theory in their train," adding that "we defend ourselves by descriptions and tame the world by generalizing" (p. 56). But just what is under attack here? For how can the writer write without describing, and how can we understand without generalizing? It is "theories" and "explanations" that are mainly at fault. For Iris Murdoch, they are almost invariably too coarse to capture the fine details that appear in the artist's vision. Theories, like fantasies, distort the truth. In Bradley's words, "Men truly manifest themselves in the long patterns of their acts, and not in any nutshell of self-theory" (p. xi).

The opposition between particularity and theory is a familiar theme in the works of Iris Murdoch. Nowhere is it more explicitly handled than in her first novel, *Under the Net*. Annandine, a character representing the thoughtful Hugo Belfounder in the dialogues written by Jake Donaghue, is made to say: "The movement away from theory and generality is the movement towards truth. All theorizing is flight. We must be ruled by the situation itself and this is unutterably particular. Indeed it is something to which we can never get close enough, however hard we may try as it were to crawl under the net."[6] The "net" that gives the book its title is Wittgenstein's metaphor for the "different systems for describing the world" (*Tractatus*, 6.341).

Following the clue from Wittgenstein's *Tractatus*, we might suppose that the metaphysics underlying the shared view of Hugo Belfounder and Bradley is *atomistic*, that is, that the particulars being sought are "atomic facts." But suggestions elsewhere, at least in *The Black Prince*, indicate that the metaphysics is *holistic* rather than atomistic. A central feature of atomism is that each "atomic fact" is logically independent of any other, yet Bradley is at pains to emphasize the close interconnections between even the most slight events in the novel, writing: "The good feel being as a total dense mesh of interconnections. My lightest whim can affect the whole future" (p. 95). For example, the kisses that he exchanges with Rachel partly, he claims, so as not to offend her and through a concern "about cutting a masterly figure," set up a chain of consequences far beyond their

6. Iris Murdoch, *Under the Net* (1954; rpt., Harmondsworth, England, 1974), pp. 80–81.

apparent significance, on which Bradley reflects: "A serious kiss can alter the world and should not be allowed to take place simply because the scene will be disfigured without it. . . . There are no spare unrecorded encapsulated moments in which we can behave 'anyhow' and then expect to resume life where we left off" (p. 95). This seems like a direct rejection of the atomistic and existentialist notion of the "acte gratuit." In a holistic world, each particular takes its place in the "total dense mesh."

What is the nature of the interconnections between these particular events? We have already noted references in the novel to the "hand of destiny." It is suggested that some events are inevitable, necessary, even predestined (pp. 170, 337). Yet it is clear that Murdoch proposes no rigid determinism in the novel. Destiny and "dark" forces are but two of the many factors that help create the "total dense mesh." Bradley is quite conscious of responsibility and guilt, yet he also asserts that "life is full of accidents" (p. 149). Mistakes, accidents, bad decisions, and fate can all set up their own chains of consequences.

The novel provides a good example of the significance that a seemingly random and chance occurrence can acquire. Bradley tried at the time to justify, he admits "absurdly," his most disastrous mistake—his failure to inform Julian of Priscilla's suicide and to return immediately to London—by arguing that it was a "pure accident, a mere contingent by-product of my carelessness, that Francis had known where to find me"; he adds that "if that terrible telephone call had been so little determined, so casually caused, it made it seem that much less real, that much easier to obliterate from history" (p. 278). But, for Iris Murdoch, the "good man" and the artist know better than to make so light of the facts, however accidental and contingent they seem. It should be the artist's aim, in his quest for truth, to give life and significance to such details, to the contingent and the particular. "Contingency is destructive of fantasy and opens the way for imagination" ("Against Dryness," p. 20).

In *The Black Prince*, much of the force of the attack on theory is directed at Freudian psychoanalysis (at least in its popularized form). Francis Marloe, a psychoanalyst, is portrayed as feeble and parasitic but, worst of all, as a theorizer. Referring to Marloe's shallow Freudianism, Bradley writes: "Francis belongs to that sad crew of semi-educated theorizers who prefer any general blunted "symbolic" explanation to the horror of confronting a unique human history. Francis wanted to "explain" me. . . . But any human being is infinitely more complex than this type of explanation. By "infinitely" . . . I mean that there are not only more details, but more kinds of details with more kinds of relations than these diminishers can dream of. You might as well try to "explain" a Michelangelo on a piece of graph paper. Only art explains, and that cannot itself be explained" (pp. xiv–xv). Perhaps the most comic part of the book is Francis's "postscript," which gives a Freudian "analysis" of Bradley and of his "novel." The glib and confident tone of the "postscript" contrasts strikingly with the hesitant, self-conscious account given by Bradley. Yet the simplicity and the detail of the events, muddles, and mistakes that Bradley describes bear an authority that makes the Freudian "explanations" seem hollow and absurd.

VI

What can we make of the two criteria, objectivity and particularity, that the novel proposes for identifying truth in art? One obvious objection arises in relation to particularity. The particulars presented in a novel are *fictional*, and how can any view, however objective, of *fictional* particulars give us truth? Ex hypothesi, it is not a view of the real world. I think Iris Murdoch might reply that good art gives us truth precisely in as much as it instructs us in how to view the world; it shows us what it is like to see things with a "just and compassionate vision." Whether the particulars seen are factual or fictional is, in this context, of subsidiary importance to the seeing itself. The artist invites us to see a set of events from a point of view (or perhaps more than one). She shows us in detail how characters, often recognizably like humans we know, confront problems, create and resolve muddles, fall in love. And, for the reader, the act of observing these characters and focusing on the smallest details of their lives is an exercise in imaginative *seeing*, which in itself might be as vivid as the seeing of actual human beings. Furthermore, the dangers of which Iris Murdoch warns the artist, namely, fantasizing or theorizing, are dangers for the reader too.

Perhaps the most serious difficulty with this account is going to be with the concept of truth involved. It might seem that what the criteria isolate has more to do with *clarity* or *perceptiveness* as modes of *vision* than with truth. Many critics, though, Iris Murdoch included, are hesitant to abandon the concept of truth in art partly because of its venerable historical ancestry and partly because it emphasizes the cognitive values of art in ways that a concept such as clarity of vision does not. But in subscribing to a truth element in fiction, we must recognize exactly what is meant by that. The emphasis is not on truth as "correspondence with the facts" but on truth as selfless sympathetic seeing. If we think of a proposition (even, in Wittgenstein's terms, the "general form of a proposition") as saying "this is how things are," we might, in the spirit of Iris Murdoch, think of literary works of art as saying "this is how to view things." It is largely a terminological matter whether to call this latter notion "truth."

I have tried to extract from *The Black Prince* a view about how art can "speak truth." But the novel is not just a treatise on truth and art. The criteria that emerge have a direct bearing on our reading of the novel as a whole. For example, as already suggested, they help justify our inclination to take Bradley's word for what happened rather than that of the "postscript" writers. Of course, convention plays a part in this, Bradley's account being the bulk of the novel, but inasmuch as we accept his criteria for truth in art, we will give more weight to his self-consciousness than to their self-centeredness and to his detail rather than their theories and explanations. "The work of art," says the "editor," "laughs last" (p. 362).

The criteria also affect our assessment of Bradley. They help isolate and clarify the nature of his efforts and failures. His relations with Arnold, Priscilla, and particularly Julian become more clear when we see them in terms of a struggle against his own ego. Bradley is in many ways an unattractive figure: his actions are histrionic and violent, but his self-consciousness is disarming and endearing. His insights into the nature of art and goodness and his unsuccessful attempts to attain these make him a sad and almost tragic figure in the end. His life exemplifies for the rest of us how difficult it is to be an artist or attain moral goodness.

VII

The Black Prince invites us to reflect on truth in relation to fiction. The concern with truth is focused on two sets of questions. First, is Bradley telling the truth? What are the characters like? What is he like? Second, what is it for art to give us truth? What is meant by such claims as "Art is concerned not just primarily but absolutely with truth"? Here, I have argued, we have two different, though related, types of truth: truth within fiction and truth about the world. Every fiction concerns us with the first type, which, at its simplest, is just a concern with what happens; many, but not all, fictions concern us with the second, as appropriately construed. What *The Black Prince* suggests, through the character of Bradley and the explicit remarks about truth, is one way in which these two concerns are related, that is, the attention required for us to come to understand fictional characters—their motives, their efforts, their failures—is precisely the attention we would, or should, use in observing people in the world. This exercise in attention and vision, rooted in the imaginative response demanded by art, spans both types of truth in fiction.

I have concentrated in this chapter on the second type of truth in fiction—the suggestion that art can in some special way express truth. Following clues from Iris Murdoch, I have pursued the thought that fiction offers unique opportunities for investing with meaning its explicit generalizations apparently about the world at large and for presenting its (fictional) particulars under a point of view or vision comparable with the "just and compassionate vision" demanded of the moral agent. Through examining many of the explicit generalizations about truth and art in *The Black Prince*, which relate to views expressed elsewhere by Iris Murdoch, I have extracted two criteria for the presence of implied or exhibited truth in works of art: these are objectivity as against fantasy and particularity as against theory. I have also suggested how these criteria might be applied to a reading of *The Black Prince*. Part of the pleasure of the novel is its curious and ingenious self-reflection. Even after all this, I am not yet confident that I have always isolated the voice of Iris Murdoch from that of Bradley Pearson.

APPENDIX

Although *The Black Prince* is arguably Iris Murdoch's clearest novelistic exploration of the idea of artistic truth, the subject comes up repeatedly in her philosophical writings and surfaces in different guises in other novels. A brief glance at this further context, especially in writings subsequent to *The Black Prince*, will reveal the complexity of the concept of "truth" which Iris Murdoch is developing.

Nowhere is the topic given closer philosophical attention than in the essay *The Fire and the Sun: Why Plato Banished the Artists*, published in 1977.[7] What is fascinating and illuminating about this essay is the way that Iris Murdoch seeks to reconcile her undisguised admiration for Plato, even sympathy with his strictures about art, and her own defense of

7. Iris Murdoch, *The Fire and the Sun: Why Plato Banished the Artists* (Oxford, 1977) (hereafter cited as *FS*).

the "truth" of art. Nor does she try to weaken or compromise Plato's hostility to art on the very question of its truthfulness; if anything, she even exaggerates it. Here is one of the summaries she gives of Plato's position:

> Artists obscure the enlightening power of thought and skill by aiming at plausibility rather than truth. Art delights in unsavoury trivia and in the endless proliferation of senseless images. . . . The artist cannot represent or celebrate the good, but only what is daemonic and fantastic and extreme; whereas truth is quiet and sober and confined. Art is sophistry, at best an ironic *mimesis* whose fake "truthfulness" is a subtle enemy of virtue. . . . Art makes us content with appearances, and by playing magically with particular images it steals the educational wonder of the world away from philosophy and confuses our sense of direction toward reality and our motives for discerning it. . . . Form in art is for illusion and hides the true cosmic beauty and the hard real forms of necessity and causality, and blurs with fantasy the thought-provoking paradox. (Pp. 65–66)

Iris Murdoch sympathizes with such an attack to the extent that she thinks Plato's warning represents the perennial danger that art faces and to which it can so easily succumb. Again, the danger is that of falling into fantasy, illusion, or consoling "charm," at the expense of objectivity, reality, and goodness. Where she follows Plato is not in his ultimate rejection of art (which she sees as a kind of self-denial, given his own deeply artistic instincts) but in his austere metaphysical characterization of objectivity, reality, and goodness. She differs from Plato only in believing that art at its best can aspire to just that transcendent reality revealed by Platonist metaphysics: "Good art, thought of as symbolic force rather than statement, provides a stirring image of a pure transcendent value, a steady visible enduring higher good, and perhaps provides for many people . . . their clearest *experience* of something grasped as separate and precious and beneficial and held quietly and unpossessively in the attention" (*FS*, pp. 76–77). The emphasis, as before, is on the metaphor of *vision*: "image," "visible," "experience," "attention." This is the realm of "truth" that art inhabits: "Art is a special discerning exercise of intelligence in relation to the real; and although aesthetic form has essential elements of trickery and magic, yet form in art, as form in philosophy, is designed to communicate and reveal" (*FS*, p. 78). Good art teaches us to *see* in a clear, objective fashion; it teaches a special "discernment" and does so at least partly through its formal qualities, the structures by which its characters and themes are presented and developed. An artist uses form to guide the imagination of an audience; the audience in turn uses awareness of form to constrain the deliverances of imagination. This is precisely how imagination in art differs from fantasy, for in fantasy, form is manipulative, relying on "trickery" and charm. Imagination, properly used, unlike fantasy, can lead to truth: "The good artist helps us to see the place of necessity in human life, what must be endured, what makes and breaks, and to purify our imagination so as to contemplate the real world . . . including what is terrible and absurd" (*FS*, p. 80).

The distinction between "fantasy" and "imagination" acquires even more central importance in her later work *Metaphysics as a Guide to Morals*, where Iris Murdoch devotes a whole chapter to imagination, extolling its virtues and tying it again to a definition of "truth" in art.[8] She describes fantasy and imagination as "two active faculties, one somewhat mechanically generating narrowly banal false pictures (the ego as all-powerful), and the other freely and creatively exploring the world, moving toward the expression and elucidation (and in art celebration) of what is true and deep" (*MGM*, p. 321). Earlier she had spoken of "trapped egoistic *fantasy*, and *imagination* as a faculty of transcendence" (p. 86). In both contexts her concern is with truth:

> "Truth" is something we recognize in good art when we are led to a juster, clearer, more detailed, more refined understanding. Good art "explains" truth itself, by *manifesting* deep conceptual connections. Truth is clarification, justice, compassion. This manifestation of internal relations is an image of metaphysics. (P. 321)

> Truth is not a simple or easy concept. Critical terminology imputes falsehood to an artist by using terms such as fantastic, sentimental, self-indulgent, banal, grotesque, tendentious, unclarified, wilfully obscure and so on. The positive aspect of the avoidance of these faults is a kind of transcendence: the ability to see other non-self things clearly and to criticise and celebrate them freely and justly. (P. 86)

Reflecting on the concept of truth involved in this characterization, we find that the truth (or otherwise) of propositions is not at issue. For Iris Murdoch, it is not propositional content (as in classical logical theories of truth) that is the bearer of truth in the context of art but something like a propositional attitude, a stance, a point of view, a way of looking. Truth has

---

8. Iris Murdoch, *Metaphysics as a Guide to Morals* (Harmondsworth, England, 1993) (hereafter cited as *MGM*).

become a *moral* concept, connected to truthfulness ("justice," "compassion," "freedom"). We recall that the "seeing" exhibited by the artist is precisely that of the moral agent: a seeing that transcends the selfish, the sentimental, the indulgent. It is a seeing informed by the imagination, not by fantasy. Truth is a property not primarily of content (character, incident) but of mode of presentation (albeit these are indissolubly linked). The artist shows truth by showing humanity, sympathy, and generosity in the development of character and theme. This kind of "truth" is far removed from that of the scientist, social scientist, or even philosopher; it is not amenable to proof, verification, or argument. We judge the truth of a work by internal criteria, its moral integrity, its descriptive clarity, its "fairness," the absence of self-indulgence, not by holding it up as a "mirror to reality."

The rejection of fantasy in art brings in the connection with Freud. Iris Murdoch has a similarly ambivalent relation to Freud, as to Plato. Attracted by much of his thought, particularly the idea of Eros, for which Freud himself acknowledges Plato and which played a major role in *The Black Prince*, she rejects his pessimistic suggestion that art is merely another mode of wish-fulfillment and fantasizing. But her own view that "art is about the pilgrimage from appearance to reality" (*FS*, p. 80) clearly echoes a more positive suggestion of Freud's that art can be "a path that leads back from phantasy to reality."

The novel *The Sea, The Sea* (1978) explores many of the same themes as *The Black Prince*, notably that of the artist caught between fantasy and truth, self-justification and objective vision, edging along the path from appearance to reality. Both novels use first-person narration, with the narrators, Bradley Pearson and Charles Arrowby, being similar in many respects: middle-aged men, aspirant artists, self-deceived lovers. Charles Arrowby tries to convince himslf, against all the evidence, that a former girlfriend of some forty years before, who he accidentally comes across at his seaside retreat, still loves him as much as he believes he still loves her. Driven by this fantasy, he kidnaps her and causes havoc in his selfish pursuit. He is unable to "see" what is happening, he is blinded by self-indulgence. By the end he reaches a cathartic weariness rather than a deep self-knowledge, yet it seems like a glimpse of truth: "Can one change oneself? I doubt it. Or if there is any change it must be measured as the millionth part of a millimetre. When the poor ghosts have gone, what remains are ordinary obligations and ordinary interests. One can live quietly and try to do tiny good things and harm no one."[9]

9. Iris Murdoch, *The Sea, The Sea* (London, 1978), p. 501.

Truth and Art

The theme of Plato's Cave resonates in the novel (as in *The Fire and the Sun*): in Plato's myth, those in the cave first see only the dancing shadows on the wall, then turn round to see the fire that casts the shadows, and finally escape to see the sun outside the cave. Charles Arrowby also speaks of a "cavern": "When I started writing this 'book' or whatever it is I have felt as if I were walking about in a dark cavern where there are various 'lights,' made perhaps by shafts or apertures which reach the outside world. . . . There is among those lights one great light towards which I have been half consciously wending my way. It may be a great 'mouth' opening to the daylight, or it may be a hole through which fires emerge from the centre of the earth. And am I still unsure which it is, and must I now approach in order to find out?" (*Sea*, p. 77). Charles's cousin James, a Buddhist with a clearer, simpler, more moral, and less self-centered vision of events, sees the truth behind Charles's fantasy: "You've built a cage of needs and installed her in an empty space in the middle. The strong feelings are all around her—vanity, jealousy, revenge, your love for your youth—they aren't focused on her, they don't touch her. . . . You are using her image, a doll, a simulacrum, it's an exorcism. Soon you will start seeing her as a wicked enchantress" (p. 442).

These themes—fantasy, the pursuit of truth, obsession, magic and enchantment, misguided love, shifting points of view—are highly characteristic of Iris Murdoch's novels; they are prominent, for example, in the more recent novel *The Message to the Planet* (1989), whose central protagonist, Alfred Ludens, though not a first-person narrator, bears similarities to Bradley and Charles. He is obsessed not with his own vision of truth but with that of the eccentric, mystical, onetime mathematical genius Marcus Vallar, who once spoke tantalizingly of "deep foundations, pure cognition, the nature of consciousness, a universal language,"[10] as if he had within his grasp a profound "message to the planet." But no such message emerges, the book that Ludens hopes Marcus will write never materializes, and after a theatrical suicide, which many people treat with relief, Marcus leaves only a tape full of incomprehensible gibberish and papers covered with meaningless scribbles, which Ludens burns without even trying to decipher. The hoped-for message, which might have revealed some ultimate truth, goes up in smoke, much like the manuscript of Ejlert Lövborg tossed into the flames by Hedda Gabler.

Ludens, like Charles and Bradley, is depicted as self-deceived, vain, obsessed, and, in the end, disillusioned in his search for some deep truth;

10. *The Message to the Planet* (1989; rpt., Harmondsworth, England, 1990), p. 13.

not only does the profound "message" elude him but the search itself is also constantly frustrated by more down-to-earth distractions, his own unsatisfactory love affair (with Marcus's daughter), his mediation in his friends' complicated marital relations, and his attempts to steer Marcus away from doctors and detractors. As for Marcus himself, we are offered innumerable perspectives on him, not all flattering: psychiatrists, priests, rabbis, mystics, New Age travelers, artists, and skeptics weigh up his supposed mystical powers and leave any final truth about him fragmented and disputed. The only final truth is that all-embracing truths are illusory: "Everything is accidental," says one character at the novel's end, "That's the message." The message for fiction, though, is more clear and more hopeful. The truths of literature lie in particularities, not in generalities—in revealing the accidental, yet giving it form. As readers we might begin with the self-centered, even grandiose, delusions of Bradley Pearson, Charles Arrowby, and Alfred Ludens, but by attending to art, we are at least offered the opportunity of taking the path back from fantasy to reality—of emerging from the cave into the sun.

7

Fear and Pity

Terror in tragedy is nothing more than being taken by surprise by
pity, whether I know the object of my pity or not. For example, the
priest at last exclaims: "You, Oedipus, are the murderer of Laius"; I
am terrified for all at once I see the righteous Oedipus unfortunate,
and immediately my pity is aroused.

> —Gotthold Ephraim Lessing, To Nicolai,
> 13 November 1756, *Correspondence*

The tragic fear and pity may be aroused by the Spectacle; but they
may also be aroused by the very structure and incidents of the play—
which is the better way and shows the better poet.

> —Aristotle, *Poetics*

I

Desdemona lies innocent and helpless on the bed. Over her towers Othello, who pronounces with solemn finality, "Thou art to die." The enormity
and horror of what is about to happen fills us with anger and dismay. Desdemona pleads for her life. But " 'Tis too late." Othello has resolved to act,
and deaf to his wife's most pitiful pleas, he suffocates and kills her.

As we watch this tragedy unfold, can we truly be described as feeling
fear and pity? Are we really *in awe* of Othello's violent jealousy and *moved*
by Desdemona's innocent suffering? But how could we be when we know
full well that what we are watching is just a play? Such questions have a
long history, but more recent discussion has thrown up a number of puzzling suggestions. It has been argued, for example, that our fear at horror
movies is only a "quasi fear" occurring as part of a "game of make-believe"
that we play with the images on the screen.[1] It has been argued, too, that
while our fear and pity might be genuine and quite natural they never-

---

1. Kendall L. Walton, "Fearing Fictions," *Journal of Philosophy* 75 (1978): 5–27; see also
Walton, *Mimesis as Make-Believe* (Cambridge, Mass., 1990).

theless involve "inconsistency" and "incoherence."[2] And, in contradiction to Aristotle, it has also been suggested that what emotional responses we do have to fiction are not only quite dissimilar from "real life emotions" but are in no way integral to a proper literary response.[3]

At the heart of the issue seems to lie a paradox about beliefs. On the one hand, it is assumed that as reasonably sophisticated adults we are not *taken in* by fiction, that is, we do not believe or come to believe, when knowingly watching a fictional performance, that the depicted sufferings or dangers involve any real suffering or danger. No one is in fact murdered in the performance of *Othello*, just as no one is in fact jealous or innocent. And we know that. On the other hand, we respond often enough with a range of emotions, including fear and pity, that seem to be explicable only on the assumption that we do believe there to be real suffering or real danger. For how can we feel fear when we do not believe there to be any danger? How can we feel pity when we do not believe there to be any suffering?

This apparent tension between the beliefs we hold about the nature of fiction and the beliefs needed to explain our responses to fiction seems to threaten at least some commonsense intuitions.[4] But another intuition, I think, tells us that our beliefs about what is real or not fade into the background when we are watching a play. Belief and disbelief do not seem to do justice to the true nature of our attention. Why is this? I suggest that the best way to reconcile our intuitions and get a clearer perspective on the matter is to shift the focus of discussion away from beliefs to the fictions themselves and correspondingly from the emotions to the objects of the emotions. I hope that the paradox of beliefs will disappear when more basic issues on these lines have been sorted out. The central question I shall address is, What are we responding *to* when we fear Othello and pity Desdemona?

Kendall Walton has reminded us of the logical oddities of our relations with fictional characters.[5] For example, we can talk of them affecting us but not, in any straightforward way, of us affecting them. They seem to be

2. Colin Radford, "How Can We Be Moved by the Fate of Anna Karenina?" *Proceedings of the Aristotelian Society* 69, suppl. vol. (1975).

3. Stein Haugom Olsen, *The Structure of Literary Understanding* (Cambridge, 1978), chap. 2.

4. Eva Schaper, in "Fiction and the Suspension of Disbelief," *British Journal of Aesthetics* 18 (1978), offers a detailed analysis of the relation between these two sets of beliefs, arguing that far from being contradictory, one set, when properly understood, can be seen to presuppose the other. Some criticisms of this view appear in B. J. Rosebury, "Fiction, Emotion, and 'Belief': A Reply to Eva Schaper," *British Journal of Aesthetics* 19 (1979).

5. Kendall L. Walton, "How Remote Are Fictional Worlds from the Real World?" *Journal of Aesthetics and Art Criticism* 37 (1978); see also Walton, "Fearing Fictions."

able to induce in us sorrow, fear, contempt, delight, and embarrassment. But we have no comeback with them. We cannot thank them, congratulate or frighten them, or help, advise, rescue, or warn them. A logical gap exists between us and them, and those who think that fiction and reality are inextricably mixed should reflect on just how wide this gap is. Exploring the nature of the gap will be at the heart of this investigation.

Walton points out what looks like an asymmetry between physical and psychological interaction between the real world and fictional worlds. No *physical* interaction across worlds, in either direction, seems to be possible. Within their world, Othello can kill Desdemona and within ours I can kill you, but a logical barrier prevents them from killing us and us from killing them. It looks as if the barrier against *psychological* interaction across worlds is more selective. Can we not be frightened, amused, and angered by beings in a fictional world? Walton advises against accepting any cross-world interaction even in the one-way psychological cases where it seems to occur. He ingeniously suggests that the apparent psychological effect on us by fictional characters takes place not across worlds but *in a fictional world*. We are not really afraid or moved but only *fictionally* so. The physical symptoms of our emotions, the clammy palms and prickly eyes, indicate merely a "quasi" emotion in this world. For Walton, to interact in any way with a fictional character, we must "enter" a fictional world.

While I am sympathetic to much of what Walton proposes and heedful of his advice not to accept cross-world interaction if we can help it, I think there is a simpler and less paradoxical way out. Rather than having us enter fictional worlds, which involves problems about just which fictional worlds we can enter and whether we can ever enter the *right* worlds,[6] it seems more satisfactory to have the fictional characters enter our world. Against Walton, then, I will argue that it is *in the real world* that we psychologically interact with fictional characters. If so, then we can, as our intuitions suggested, be really afraid and really moved.

II

How can fictional characters enter our world? What is it in our world that we respond to when we fear Othello and pity Desdemona? My suggestion, drawing on the theory developed in Chapters 2 and 3, is that fic-

---

6. See Robert Howell, "Fictional Objects: How They Are and How They Aren't," *Poetics* 8 (1979), who raises difficulties for Walton's account along these lines.

tional characters enter our world in the mundane guise of descriptions (or, strictly, the senses of descriptions) and become the objects of our emotional responses as mental representations or, as I shall call them, thought contents characterized by those descriptions. Simply put, the fear and pity we feel for fictions are in fact directed at thoughts in our minds.

First a word about thoughts. Adopting something like the scholastic distinction between the "formal" reality of a thought and its "objective" reality, I will distinguish, in my own terms, between thoughts as states of consciousness and thoughts as representations. As states of consciousness, thoughts are individual and unique; they are properties of a person at a time, probably properties of the brain. As representations, thoughts are types; they can be shared and repeated. As such, they are "intentional" in that they are directed toward an object: they are *of* or *about* something. To avoid confusion in the context of a discussion of fiction, I prefer to talk of the *content* of a thought rather than its *object*. Two thoughts as representations are identical if and only if they have the same content. The content of a thought is identified under some description such that two thoughts have the same content if and only if they are identified under the same description. Identifying descriptions of thought contents can be of two kinds, which I shall call "propositional" and "predicative." The thought "the moon is made of green cheese" has a content identified under a propositional description, the thought "a piece of cheese" is identified under a predicative description. By allowing both types of descriptions, I intend to admit as thoughts everything we might consider as mental contents, including mental images, imaginings, fantasies, suppositions, and all that Descartes called "ideas." It is arguable that epistemologically we have privileged access to our thoughts only as representations, with regard to content-identifying descriptions, not as states of consciousness.[7]

It is important to notice the relations between a thought content, as here conceived, and truth-value and belief. Strictly speaking, a thought content, even if identified under a propositional description, is not assessable as true or false. Certainly, the very same propositional content could be incorporated in a judgment or assertion and as such have a truth-value.[8] But as an identifying property of a thought, the proposi-

7. For a discussion of related points, see Daniel Dennett, "On the Absence of Phenomenology," in *Body, Mind, and Method*, ed. D. F. Gustafson and B. L. Tapscott (Dordrecht, 1979).

8. The notion here of propositional content comes from J. R. Searle, *Speech Acts* (Cambridge, 1969), chap. 2.4; see also J. R. Searle, "What Is an Intentional State?" *Mind* 88 (1979), and Searle, *Intentionality* (Cambridge, 1983).

tional description involves neither judgment nor assertion. For this reason it might be misleading to report the occurrence of a thought by the expression "A thinks that p," which would normally be taken to imply that A believes or is willing to affirm that p. In our required sense, no such belief or willingness need be present. "Having a thought that p" means only being in a mental state characterized by the propositional description "that p." A thought content differs from a belief. Belief is a psychological attitude held in relation to a propositional content. It is one among many attitudes—including disliking, rejecting, remembering, and contemplating—that we might take to the contents of some of our thoughts. This distinction between thought and belief is important in what follows, for the thought contents derived from fictions do not have to be believed to be feared.

Thoughts as representations can be the proper objects of emotional responses such as fear and pity. What is it to be an object of fear? Not everything that we fear exists or is real; we might fear ghosts, leprechauns, or Martians. It is helpful to distinguish between being frightened *of* something and being frightened *by* something. "A is frightened by X" normally implies the existence of X; it is X that in fact arouses the fear, though it might be unknown to A. "A is frightened of Φ" does not imply the existence of Φ, though "Φ" would be one of the descriptions under which A identifies what he or she is frightened of. What we are frightened *by* I will call the "real" object of our fear; what we are frightened *of* I will call the "intentional" object.[9] It is my contention that the real objects of our fear in fictional cases are thoughts. We are frightened *by* thoughts, though we are not frightened *of* thoughts, except in special circumstances. There are parallels with the objects of pity. Our feelings of pity can have real and intentional objects. The real object of our pity, what we are moved *by*, is what arouses our emotion. As with fear, this too can be a thought. The intentional object of our pity will be the direct object of the verb "pity" and will be identified under some intentional description. We do not pity thoughts, but thoughts can be pitiful and can fill us with pity.

The introduction of thoughts as the real objects of our responses to fiction arises out of our earlier paradox of belief. It is not meant as a general explanation of intentional objects. Suppose we claim to be frightened of Martians and Martians do not exist. If we believe that they exist, then it is no help to introduce *thoughts* of Martians as an attempt to

---

9. The account of "intentional object" here is similar to that in G. E. M. Anscombe, "The Intentionality of Sensation: A Grammatical Feature," in *Analytical Philosophy*, ed. R. J. Butler (London, 1965), 2d series.

eliminate intentional objects. For the belief itself has already landed us with such objects. But if we do not believe that Martians exist but still claim to find them frightening, then the introduction of thoughts as an intermediary has genuine explanatory value. This value stems partly from the independence of thought and belief. We can be frightened by the thought of something without believing that anything real corresponds to the content of the thought. We find the thought frightening and might believe it to be frightening, but that belief raises no paradox in relation to our other beliefs about fiction.

I want to make four points about being frightened by thoughts. First, the propensity of a thought to be frightening is likely to increase in relation to the level of reflection or imaginative involvement that is directed to it. In addition, thoughts can differ among themselves with respect to *vividness,* and our reflection on thoughts can be graded with respect to *involvement.* Part of what I mean by involvement with a thought is the level of attention we give to it, which can be increased, for example, by bringing to mind accompanying mental images or by "following through" its consequences. For this reason it is often not so much single thoughts that are frightening (though they might be disturbing or worrying) as thought clusters. One has to be in the right "frame of mind" to find a thought frightening, which is partly indicated by a tendency to develop thought clusters.

Second, I can be frightened by a thought or a thought cluster at a time when I am in no actual danger and do not believe myself to be in danger. At this moment I am in no danger of being mauled by a lion, which is no doubt good reason for saying that it would be absurd and irrational for me to be afraid at this moment of being mauled by a lion. But it is not absurd or irrational but natural and likely that I might be frightened here and now by the thought of being mauled should I bring to mind snarling teeth, the thrashing of claws, searing pain, and so on.

Third, it need not be even remotely probable or likely that I will ever face the danger envisaged in a frightening thought, and I need not believe it to be probable. I might find the thought of being stranded on a distant planet or being a monarch deposed in a military coup frightening without supposing that this will, or even could, happen to me.

Finally, the fear associated with a frightening thought is a genuine, not a "quasi" or fictional, fear. This brings us back to Walton, for whom the fears associated with fictions are not real fears. Does anything argued by Walton count against thought contents evoking real fears? He imagines Charles, who is like you and me, watching a horror movie about a terrible green slime. Charles shrieks and clutches his chair as the slime oozes relentlessly toward him. First, Walton argues that because *Charles is fully aware that the slime is fictional,* we cannot say that he is genuinely afraid. At best Charles is fictionally or make-believedly afraid. The argument here, though, does not affect the fear associated with a frightening thought; this fear is the real thing. We have seen in the second and third points that we can be frightened by a thought regardless of whether we believe ourselves to be in any danger and regardless of whether we believe the content of the thought to be either true or probable. Walton's argument might establish that Charles is not—and cannot be, given his beliefs—afraid *that the slime is threatening him* or *that he is in danger from the slime,* but it does not show that he is not frightened. We need to distinguish between Charles's being frightened *by the slime* and his being frightened *by the thought of the slime.* The former presupposes the reality of the slime, so it cannot be true; but neither the reality of the slime nor Charles's belief in its reality is presupposed by the latter. The thought of the slime, made vivid by the images on the screen, is a frightening thought for Charles, and he is frightened.

The second part of Walton's argument to show that Charles is not genuinely afraid is that he does not manifest the behavioral evidence we would expect from someone who is genuinely afraid of the slime; he does not call the police or warn his friends. Indeed not, for he knows well enough that no real slime exists for the police to investigate. Nevertheless, there might be behavioral evidence that he is frightened by the thought of the slime. He might close his eyes and try to bring other things to mind, a common practice among audiences at horror films. It is a clue, I think, that we are on the right line in identifying thoughts as the proper objects of our fear of fictions.

My conclusion at this stage of the argument is that mental representations or thought contents can be the cause of emotions such as fear and pity quite independently of beliefs we might hold about being in personal danger or about the existence of real suffering or pain. This is the first step toward resolving our original paradox of belief.

III

What I must now argue is that when we fear Othello or the slime or we pity Desdemona, our fears and tears are directed at thought contents. I must also show how these are derived from the fictions and thus how the relevant thought contents can be identified. In general, my claim will be that the explicit or implicit propositional content of a fictional presentation determines and identifies the thought contents to which we react. A further claim will be that this content stands to truth and assertion in much the same relation as that of the content of thoughts to truth and belief. I also hope that a clear understanding of the logic of fiction, as proposed in earlier chapters, will provide an explanation of the logical gap that exists between us and fictional worlds.

All that we know about the fictional worlds of novels and stories is ultimately derived from the descriptive contents of the fictional works themselves. What determines fictionality is not a special kind of meaning or propositional content but the "force" or intention with which the content is presented, conforming to the conventions of a practice of storytelling. These conventions dictate the "point" of fictive utterance, the way it prompts a complex response of imaginative supplementation. Standard speech act conventions are suspended. An author does not assert the content as true and in turn an informed reader does not believe it to be true but rather imagines it to be so.

When we ask for the reference of the names "Othello" and "Desdemona," we are asking about either *internal* or *external* reference, that is, what the names refer to in the world of the fiction, from the internal perspective, or what they refer to in the real world, from the external perspective. In the play (in the fictional world depicted by the play), the names stand for those very persons whose tragic fate imaginatively engages us. On the external perspective, assuming the fictionality of Othello and Desdemona, the references are to fictional characters. Characters, from that perspective, are abstracted sets of qualities corresponding to the descriptive content (and appropriately derived content) of the narratives that introduce them. Such was the theory developed in Chapters 2 and 3.

We recall the Fregean suggestion that when we truly assert "In Shakespeare's play, Othello kills Desdemona," the names "Othello" and "Desdemona" refer only to their senses (in the play), not to any nonexistent objects as referents. The sense of the names will be given by those descriptions used in the fiction, or derivable from it, which characterize and identify its internal reference. Thus the sense of the name "Desdemona" is given by such descriptions as the person who is named "Desdemona" in Shakespeare's play *Othello*, who loses her handkerchief, who talks innocently to Cassio, who is killed by her jealous husband, and so on. Only the sense of these descriptions survives in the real world, not the reference to a person. Stated baldly, when Desdemona enters our world, she enters not as a person, not as an individual, not even as an imaginary being, but as a complex set of descriptions with their customary senses.

Here, then, we have an explanation of the logical gap between our world and fictional worlds. Fictional, or internal, references are blocked as real-world references either in virtue of occurring as pretended references in fictive uses of sentences or in virtue of occurring within the scope of intensional prefixes such as "In the play ____," which transform fictional references into nonfictional references and thus into senses. Fictional characters as such can never cross these logical barriers. In the fictional world they exist as people; in the real world they exist only as the senses of descriptions. The word *character* is a convenient but endlessly confusing device for talking of senses under the pretense of referring to people. "Referring to a character" just means either pretending, through the conventions of storytelling, to refer to a person or actually referring to meanings found in or derivable from a work of fiction.

IV

Now we have all the logical apparatus needed to show that when we fear and pity fictional characters, our emotions are directed at real, albeit psychological, objects. We do not have to postulate either that the emotions are fictional or that they are directed irrationally at nothing at all. Nor do we have to postulate beliefs that we know to be false in order to explain the emotions. We have, on the one hand, the notion of a thought content, which can be the proper object of emotion. On the other hand, we have the propositional contents of fictional sentences in which, through the mediation of suspended illocutionary intentions (in an author's use) or implicit intensional operators (in an informed reader's use), the senses of the fictional names have replaced the fictional references. The final hurdle is to show what relations obtain between the thought contents in our minds and the propositional contents of the fictions.

To what thought contents must we respond for us to be said to be truly fearing Othello or pitying Desdemona? Not any tears are tears for Desdemona, and not any thoughts are thoughts about Othello. Strict criteria must be applied to identify the right thoughts and thus the right tears. The following seem to be important.

In general there must be both a causal and a content-based connection between the thoughts in our minds and the sentences and descriptions in the fiction. A causal connection is needed to rule out the possibility of our responding to descriptions identifying properties which as it happens belong to a fictional character but which have come to our attention from a quite different, even nonfictional, source. Not even tears for the thought of an innocent wife killed by a jealous husband who happens to be a Moor of Venice are ipso facto tears for Desdemona. It seems to be a necessary condition that there be a causal route back from the thought to Shakespeare's play. That is, Shakespeare's play must have some explanatory role in accounting for the genesis of the thought.

A causal connection, though, is not sufficient. There must also be a closer link connecting the senses of Shakespeare's sentences and the thoughts to which we respond. The paradigm connection would be one of identity of content where the very propositions expressed or predicates employed by Shakespeare also identify our thoughts, such that in grasping the sense of his sentences we directly acquire corresponding mental representations identified through his own propositional or predicative descriptions. Such a direct link would be sufficient to secure the appropriate thoughts but is not necessary. More often than not we acquire the relevant thoughts from a combination of our own descriptions and a suitable subset of an author's descriptions.

Deviation from this paradigmatic, content-based connection can occur in different ways. First, suppose we have never read or even heard a word of Shakespeare's *Othello* and we come to learn of Desdemona's tragic plight only through a retelling of the story—or part of it, in summary or paraphrase—which perhaps involves none of the descriptions written by Shakespeare. Are our tears then tears for Desdemona? Much will depend on the retelling. I think we can say at least this: if the descriptions are logically implied by some relevant descriptions in the play, then the thoughts identified via these descriptions would qualify as thoughts about Desdemona.

We can go further than that, however, for much that we believe to be fictionally true about Desdemona will not be derived directly from either the sense of Shakespeare's sentences or the sense of sentences logically implied by those sentences. For we read fictional prose, or poetry, against an intellectual and imaginative background, and much that we call understanding a work of fiction involves supplementing the explicit content with information drawn from this background. So the imaginative reconstruction that readers or producers put on the events and personalities leading up to Desdemona's death might issue in mental representations far different from those directly or logically related to the propositional contents expressed in the original text. Yet these divergences might be licensed through looser forms of implication arising from conventions governing appropriate response to fiction. We cannot deny a genuine indeterminacy in some of our claims to be reacting to particular fictional characters and events. At these more distant reaches from the paradigm, no simple formula can settle the question whether our fear and pity are for Shakespeare's Othello and Desdemona or merely for some imaginative constructs of our own. But our concern here is only to show how these emotional responses are possible. On the view proposed, the question now becomes whether we are responding to thoughts identifiable under descriptions appropriately derived from those offered in the play. The connection back to the original sentences must be maintained. Some of the criteria for the appropriate supplementation of fictions were discussed in Chapter 4. In practice, it is a matter that can call for acute critical sensitivity, as can the detailed unraveling of the senses of some fictional sentences. In general, though, we can say that we are responding to a fictional character if we are responding to thoughts, with the required causal history, that are identified through the descriptive or propositional content either of sentences in the fiction or of sentences logically derived from the fiction or of sentences supplementing those of the fiction in appropriate ways.

A higher-order supplementation of fiction exists in the form of literary interpretation, which is concerned with the aesthetic significance of the content of fictional sentences. It might be that the higher-order descriptions occurring in interpretations—as when we say, for example, that *Othello* is about Machiavellian sophistication and the destruction of innocence—could themselves give rise to thought contents that in turn evince further emotions. Our responses at this level are important but should not be allowed to obscure our responses at a more basic and more particular level.[10]

V

My conclusion, then, is simple: when we respond emotionally to fictional characters, we are responding to mental representations or

10. M. Weston, "How Can We Be Moved by the Fate of Anna Karenina?" *Proc. Arist. Soc.* 69, suppl. vol. (1975), has been criticized in both Colin Radford, "Tears and Fiction: A Reply to Weston," *Philosophy* 52 (1977), and B. Paskins, "On Being Moved by Anna Karenina and *Anna Karenina*," *Philosophy* 52 (1977), for trying to account for our responses at a thematic level. But the specificness of the responses that Radford and Paskins look for is obtained on the present account.

thought contents identifiable through descriptions derived in suitable ways from the propositional content of an original fictional presentation. I think this conclusion, given the arguments leading up to it, affords explanations of a number of puzzling features of fictions. It shows, for example, how we can know something is fictional but still take it seriously without having to believe or even partly believe it. We can reflect on and be moved by a thought independently of accepting it as true. This in turn accounts for the intuition that belief and disbelief stay in the background when we are engaged with fiction. Vivid imagining replaces belief. It explains any apparent dissimilarity between our emotional responses to fiction and "real-life emotions." Although we do not react to the killing of Desdemona as we would to a real killing before our eyes, we do react much as we would to the thought of a real killing. The thought and the emotion are real. Also, although it incorporates a *de dicto* account of fictional characters (as linguistic constructs), it acknowledges the pull of *de re* accounts (as possible objects). Fictions are made up of sets of ideas, many having correlates in reality, and these ideas invite an imaginative supplementation and exploration. In connection with fictional characters, this "filling in" process is not unlike that of *coming to know another human being*: hence the sense of the "roundedness," "completeness," "objectness" of characters. Further, it explains the logical asymmetry in our psychological interactions with fictional characters, why we can fear but not rebuke them, admire but not advise them: their transformation into mental representations determines these constraints.

We can push the conclusion a bit further and use it to explain why our responses to fictional characters are so closely bound up with our responses to the whole work in which they appear. The answer lies partly in the shift from reference to sense in fictional names. It is not just that *someone* is killed by a jealous husband that gives the emotive power to *Othello* but that the description of the killing is connected in a quite particular way with a great number of other descriptions in the play, including those of Desdemona. The cluster of descriptions that give sense to "Desdemona" will tend to issue in just those clusters of thoughts which I earlier suggested can increase our involvement with a thought and thus the intensity of our response to it. I think, finally, this point opens up a whole new area of interest where we see the structural ordering of language in a literary work as determining the ordering of thoughts in a reader. Much of the value of literature, both aesthetic and cognitive, lies in its power to create complex structures of thought in our minds.

Fear and Pity

APPENDIX

The theory of emotional response to fiction outlined above has been endorsed by some in the philosophical community[11] but has not found favor with all. Here I will address two objections that raise questions about central features of the theory. The first, pressed by Kendall Walton himself, is that *thoughts* are not plausible candidates for the objects of fear in cases where spectators—say, of a horror movie—purport to be "afraid." The second, pressed by Bijoy Boruah, for example, is that on *de dicto* accounts of fiction, emotional responses to fictional characters will always have as their objects items characterizable in *general* terms, thus losing the desired specificity of such emotions. Having looked at these objections, I will return at the end to the historical context of the debate.

I

Walton insists that Charles, representing the typical movie goer, "does not consider the thought [of the depicted slime brought to mind by a slime horror movie] dangerous or treat it as such, nor does he experience even an inclination to escape from it."[12] Thus thoughts cannot be the object of fear in these cases. Walton, however, accepts that Charles might have genuine fear arising from the movie: he might, for example, fear the existence out in the world of real slimes *like* the fictional one. Walton's point is only that *Charles does not fear the slime* because he knows there is no such thing. But on that we agree. It cannot be literally true that Charles fears the slime, for the reasons Walton gives. I also agree that Charles's experiential-cum-behavioral manifestations—which Walton calls "quasi fear"—are not sufficient to establish genuine fear. My claim is only that the fictionality of the slime (along with clear recognition of that) is no bar to Charles's having real fear. Walton accepts that works of fiction can cause genuine feelings or moods. A reader might be made cheerful or gloomy through reading a work, which, in turn, interestingly, makes it fictional that he feels cheerful or gloomy.[13] So some psychological states survive across worlds. Being frightened, I maintain, can be just such a state, given certain readily satisfiable conditions.

11. Notably by Noël Carroll in *The Philosophy of Horror, or Paradoxes of the Heart* (London, 1990).

12. Walton, *Mimesis as Make-Believe*, p. 203.

13. Ibid., p. 253.

Walton's premise is that Charles is "playing a game of make-believe" with the images on the screen. I accept the premise at least to the extent that it means that Charles imagines himself in a world with the green slime and (in Walton's idiom) it is fictional that the slime is getting nearer. But this participation can, I argue, with a suitable degree of imaginative involvement, *cause real fear* in Charles. Like all fear, it can motivate evasive action: if too frightened Charles will *stop participating*, by thinking of something else, concentrating on technical aspects of the film, closing his eyes, or walking out.

Charles's imaginings, his mental representations, frighten him. But what is he afraid of? He is not, as I said, strictly speaking, afraid of *the slime* because he does not believe it to be real. Nor is he afraid of *imagining the slime*, in the sense in which a psychoanalytic patient or someone with a heart condition might be. As pressed earlier, we need to distinguish what Charles finds frightening, which specifies either a general type (slimy things) or some feature of the particular instance; what he is frightened *by*, which specifies the cause of the fear; and what he is frightened *of*, which specifies the intentional content of the fear. The thought of being devoured by the slime is a frightening thought for Charles. He is frightened by that thought, made vivid by the images in the movie. What he is frightened of is *the imagined slime*, which is not a mysterious "fictitious entity," certainly not a kind of slime, but a kind of imagining. "Slime" characterizes the intentional content of his fear (and his imaginings); it is a slime-fear, not, say, a vampire-fear. No doubt if Charles did not have a disposition to find slimy things frightening, he would not be frightened by the thought of this slime. Perhaps the movie triggers some deep (primeval) fear in Charles, perhaps a psychoanalytic basis exists for Charles's fear, perhaps there could even be an evolutionary explanation for why Charles, as a human being, should be frightened of slimy things; but these are largely empirical elaborations evoked to explain a particular example. After all, it is not as if all viewers must respond as Charles does. The point is only that nothing, given the data of the case, counts theoretically against Charles having real fear.

Walton dismisses the theory on the grounds that only in special cases—for example, if he had a heart condition—might Charles be said to "fear the thought of the slime."[14] But the person with the heart condition fears the *act* of thinking about the slime, not the *content* of the thought. Nor is it right to object that "his experience simply does not feel

14. Ibid., p. 203.

like fear of a thought,"[15] for when Charles is kept awake at night by the recurring horrific images of the slime, it must indeed feel like fear of a thought but still seems phenomenologically identical to what he feels in the theater. Finally, of course Charles *says* he is afraid of the slime; he does not need to spell out its imaginary nature.

What is at issue here? It is not the phenomenology of watching horror movies, for Walton acknowledges, in the idea of "quasi fear," all the sensations of the frightened viewer. It is not the nature of emotions; no weakening of the idea of emotion is needed to sustain the reality of Charles's fear, nor is it difficult to find appropriate cognitive states for Charles. The real issue concerns the bounds of pretense, the scope of the "game" that Charles is allegedly playing with the movie. To what extent are responses to fiction properly thought of as "game playing?" We have a paradigm of "make-believe emotions"—children who play at being sad or angry or frightened—but Charles's condition seems nothing like that.

The question is, How are we to understand Charles's remark "I am terrified of the slime"? Both Walton and I agree that it is not literally true, so some interpretation is required. For Walton the utterance expresses the fact that it is fictional that Charles is afraid of the slime, that Charles imagines being afraid of it. Walton sees a direct parallel with other remarks of Charles's such as "the slime is heading this way." That utterance again, on Walton's view, is Charles's way of expressing the fact that it is fictional that the slime is heading toward him, that he imagines it doing so. The trouble with this parallel, though, is that embedding both the beliefs and the emotions in imagining leaves Charles's behavioral manifestations a mystery. Why should imagining being afraid of something produce symptoms of "quasi fear"? On my alternative analysis, when Charles says "I am terrified of the slime," he does so because he is terrified and wants to report that; and he knows that the cause of his fear is the slime image on the screen, and he does not need to remind his interlocutor that the slime is just fictional. Then his symptoms of fear cease to be mysterious and are what they seem to be: he is genuinely afraid.

No doubt more needs to be said about the "afraid of" idiom. Normally when people are afraid of something, they are afraid that something bad is about to or might happen to them. It is not immediately clear what Charles thinks is going to or might happen to him there and then in the cinema. Knowing that the film is fictional, he does not *believe* that he is in any immediate danger. Can we find a relevant propositional content

15. Ibid.

for Charles's fear as well as an intensional object? It is not that he is afraid that *this* (slime) will devour him, because he does not believe what he is seeing is real. The clue again must lie in what Charles brings to mind— *being attacked by a ferocious slime*. He vividly imagines *that he is being or is about to be attacked by such a slime*, and that imagined content is also the content of his fear. It seems a short step from entertaining the thought that something bad (being devoured by slime) *might* happen to him and imagining it *actually happening* to him. The content *being attacked by a ferocious slime*, having no indexical or referential component, is general in nature and does not presuppose the existence of some actual slime (or belief in its existence).

II

The second objection, which moves us from fear to pity, takes off from this last point in criticizing the appeal to such generality, seeing it as undermining the essential specificity of emotional response to fiction. Colin Radford, for example, has often stressed the point that our responses to Anna Karenina cannot be directed to just anyone who happens to be like her or to share her salient properties (perhaps someone the reader knows) because then it would not be a response specifically to *Anna* herself: "The feelings of pity, etc., which we have for Anna as we read, or reflect on the book, are for *her* (and so not for any real persons who might be similarly placed of course). Since this is a tautology, little needs to be, or indeed can be, said in its defence."[16] Bijoy Boruah has pressed a similar point against my position:

> To say that our response is directed towards the senses of thoughts or ideas about life is to imply that the object of a fictional emotion is always general. For example, when we respond to Anna Karenina with sadness, what we really respond to is not Anna but the general idea that it is unfortunate and regrettable that a woman should be in such a miserable condition as described by Tolstoy. This interpretation does not allow the fictional character to be the focus of attention of our emotional state. . . . It diffuses the so-called character into a set of ideas: the character is reduced to the illustration of the possibility of a certain kind of life. But this does not seem right.[17]

16. Colin Radford, "The Essential Anna," *Philosophy* 54 (1979): 391.
17. Bijoy H. Boruah, *Fiction and Emotion* (Oxford, 1988), p. 44.

But the objections of Radford and Boruah do not present much of a problem for the view I wish to defend. Although a fictional character is analyzed—from one perspective—into a set of properties roughly corresponding to the characterizing descriptions in and derivable from a work of fiction, it by no means follows that a character becomes merely an "illustration of the possibility of a certain kind of life." Nor is it part of my theory on emotional responses to fiction that they are directed to just *someone or other* who happens to possess the relevant properties. The specificity of fictional characters, as required to explain the appropriate cognitive and emotional attitudes, resides in a number of factors: in the specificity of the characterizing (descriptive) content, in the causal connectedness of thoughts "about" fictional characters to particular works (that is, those in which the descriptions or images originate), and, above all, in the imagining itself. The "particularity" of Anna Karenina—the thought that she is a particular person in a unique set of circumstances—rests on the fact that readers *imagine* precisely one unique individual whose (true) story is being told; that is what I have called the "internal" perspective on a fictional world. Within the world being imagined, Anna has all the particularity of any real human.

Radford and Boruah are right that when we respond emotionally to Anna Karenina, the explanation must in some sense refer specifically to *Anna*. But as she is a fictional character—like the slime—some further explanation is needed for what is meant by the claim that a reader "pities Anna," for just as it cannot be literally true that Charles "fears the slime," so (as it seems) it cannot be literally true that Smith (a reader) "pities Anna." The answer, as suggested earlier, is to invoke the *thought* of Anna and her predicament (a thought that is not itself fictional or unreal), enhanced by a sympathetic imagining of what it would be like to be in just such a predicament. Genuine pity can attend such imagining, and it is not merely directed vaguely at *someone or other* who might share common properties with Anna but is aroused by imagining precisely *this* set of circumstances happening to *this* person.[18] It is only from the "external" perspective that Anna becomes a fictional character describable in general

---

18. For a detailed and persuasive account of how we can feel pity for fictional characters, see Alex Neill, "Fiction and the Emotions," *American Philosophical Quarterly* 30 (1993): 1–13. Neill argues in another paper, "Fear, Fiction, and Make-Believe," *Journal of Aesthetics and Art Criticism* 49 (1991): 47–56, against Kendall Walton, that viewers at horror movies have neither real nor make-believe fear; if anything, they experience only noncognitive reactions such as shock or alarm.

terms without commitment to the existence of any individual instantiating the defining properties.

What the discussion of generality and particularity shows is how important to the institution of fiction (and literature) is Iris Murdoch's idea, developing that of Aristotle, that the particularities of fiction can support a universality of vision. Indeed, it should now be clear how fictional characters combine both the particular and the universal, given the different perspectives that can be adopted to them. By *seeing* (through imagination) the lives of fictional characters finely drawn in all particularities by an artist, we are offered an opportunity to reflect more universally and objectively on comparable matters in the real world. Imaginatively we bring to mind unique individuals; intellectually we recognize the presentation of universals. So it is with our emotional responses to fiction, which, from the twin perspectives, are directed both to the details of imagined individual lives and to thoughts of an intrinsically general nature which reach beyond imaginary worlds back into the real world.

III

It is a long way from Walton's slime back to Sophocles's Oedipus, and it is not obvious that discussion of the one has much bearing on an understanding of the other. But the central place that Aristotle gives to fear and pity in our response to tragedy suggests that a general account of these emotions in relation to fiction must have some relevance to an account of tragedy. As Aristotle says, "The plot [of a tragedy] in fact should be so framed that even without seeing the things take place, he who simply hears the account of them shall be filled with fear and pity at the incidents; which is just the effect that the mere recital of the story in *Oedipus* would have on one."[19] The implication seems to be that simply reflecting on the story, properly told—even apart from seeing it acted on stage—is enough to stir those emotions. On that view, again, prominence is given to *thoughts* in explaining the emotional response. But more problematic in Aristotle's account is the nature of the "fear" associated with a character like Oedipus. In Walton's case of Charles and the slime, the fear is centered on Charles himself; in as much as Charles feels fear, it is fear *for himself.* Yet in the case of Oedipus, an audience feels fear *for Oedi-*

19. Aristotle, *Poetics* 1453b, 2–3.

pus, as the terrifying revelations unfold. Perhaps, then, after all, the cases are not particularly close.

The matter, however, is more complex and interesting than it at first appears. On the one hand we have Aristotle's own account of fear, which does suggest that he sees it as essentially self-regarding; on the other we have his remarks about the "universal" nature of poetry, which suggest that he sees depictions of characters like Oedipus as focused quite differently from the individual-centered descriptions of history. In combination these points yield an important insight into the so-called tragic emotions.

In the *Rhetoric* Aristotle defines fear as "a pain or disturbance due to imagining some destructive or painful evil in the future. For there are some evils, e.g. wickedness or stupidity, the prospect of which does not frighten us: only such as amount to great pains or losses do, and even these only if they appear not remote but so near as to be imminent."[20] Pity is "a feeling of pain at an apparent evil, destructive or painful, which befalls one who does not deserve it, and which we might expect to befall ourselves or some friend of ours, and moreover to befall us soon."[21] The relation of fear and pity is symmetrical: we pity those suffering just such pains that would make us feel fear, and we fear just what would make us feel pity for others. There is also an element of self-directness in pity, as the definition shows. The idea of "imagining" (*phantasia*) some imminent evil implies only that the evil is brought to mind, not that it need turn out to be actual. Both fear and pity are caused by the thought of what *might* happen.

Tragedy, of necessity, involves "imagining some destructive or painful evil." But is it an evil that the spectator associates with himself? The answer seems to be yes, albeit in an indirect manner. First, a tragic character must be "like ourselves" (*Poetics* 1453a, 4) in significant respects, for that is what makes the incidents especially fearful and pitiful; to show either the morally perfect or the morally wicked suffering a tragic downfall would not raise the appropriate feelings (the former would simply be "shocking"). Then, second, because tragic poetry is more "universal" than history, showing what "might happen" rather than what has happened, the subject matter gives focus to "what such or such a kind of man will probably or necessarily say or do" (*Poetics* 1451b, 4); it thus carries us beyond the immediate particularities to a consideration of "kinds" of per-

20. Aristotle, *Rhetoric* 2.5.1, 1382a, 21–23.
21. Ibid., 2.8.1, 1385b, 12–16.

sons, to which we, of course, might belong. This is not to deny Radford's point that the emotions are directed at the specific persons and incidents depicted, but it serves to emphasize, once again, that those incidents and persons take on a more "universal" aspect when viewed as constituents of poetic art. The terrifying fall of Oedipus, through no unequivocal fault of his own, is a stark reminder to us of how vulnerable we are to the whims of chance. Our close sympathetic and imaginative involvement with the drama of Oedipus heightens our "pity" for him and our fear for ourselves, at least indirectly, when we conceive of ourselves as relevantly similar.[22]

This account of "fear" in connection with tragedy is not inconsistent with Walton's view. Although Walton denies that Charles "fears the slime," he readily acknowledges that real fears might arise from the movie; Charles "may genuinely fear . . . suspected actual dangers."[23] It is such genuine fears about their own fate that spectators experience while watching tragedy. As I see it, however, the attraction of the account given above—invoking thoughts brought to mind through imaginative involvement—is that it offers a uniform explanation of all these cases: fearing for others and fearing for oneself, focusing on the characters and looking beyond them. It does not need to appeal to a special category of "quasi fear" to accommodate the differences.

IV

I will end with some brief remarks about another historical application of this debate which comes in an intriguing exchange from the eighteenth century between Dr. Johnson and William Kenrick and which nicely anticipates some of the issues in the modern debate. It is relevant as well to the discussion of tragedy in the next two chapters. Here is Dr. Johnson:

> It will be asked how the drama moves, if it is not credited. It is credited with all the credit due to a drama. It is credited, whenever it moves, as a just picture of a real original; as representing to the auditor what he

22. I am indebted here to Alexander Nehamas's argument in "Pity and Fear in the *Rhetoric* and the *Poetics*," in *Aristotle's "Rhetoric": Philosophical Essays*, ed. D. J. Furley and Alexander Nehamas (Princeton, N.J. 1994). See also Martha C. Nussbaum, *The Fragility of Goodness* (Cambridge, 1986), p. 386.

23. Walton, *Mimesis as Make-Believe*, p. 202.

would himself feel, if he were to do or suffer what is there feigned to be suffered or to be done. The reflection that strikes the heart is not that the evils before us are real evils, but that they are evils to which we ourselves may be exposed. If there is any fallacy, it is not that we fancy the players but that we fancy ourselves unhappy for a moment; but we rather lament the possibility than suppose the presence of misery, as a mother weeps over her babe when she remembers that death may take it from her. The delight of tragedy proceeds from our consciousness of fiction; if we thought murders and treasons real they would please no more.

Imitations produce pain or pleasure not because they are mistaken for realities but because they bring realities to mind.[24]

Johnson's rationalistic suspicion of the imagination makes him scorn the idea of an audience becoming "swept up" by a fictional representation, and his adherence to a classical mimetic (or "imitation") theory of poetry allows him to locate poetic value only in the capacity to "picture" reality. These two elements together lead to an austere externalist view of drama which emphasizes the "consciousness of fiction" over imaginative empathy with its characters and which in turn has the consequence for Johnson, as shown in the above passage, that such emotional responses as are experienced from drama are always self-directed. Audiences are made to reflect on what evils might await them or what it might be like for them to be faced with similar predicaments. Although there is an element here of Aristotle's account of the tragic emotions (their self-directedness), Johnson seems to leave no room for that other element of Aristotle's theory: the sympathetic identification with tragic characters.

The critic, and contemporary, William Kenrick tackles Johnson on just this point. Kenrick highlights the internalist perspective under which spectators are "swept up" in fictional drama: "We do not pretend to say that the spectators are not always in their senses; or that they do not know (if the question were put to them) that the stage is only a stage, and the players only players. But we will venture to say that they are often so intent on the scene as to be absent with regard to every thing else. A spectator properly affected by a dramatic representation makes no re-

---

24. Dr. Johnson, "Prefaces to Shakespeare's Plays," in *Shakespeare: The Critical Heritage*, ed. Brian Vickers (London, 1974), 5: 71. Johnson's comments occur within a discussion of the unities (of time and place) in drama, particularly the question of whether Shakespeare conforms to the unities as originally conceived by Aristotle in the *Poetics*. Johnson's view is that the unities are needed only to make drama "credible," but those who "credit" drama (i.e., believe in its veracity) are suffering a naïve delusion. Thus, in that sense, the unities are pointless.

flections about the fiction or the reality of it."[25] He goes on to say that spectators are taken in or "deceived" at the level of the emotions: "The spectator is unquestionably deceived, but the deception goes no further than the passions, it affects our sensibility but not our understanding; and is by no means so powerful a delusion as to affect our *belief.*"[26] Kenrick appears to hold a causal account of the emotions: "The audience are moved by mere mechanical motives; they laugh and cry from mere sympathy at what a moment's reflection would very often prevent them from laughing or crying at all. . . . We are in this case merely passive, our organs are in unison with those of the players on the stage, and the convulsions of grief or laughter are purely involuntary."[27] Although the causal emphasis perhaps unduly plays down the role of cognition in emotional response, Kenrick's position otherwise seems more persuasive than Johnson's if only in acknowledging the emotional involvement of spectators in fictional drama. The problem for Kenrick would be how to elaborate a tenable theory of the emotions which allows for them to be "deceived," regardless of beliefs. It might well be that the only tenable account would involve postulating a special class of "quasi emotions" along Waltonian lines. But, then, as we have seen, such an account loses the genuine fear and pity that Kenrick and others are out to explain.

In the end, the correct solution, I believe, must lie in an Aristotelian "happy mean," which balances the strict externalism (intellectualism) of Johnson and the internalism (deceptivism) of Kenrick. I hope that the theory presented in this chapter helps lay the foundation for such a solution. Now we can turn in the next two chapters to tragedy itself, where some of these ideas can be further consolidated.

25. William Kenrick, in Vickers, *Shakespeare*, p. 190.
26. Ibid., p. 191.
27. Ibid., p. 192.

8

Tragedy and Moral Value

The second order of the art [of drama] is that, where in dramatic representations . . . there is displayed a deep knowledge, not of individuals and their affairs alone, but of our whole species, of the world and of life. . . . But in my opinion the art of the dramatic poet has, besides all this, yet another and a higher end. The enigma of life should not barely be expressed but solved.

> —Carl Wilhelm Friedrich von Schlegel,
> *Lectures on the History of Literature*

Real life is not tragic. Religion is not tragic. . . . Strictly speaking, tragedy belongs to literature. Tragedies are plays written by great poets.
> —Iris Murdoch, *Metaphysics as a Guide to Morality*

I

Philosophers have long been intrigued by tragedy. Aristotle sought to define and defend it, Hume wanted to account for the peculiar pleasures it affords, and Schopenhauer and Nietzsche were attracted by the view of life it implies. Those who study tragedy do so perforce from some perspective or other, with some particular interest in mind. The thought that tragic drama gives moral insight or teaches a moral lesson is one such familiar perspective. But it is one, I suggest, that we should treat with care if not suspicion.

The danger of the search for moral wisdom in the great works of tragedy is that it can become just another form of appropriation, in which one loses sight of what is truly distinctive about tragedy conceived as literature or art. No doubt there is something intrinsically uplifting or disturbing about the stories, however told, of Antigone or Agamemnon or King Lear such that reflection on these characters' more or less disastrous responses to a personal crisis can stir us to think again about our own moral precepts. But that seems to ignore the mode in which the stories are presented, the role of representation—of art itself—in what the stories have to tell. What needs exploring is the distinctive literary response to the works and how that might engage with moral content.

The focus for my discussion will be the question of why and how the representation of human suffering and disaster can have value and, specifically, moral value.[1] Clearly not any representation of human suffering is morally valuable; indeed, some representations are quite the opposite, being actually immoral, morally depraved, or morally exploitative. So how can we distinguish between those representations which, as it might be put, merit our sympathetic involvement and those which do not, being wantonly cruel or self-indulgent or voyeuristic or pornographic?

The representations that are valuable, we say, are works of art: they have some higher purpose, aesthetic or moral or both. Their mode of representation offers some special insight into the nature of human despair and human tragedy. But what does this claim amount to?

First, there is a constraint on subject matter: the suffering associated with tragic drama is of a distinctive kind. It is not just that someone suffers a disastrous reversal of fortune. Not just any piece of bad luck is tragic, nor is any unhappy ending. For one thing, circumstances must be largely outside the agents' control, for which they are not wholly culpable, and which bring about their downfall. But more than that, as Aristotle insists, the person who suffers in this way must be worthy of our respect, must have morally admirable qualities, such as to elicit pity and sympathy at his or her demise. It is wrong to think of the Aristotelian hamartia as a "fatal flaw" in the character, in a purely negative sense, for then the character would be somewhat less deserving of our sympathy. Rather, as Aristotle conceives it, hamartia is best thought of as a contingent by-product of otherwise admirable character traits—for example, the tendency of the courageous soldier to take especially unwise risks.[2] Inasmuch as we admire courage, it would be misleading to describe a risk-taking disposition as a "flaw" in the courageous soldier. Often hamar-

---

1. The focus is not the same as that of Hume's "Of Tragedy," where Hume is concerned with "the unaccountable pleasure which the spectators of a well-written tragedy receive from sorrow, terror, anxiety," in *Essays: Moral, Political, and Literary* (Oxford, 1963), p. 221. No doubt *part* of the value of tragedy can be explained in terms of the pleasure it gives, but I suggest that the pleasure (properly defined) is as much a consequence of its moral value as an explanation of it. My account of moral value will, I hope, go some way toward shedding light on the appropriate kind of pleasure.

2. I have taken the point from Amélie Oksenberg Rorty, "The Psychology of Aristotelian Tragedy," in *Philosophy and the Arts*, Midwest Studies in Philosophy, ed. P. French, T. Uehling, and H. Wettstein, no. 16 (Minneapolis, 1991), pp. 61–63.

tia involves not knowing or not acknowledging one's true identity either, as in the case of Oedipus, through a more or less excusable ignorance or, in the case of Phaedra in her fatal passion for Hippolytus, through some overwhelming emotion, not entirely within her control.

Nevertheless, the description of the tragic hero as morally admirable only compounds the problem of why the representation of such characters suffering reversals of fortune should have any moral or aesthetic value. Perhaps the most common line of thought which seeks to explain the moral seriousness of tragedy—which is part of a long tradition on the subject—is the notion that the dramatic portrayal of tragic events expresses, even epitomizes, metaphysical or religious views of the world which are of independent moral significance. It is part of Christian theology, for example, that suffering is the path to redemption, that all human suffering is prefigured in the story of Christ's Passion, that Christ died that man might be saved. Many tragic dramas—though not all—represent suffering and death as a kind of purging, a way of ushering in a new order, of laying a foundation for renewal and hope, even of resurrection. When Fortinbras enters at the end of *Hamlet,* he holds out the promise of a new order in the face of death and destruction.

Even in the non-Christian tradition, the value of tragedy is commonly seen to reside in a metaphysical picture of the world, albeit a bleaker, less consoling kind. Characteristically it is a metaphysics of a world governed by fate or natural law which is depicted as blindly indifferent to human suffering and to human conceptions of fairness and benevolence. Portraying humans in the grip of such metaphysically terrifying forces is seen as a salutary moral reminder of human frailty within an indifferent world—or simply as a revelation of cosmic justice that far transcends the narrow confines of human pity. The romantic metaphysicians of the nineteenth century—notably Hegel, Schopenhauer, and Nietzsche—all see the value of tragedy in the image it presents of human life overwhelmed by these uncontrollable, barely understood forces. Of the three, only Hegel manages to extract from tragedy any glimmer of optimism, seeing it as a reaffirmation of an absolute morality in the face of apparent moral conflict, even if the terrible price is the destruction of those who initiate the conflict (he takes Sophocles' *Antigone* as his paradigm). Schopenhauer presents an exactly opposite view; what tragedy offers—what makes it the "highest poetical achievement," is not any grand poetic justice but a stark confrontation with what he calls the "terrible side of life": "The unspeakable pain, the wretchedness and misery of mankind, the triumph of wickedness, the scornful mastery of chance, and the irretrievable fall of the just and the innocent are all here presented to us; and here is to be found a significant hint as to the nature of the world and of existence." The response it produces, he suggests, is one of "resignation, the giving up not merely of life, but of the whole will-to-live itself."[3] Nietzsche's position, though owing much to Schopenhauer, stands somewhere between the two—the source of tragedy, he claims, is not some remote external force but a conflict between two deeply rooted facets of humanity represented by the Apollonian rational order of phenomena, on the one hand, and the Dionysian irrational ecstatic order of things-in-themselves, on the other. The destruction of the Apollonian individuality of the hero in the Dionysian abyss serves to reaffirm the transitory and parochial nature of values in a valueless universe.[4]

Although my sketchy outline does scant justice to such religious and metaphysical conceptions of tragedy, I think they tell only part of the story at best. Because they apply only to particular tragedies within clearly defined traditions (in the case of the metaphysical view, principally to Greek tragedy and Sophoclean tragedy at that), they do not seem to answer in principle the question we have posed, which is far more general in nature, namely, What moral value *can* reside in depictions of human suffering, and what makes some but not all such representations morally valuable? It is not sufficient to locate this value in an independently statable metaphysical view of the place of man in nature even if there are characteristic themes in tragic drama which reinforce some such general vision. For what gets left out of the account is the specific means by which this vision, or these themes, are represented in literary works and the special achievement of this mode of presentation. The interesting question is not just what visions of human life underlie tragic drama but also what special contribution is made by the imaginative realization of such visions in works of literature. Here I believe that Aristotle is a better guide than the romantic metaphysicians, not least because he stresses the poetic character of tragedy (contrasting it, for example, with the narratives of history) and the peculiar range of responses that are appropriate to poetic mimesis, especially involving the emotions.

My own approach can be called humanistic in that I am inclined to suppose, like Aristotle, that the great tragic dramas retain an enduring human interest because they develop themes of a more or less universal

3. Arthur Schopenhauer, *The World as Will and Representation*, trans. E. F. J. Payne, vol. 1 (New York, 1958), p. 253.

4. For a succinct philosophical account of these metaphysical views, see Anthony Quinton, "Tragedy," *Proceedings of the Aristotelian Society* 34, suppl. vol. (1960): 145–164.

nature; they have a "moral content," in a sense to be explained, that, while not necessarily offering moral solutions, engages imaginatively with some of the deepest concerns of human beings in their attempts and repeated failures at living a moral life. The interest of this conception lies, of course, less in its general formulation than in the way it is *worked out* and, specifically, the way it is located among other conceptions: that of literature, of moral content, of fiction, of the imagination. In this chapter I will take a few steps toward that further working out.

II

The humanistic view of tragedy has no commitment, as I would defend it, to the belief that tragedy (or any literature for that matter) inevitably heightens the moral sensibilities of its readers or brings them to lead morally better or more fulfilling lives. Whether watching tragic drama or reading literature has such effects is a purely contingent and causal matter; and little empirical evidence exists for the morally beneficial effects of the study of literature (the same holds for the study of philosophy or social science). Sometimes Martha Nussbaum, for example, following in the footsteps of Matthew Arnold, F. R. Leavis, or even Nietzsche, seems to suggest a more essential link between literature and living a moral life.[5] But that is no part of my view. I do, however, hold that works of literature occupy an indispensable place in any literary culture and that all things being equal it is better to read the great works of literature than not. The reasons for this will partly emerge from a consideration of what might be meant by "moral content," as conceived in connection with a humanistic conception of literature.

Traditionally, we can identify two strands of thought about moral content in literature or in tragedy in particular. One is the idea of a *moral lesson* or moral principle derivable from a work; the other is the idea of a *moral vision* expressed in a work. The first idea, that of a moral lesson, can probably be traced back to the tradition of folktales or parables, whose purpose was to illuminate or teach a *moral* that gives meaning and interest to a narrative. It might be thought that this paradigm is too naïve or too remote from current conceptions of literature to merit much serious

5. In *Love's Knowledge: Essays on Philosophy and Literature* (Oxford, 1990), Martha Nussbaum writes, for example, "A novel, just because it is not our life, places us in a moral position that is favorable for perception" (p. 162), and "The universalizing tendency of the moral imagination is encouraged by the very activity of novel-reading itself" (p. 166).

attention. But the idea of a moral lesson has more sophisticated formulations, and again, the interesting question is not whether moral lessons or principles can be drawn from great works of literature—for it is always easy enough to do so—but what status should be given to them or, as I shall put it, where they should be located within an adequate theory of literary appreciation. In some respects the generalizations about tragedy found in the work of Hegel, Schopenhauer, and Nietzsche—and unlike those of Aristotle, who is concerned with more formal features—can be thought of as statements of the moral lessons to be drawn from tragedy.

Consider, though, a much simpler example from George Orwell in his essay "Lear, Tolstoy, and the Fool," written in 1947. Orwell argues that *King Lear* has two morals, one explicitly stated, one merely implied:

> First of all, . . . there is the vulgar, common-sense moral drawn by the Fool: "Don't relinquish power, don't give away your lands." But there is also another moral. Shakespeare never utters it in so many words, and it doesn't very much matter whether he was fully aware of it. It is contained in the story, which, after all, he made up, or altered to suit his purposes. It is: "Give away your lands if you want to, but don't expect to gain happiness by doing so. Probably you won't gain happiness. If you live for others, you must live *for others*, and not as a roundabout way of getting an advantage for yourself."[6]

Orwell is no doubt right that at one level such homespun lessons about what to expect if you give away your lands *can* be derived from *King Lear*. But the patent inadequacy of this account to explain either the literary interest of the play or its moral seriousness points up a general weakness of the moral lesson view of moral content. Perhaps the problem can be summarized like this: either the moral lesson is too close to the work, tied too specifically to the characters and incidents in the work, in which case it cannot function as an independent, generalizable moral principle, or the moral lesson is too detached, too loosely connected to the specifics of the work to be perceived as part of the literary content or meaning that the work expresses. The tension here is precisely between the *derivability* of the moral principle and its *independence* as a general moral truth.

It is important to see that the problem is not just that of how to formulate a moral lesson in some derived statement. For literary works all

6. Orwell, *The Collected Essays, Journalism, and Letters of George Orwell*, vol. 4, ed. Sonia Orwell and Ian Angus (London, 1968), p. 298.

too often provide such statements themselves. The closing speech by the Chorus in the *Antigone* would be an obvious example:"Wisdom is the supreme part of happiness; and reverence towards the gods must be inviolate. Great words of prideful men are ever punished with great blows, and, in old age, teach the chastened to be wise."[7]

But to extract this moral homily from the play, independently of its specific literary function, would be utterly misleading. For the literary interest of the Chorus's words is much more subtle: although supposedly alluding to Creon as growing wise through suffering, they hint that they are referring to themselves as well. The Chorus's own stance with regard to Creon and Antigone shifts during the play—as the elders of Thebes, they have a vested interest in the power of the state, represented by Creon, yet in the light of Tiresias's warning, they come to fear for their city and to blame Creon for undermining its stability. Many of the conflicts in the play are mirrored in the attitudes of the Chorus, a detailed account of which would need to explore the shifting dynamics of power and justice and fear and arrogance in the relations of the Chorus to the main protagonists. The moral lesson drawn by the Chorus reflects inward more than outward; it prompts us to think again about the kind of wisdom both they and Creon have acquired and the different forms that "chastening" has taken throughout the drama.[8]

When derived moral lessons are relativized in this way to interpretive frameworks (not least by the workings of irony), they come to acquire a status quite different from that of independent moral truths, that is, they acquire the status of thematic statements or descriptions. Here is Wilson Knight, in *The Wheel of Fire*, arguing that *King Lear* can be interpreted as what he calls "comedy of the grotesque": "Though love and music—twin sisters of salvation—temporarily may heal the racked consciousness of Lear, yet, so deeply planted in the facts of our life is this unknowing ridicule of destiny, that the uttermost tragedy of the incongruous ensues, and there is no hope save in the broken heart and limp body of death."[9]

Knight uses the concepts "ridicule of destiny" and "tragedy of the incongruous" not as components of a moral lesson which can be learned from the play and applied independently of it but as thematic concepts for an enhanced understanding of the play. Although he might appear to be making a generalizable comment about the role of ridicule and the

7. Sir Richard C. Jebb, *The Tragedies of Sophocles* (1904; rpt., Cambridge, 1957), p. 172.

8. On the Chorus's role in *Antigone*, see R. W. B. Burton, *The Chorus in Sophocles' Tragedies* (Oxford, 1980), chap. 3.

9. G. Wilson Knight, *The Wheel of Fire* (London, 1972), p. 175.

comic in tragic situations, the interest of his analysis is grounded in what light it can shed on specific scenes in *King Lear*. It is a commonplace that moral concepts and moral propositions can appear in thematic descriptions, but it is not always recognized that moral content *as it figures in thematic statements* and moral content *as it figures in independent moral principles* are performing two radically different functions and are thus assessable in radically different ways.[10]

III

Let me turn next to moral content conceived as moral vision. Here the idea is that the moral value of tragedy lies in what it *shows* (to use Wittgensteinian terminology), not in what it *states* or *implies* propositionally. The metaphor of a picture or view or vision of the world is widely used in this context. Thus Iris Murdoch writes, in a passage we looked at in Chapter 6, "The study of literature . . . is an education in how to picture and understand human situations."[11] As we saw in that chapter, it is Murdoch's view that great art helps us acquire a more detached, objective, and selfless perspective on the world which is always threatened by the essentially egocentric outlook of our ordinary lives. "The tragic poet breaks the egoistic illusory unity which is natural to art and is able to look at human evil with a just and steady eye."[12]

In a related strand of argument, the idea of moral vision in contrast to a moral lesson has been thought to embody an insight into ethics itself, as well as the connection between literature and ethics. This is notable in the Wittgensteinian school as represented, for example, by D. Z. Phillips and R. M. Beardsmore, who have both argued that the central task of ethics is not to formulate and apply general principles but rather to stress the particularity of moral situations and the idea that profound moral disagreements reside not in a difference of *beliefs* but in different ways of *looking* at the world.[13] The argument is then brought to bear on literature with a parallel drawn more or less explicitly between a moral agent on the one hand and a competent reader on the other. The idea is that the

10. For a detailed discussion, see Peter Lamarque and Stein Haugom Olsen, *Truth, Fiction, and Literature: A Philosophical Perspective* (Oxford, 1994), Chap. 13.

11. Iris Murdoch, *The Sovereignty of Good* (London, 1970), p. 34.

12. Iris Murdoch, *Metaphysics as a Guide to Morals* (Harmondsworth, England, 1993), p. 117.

13. See, for example, D. Z. Phillips, *Through a Darkening Glass* (London, 1986), and R. M. Beardsmore, *Art and Morality* (London, 1971).

moral agent and the reader both confront complex moral situations, with both called on to adopt an imaginative perspective on those situations which should yield in the one case a moral judgment or appropriate action and in the other a moral insight or revised way of seeing. A competent reader might hope to learn from the literary work not by formulating a derived moral principle but by acquiring a new vision or perspective on the world.

A not dissimilar position is taken by Martha Nussbaum and Hilary Putnam as part of a general argument toward the assimilation of particular works of literature into moral philosophy as essential components of moral reasoning. Nussbaum states: "If the enterprise of moral philosophy is understood . . . as a pursuit of truth in all its forms, requiring a deep and sympathetic investigation of all major ethical alternatives and the comparison of each with our active sense of life, then moral philosophy requires such literary texts, and the experience of loving and attentive novel-reading, for its completion."[14] And according to Putnam: "Literature does not, or does not often, depict *solutions*. What especially the novel does is aid us in the imaginative re-creation of moral perplexities, in the widest sense. . . . If moral reasoning, at the reflective level, is the conscious criticism of ways of life, then the sensitive appreciation in the imagination of predicaments and perplexities must be essential to sensitive moral reasoning. Novels and plays do not set moral knowledge before us, that is true. But they do (frequently) do something for us that must be done for us if we are to gain any moral knowledge."[15]

Again it seems beyond doubt that literary works—including perhaps par excellence works of tragedy—have the capacity to foster "sensitive appreciation in the imagination of predicaments and perplexities." And no doubt there is a moral aspect to this. But the danger with this whole line of thinking is that too much gets run together too fast. The imaginative and moral and literary dimensions blur into one another in a way that threatens to weaken such insights as we might hope to gain about the moral value of tragedy or the literary representation of suffering. But I do think we can build on the simple intuitions that govern both the "moral lesson" and "moral vision" views of moral content.

14. Nussbaum, *Love's Knowledge*, pp. 26–27.
15. Hilary Putnam, "Literature, Science, and Reflection," in *Meaning and the Moral Sciences* (London, 1978), pp. 86–87.

IV

First, we need to acknowledge at least a prima facie distinction between a *fictive* dimension, a *literary* dimension, and a *moral* dimension in works of tragedy. Explaining how these are distinct and also how they interrelate will be the basis of the account that follows. My suggestion is that these dimensions are not interchangeable, not coextensional, and not reducible one to the other but that if we want to find a general explanation of the moral values of tragedy, we need reference to all three.

The fictive dimension might seem problematic in relation to tragedy on the grounds that the subject matter of tragic drama was traditionally based on true stories—or at least stories assumed to be true—involving actual individuals, families, dynasties, emperors, or kings on whom misfortune had fallen. Even if that is right, however, though it is not part of a definition of tragedy, it is still appropriate to speak of a fictive dimension in the sense I intend. For the fictive dimension, as explained in Chapters 2 and 3, involves a mode of storytelling, not a kind of story told. Real events can be fictionalized by being represented in a certain way. Fictiveness in this sense is a mode of utterance, one that invites and elicits an imaginative response rather than a response grounded in belief and verification.[16] Fictive storytelling disengages standard conditions of assertion, it invites imaginative rather than belief-based involvement, it creates worlds and characters, and it encourages participation, not a concern for correspondence with the facts. The fictive dimension is value-neutral. There is no inherent value in the fictive mode, only instrumental values.

The literary dimension is different in several respects. For one thing it is not value-neutral. To identify a literary dimension in a work is to identify something of value in the work, some special interest that it promises, some expectation that it will reward a certain kind of attention. To appreciate a work for its literary values is to attend to its aesthetic qualities but especially to the way that it sustains and develops a humanly interesting content or theme,[17] ideas I will develop further in Chapter 12. We have already seen how such a theme might have a moral content, that is, how it might be expressed in a proposition apparently of the same form as a moral principle or injunction. Themes can take other forms as well. But a description of a theme with moral content is not functioning as a

16. For more details of this account of fiction, expanding on Chapters 2 and 3, see Lamarque and Olsen, *Truth, Fiction, and Literature*, pt. 1.

17. Again, for a fuller account, see ibid., pt. 3.

description of an independent moral principle but offers a way of identifying some central focus or unity in the work (it points inward, not outward). There is no implication that a work must sustain some one determinate theme. *King Lear* invites any number of interpretations, including what Jonathan Dollimore has called a "materialist reading" whereby the focus of the play is seen to be "power, property and inheritance": "The cherished norms of human kindness [are] shown to have no 'natural' sanction at all. A catastrophic redistribution of power and property . . . disclose[s] the awful truth that these two things are somehow prior to the laws of human kindness rather than vice versa."[18] This interpretation need not preclude that given by Knight, for example: both readings conform to the conventions of literary appreciation, both seeking to identify some thematic coherence that makes the play rewarding as a work of art.

The fictive and the literary dimensions can be explained in terms of a certain kind of attention given to a work: a certain perspective on the work, conventionally determined. The fictive dimension invites what might be called a fictive stance—that of imaginative involvement and cognitive distance—whereas the literary dimension invites a related, but distinct, literary response—the attempt to define a unifying aesthetic purpose in the work through thematic interpretation.

So it is, third, that a work can have a *moral dimension*, not reducible to the other two, which facilitates some further moral appropriation of the work's content, either as a contribution to moral philosophy or as illustrative support for some broader metaphysical picture or just for clarifying one's own moral precepts. Thus when Dollimore goes on to say about *Lear*, "Human values are not antecedent to these material realities but are, on the contrary, in-formed by them,"[19] he is both talking about the play and making a statement about the nature of moral values as he sees them. Similarly, the moral vision theorists such as Murdoch or Phillips or Nussbaum (or even Schopenhauer and Nietzsche) appropriate the vision (moral content) of tragic drama into their own independent moral theories. Their mistake, I have suggested, is to suppose that the moral dimension is simply subsumed under the literary dimension, that there is a seamless transition from being literary critics to being moral philosophers; that in identifying a literary theme of a moral nature, they have ipso facto established a moral insight.

18. Jonathan Dollimore, "*King Lear* and Essentialist Humanism," in *Shakespearean Tragedy*, ed. John Drakakis (London, 1992), p. 201.
19. Ibid.

Fictional Points of View

To bring out more precisely how the fictive, literary, and moral dimensions interrelate—and thus how it is that representations of suffering in tragedy can merit our moral interest and involvement—I will briefly bring in one further and final distinction, which has come up already in different contexts: that between internal and external perspectives on imaginary worlds. This distinction is absolutely fundamental to understanding the values we attribute to fictional representations.

The internal perspective on an imaginary world is paradigmatically that of the fictive stance, namely, direct imaginative involvement with the subject of a work. Readers or viewers can project themselves into a fictional world and become, so it seems, participants or observers in that world. In contrast, the external perspective involves no imaginative projection; it focuses on the fictionality of the worlds depicted, on modes of representation, on literary devices and narrative structure, on theme and genre, on possible interpretations. Under the internal perspective, fictional characters are imagined to be fellow humans in real predicaments, objects of sympathy and concern, similar to ourselves in many respects; under the external perspective, they are viewed as fictional characters, linguistic or ideological constructs, whose nature and qualities are grounded in the descriptive modes by which they are presented.[20] The two perspectives nicely interact. Take our reaction to the death of Cordelia in *King Lear*, internally and imaginatively, viewers are dismayed by so futile and tragic a loss. Yet, from the external perspective, few would welcome Nahum Tate's rewriting of the play where Cordelia is saved. Cordelia's death, as we come to see, is essential to the tragic structure of the play. From the internal perspective, we might wish her spared; from the external perspective, we want the play just as it is.[21]

There are deeper connections still. Our imaginative response to, say, Lear and Cordelia is not just a response to them as persons in a tragic

20. More on internal and external perspectives on fiction can be found in Lamarque and Olsen, *Truth, Fiction, and Literature*, chap. 6. We saw in Chapter 1 some of the similar, though not identical, conceptions of internal and external ways of reflecting on characters proposed, for example, by Kendall Walton, Peter van Inwagen, and Frank Palmer. A rather different distinction is that between a first-order response to tragedy and a "metaresponse," that is, a response to the first-order response. This distinction has been used by Susan Feagin to account for the pleasures of tragedy. A metaresponse is not the same as the external perspective, for the latter is a way of contemplating a *work* (and its content), whereas the former is directed to a reader of the work. See Susan L. Feagin, "The Pleasures of Tragedy," *American Philosophical Quarterly* 20 (1983): 95–104; and Sally Markovitz, "Guilty Pleasures: Aesthetic Meta-Response and Fiction," *Journal of Aesthetics and Art Criticism* 50 (1992): 307–316.

21. Although in a different theoretical setting, the account is similar to that in Kendall L. Walton, *Mimesis as Make-Believe* (Cambridge, Mass., 1990), pp. 258–259.

predicament but a response to them *as represented* in a dramatic context. As Flint Schier puts it, "Our reaction is necessarily governed by *how* they are represented, and the kind of emotion that it is appropriate to feel is determined by the quality of the representation."[22] Not all kinds of representation, even of ostensibly the same subject matter—for example, sentimental, sensational, melodramatic kinds—merit emotional involvement. The same point can be put like this: the external perspective, an awareness of modes of representation, dictates the kind of involvement appropriate from the internal perspective. If that is right, it follows that the responses of pity and fear which are so central to Aristotle's account of tragedy are not just vague and contingent reactions to characters conceived as real people but are also an integral part of an imaginative engagement with the tragedy's representational content; a failure to respond in that way is partly a failure of understanding. *Katharsis* can then be seen not merely as a clinical "purging" of the emotions but as a further kind of self-knowledge, one involving a clarification or "working through" of the emotions, revealing their proper objects.[23]

The distinction between internal and external perspectives can also help explain how literary tragedy differs from fantasy or horror. One difference in modes of imagining is this: sometimes we simply *find ourselves* in a certain state of mind, sometimes we adopt a state of mind because we recognize we are being invited to do so. Fantasy belongs with the former, art with the latter. In the case of works of art, we respond in a certain way to the fictive presentation at least partly because we recognize a reason for doing so, within the structure of the work. In contrast, the imaginings of fantasy are purely manipulative; attitudes and responses are the products of causes, and we adopt a point of view, as we might say, *in spite of ourselves*. We have only a minimal awareness of the representational modes in which the fantasy is embodied. In fantasy, then, unlike in art, the internal perspective on an imaginary world overwhelms the external perspective.

What is valuable about artistic representation is the careful mediation of the two perspectives, the guidance of imaginative response by the very structures of representation itself. An appropriate response to the speech by the Chorus at the end of the *Antigone* is dictated by the function it is seen as serving in the structure of the play, that is, as more than just a

22. Flint Schier, "Tragedy and the Community of Sentiment," in *Philosophy and Fiction: Essays in Literary Aesthetics*, ed. Peter Lamarque (Aberdeen, 1983), p. 85.

23. The idea of "working through" emotions comes from Amélie Rorty, "Psychology of Aristotelian Tragedy," p. 66.

moral homily offered for our edification. The matter is normative, for one who fails to respond has not only failed imaginatively but also in understanding.

Returning then to the moral content of tragedy, we can see different interlocking elements. Taken as a literary work, a tragic drama will invite an interpretation of its central themes, characterizable often, if not always, in moral terms. This interpretation will be specific to the work; it is a way of redescribing and unifying elements of the work's subject matter and must be sensitive to the modes in which that subject matter is presented. But tragedies are also dramatic productions that engage viewers imaginatively. Aristotle's emphasis on action rather than character, on dramatic form rather than narrative form, highlights the importance of first-person performance, not third-person narration, in tragedy: the direct presentation of the suffering hero, not just a report about him or her.[24] The dramatic presentation both elicits and controls a sympathetic and imaginative response that serves to make the moral themes more immediate. Only at this point is the further appropriation of the moral content of tragedy possible or valuable—be it in support of a Schopenhauerian pessimism or the cultural materialism of Jonathan Dollimore or in debates in moral philosophy. Generalizations on the theme of people of good character suffering terrible reversals of fortune can yield an important moral perspective on human life only in the light of a full assimilation of the sympathetic, imaginative response to the particularities of tragic drama, mediated by some overall conception of how the elements of the drama cohere within a thematic interpretation. Once again, what is further reinforced is the Murdochian-cum-Aristotelian view of the universal emerging from the particular in poetic art.

It is the interrelation between the moral and the literary which is of special interest; for one consequence of the account given—and surely a desirable consequence—is that a different kind of moral appropriation will be available under different thematic interpretations of a work. To take an extreme and trivial example: were *Othello* to be interpreted or performed as comedy, say, or as racialist propaganda, then the sympathetic engagement with the imaginary world dictated by its tragic elements would be diluted or made fun of and any corresponding moral insight would be lost or perverted. Only *under a certain description* does tragedy merit and reward a moral perspective.

24. The importance of the dramatic and "first-person" nature of tragedy is emphasized by Ruby Meager in "Tragedy," *Proceedings of the Aristotelian Society* 34, suppl. vol. (1960): 165–186.

Tragedy and Moral Value

The moral value of tragic drama is *constituted* by the fact that certain modes of representing tragic events afford controlled imaginative access to themes of human failure and disaster. This access is uniquely available to art in the way that it exploits and balances the tension between internal and external points of view. There is no simple answer to why we should want such access to human suffering (we will explore one suggestion in the next chapter). But, in general, surely no explanation is needed for why matters of such central human concern should be of enduring human interest.

9

Tragedy and Skepticism

There are bleak tragedies, tragedies that end on a note of wintry quiet, where the only consolation seems to be that life is finite, suffering must have an end—the story is almost over. This is the atmosphere of Schubert's song cycle *Die Winterreise.* The power of this cycle, its command of our rapt attention, cannot lie in any consoling vision of the world. On the contrary, winter has occupied the haunts of summer, and all that is left is reflection on the winter within the poet's soul—reflection, wandering, madness and death. The power of such an experience must reside in the intimacy of it. We do not witness the suffering from without, but rather from within the very soul of the sufferer. The value that we attach to this experience and the reason we seek it is undoubtedly just this: that it gives us an imaginative sense of what it is like to feel, see and live in a certain way. No mere perception of grief from without could give us so strong a sense of the subjective reality of grief.

—Flint Schier, "Tragedy and the Community of Sentiment"

. . . my identification of you as a human being is not merely an identification *of* you but *with* you.

—Stanley Cavell, *The Claim of Reason*

I

Perhaps the most original, certainly the most striking, aspect of Stanley Cavell's philosophy is the connection he draws between tragedy and skepticism. Here we see all the hallmarks of Cavell: the merging of philosophy and literature, the interdisciplinary virtuosity, the eye for the unusual. The idea first came up in his book *Must We Mean What We Say?* (1969), in which he juxtaposed a chapter on other minds ("Knowing and Acknowledging") with a reading of *King Lear* ("The Avoidance of Love"). He admitted later that he was unclear at that time about the implications of this juxtaposition;[1] but he followed

---

1. Stanley Cavell, *The Claim of Reason* (Oxford, 1979), p. 389.

it up in *The Claim of Reason* (1979) with an extensive discussion of skepticism about other minds this time including a reading of *Othello*. Finally, in 1987 he published a collection of six of his own essays on Shakespeare (including the ones on *Lear* and *Othello*). In his lengthy introduction to *Disowning Knowledge: in Six Plays of Shakespeare*, he explained and justified what he called "an epistemological reading of Shakespearean tragedy" according to which skepticism is a central theme in certain of the major plays.

So what is the connection? As with all Cavellian exegesis, the answer is not simple but contains many overlapping strands of thought. What is clear is that Cavell sees the connection working in both directions: skepticism, in particular about other minds, is a kind of tragedy, and tragedy is, as he puts it, "obedient to a skeptical structure."[2] Let us look at both equivalences, beginning with the claim about skepticism itself. I will look later at the details of Cavell's discussion of skepticism about other minds. But one general feature of his approach is to see philosophical doubts about other minds—what he calls the "skeptical recital"—as a real psychological phenemonon, or grounded in such, based on actual relations that people stand in one to another. Cavell feels the skeptic's predicament deeply; for him, it is not merely an idle philosophical thought experiment to raise all-embracing or "world-consuming" doubts but something we "live," something distinctively and unavoidably human. Indeed, it is as human as tragedy and like tragedy as universally seductive. He writes, "Skepticism's 'doubt' is motivated not by (not even when it is expressed as) a (misguided) intellectual scrupulousness but by a (displaced) denial, by a self-consuming disappointment that seeks world-consuming revenge."[3] Elsewhere, he makes the equation with tragedy explicit: "Skepticism concerning other minds is not skepticism but is tragedy."[4] Both tragedy and skepticism reveal the fragility of our relations with the world: the craving for certainty and the disappointment at its loss. Both "conclude," he says, "with the condition of human separation"; what both show is that "the alternative to my acknowledgment of the other is not my ignorance of him but my avoidance of him, call it my denial of him."[5]

Turning to the second part of the equivalence, the thought that tragedy (tragic drama) exhibits the same structure as skepticism, we

2. Stanley Cavell, *Disowning Knowledge: in Six Plays of Shakespeare* (Cambridge, 1987), p. 5.
3. Cavell, *Disowning Knowledge*, p. 6.
4. Cavell, *Claim of Reason*, p. xix.
5. Ibid., p. 389.

find a detailed application of Cavell's redescription of skepticism to themes in certain Shakespearean plays. In *King Lear*, Cavell characterizes the relation between Lear and Cordelia—and to a lesser extent that between Gloucester and Edgar—through the theme of the "avoidance of love." Lear's denial of Cordelia, his failure to "acknowledge" her in the face of such manifest and deep love between them is, as Cavell puts is, "an instance of the annihilation inherent in the skeptical problematic."[6] But perhaps the example of *Othello* is even more striking given the explicitness of doubt or uncertainty in the relation between Othello and Desdemona. The novelty of Cavell's reading of the play is its emphasis on the self-destructiveness of Othello's love for Desdemona, which makes demands, like the skeptic's, that can never be met:

> Othello's radical, consuming doubt is not caused by Iago's rumoring. Othello rather seizes upon Iago's suggestions as effects or covers for something the object has itself already revealed, and claimed, despite its most fervent protestations to the contrary. In this way Othello's jealousy itself is an unstable, turned concept. He seeks a possession that is not in opposition to another's claim or desire but one that establishes an absolute or inalienable bonding to himself, to which no claim or desire *could* be opposed, could conceivably count; as if the jealousy is directed to the sheer existence of the other, its separateness from him. It is against the (fantasied) possibility of overcoming this hyperbolic separateness that the skeptic's (disappointed, intellectualized, impossible, imperative, hyperbolic) demand makes sense.[7]

When Cavell speaks of the "skeptical structure" of tragedy, one thought he has in mind is what he calls the "precipitousness of skepticism's banishment of the world," which he sees figured, for example, in the "precipitousness of the Lear story, the velocity of the banishment and of the consequences of the banishments."[8] One feature of classical tragedy, in its Aristotelian form, is that the tragic outcome has a formal inevitability about it, conforming to the dictates of necessity and probability. From the start the seeds of disaster are sown, in the hamartia deep within the character of the central protagonist, and the drama is structured around a peripeteia, or reversal, in the plot, following which a rapid, inexorable

6. Cavell, *Disowning Knowledge*, p. 6.
7. Ibid., pp. 8–9.
8. Ibid., p. 5.

descent leads to the tragic denouement. As Cavell points out, for example, from the moment that Othello starts demanding "ocular proof" (III, iii, 360) "he is lost":[9]

> By the world
> I think my wife be honest, and think she is not,
> I think that thou art just, and think thou art not;
> I'll have some proof.
>
> (III, iii, 384–387)

Similarly, once the skeptical recital is begun, with its own parallel waverings, contradictions, and demands for proof, its own inner logic makes it unstoppable.

If skepticism is a species of tragedy and tragedy is a figuration of skepticism both thematically and structurally, a third connection can be found in Cavell which concerns the relation of the reader or viewer of tragedy and the protagonists in it. It is ultimately that connection which I want to pursue in the light of the other two. For it is here we find a further application of the key term *acknowledgment*; on Cavell's thesis, tragedy and skepticism result from the failure of acknowledgment, the denial of the other, the avoidance of love. Likewise, a viewer of tragedy can fail, perhaps initially must fail, in the acknowledgment of the protagonists; and this failure can mirror the failure in the dramatic events which gives rise to the tragedy, thus serving, as Cavell sees it, to implicate the viewer in the tragedy.[10] In "The Avoidance of Love," Cavell gives a long account of the problems arising from the fictionality of a drama such as *King Lear* (pp. 97–110). How can we *mind* what happens to Lear and Cordelia, when they are merely fictional characters? How can we know them or acknowledge them when they do not exist in reality? Although Cavell doesn't develop the idea, part of the answer, which I shall pursue as we go on, is that we are called on to use our "empathetic projection" (to use Cavell's own term) in engaging with the characters, and it is just that capacity for imaginative projection that will save us from the madness of radical skepticism about other minds.

9. Ibid., p. 128.

10. Cavell writes, "In failing to see what the true position of a character is, in a given moment, we are exactly put in his condition, and thereby implicated in the tragedy," in ibid., pp. 84–85.

II

In discussing skepticism, Cavell is interested in skeptical scenarios, offering a string of subtle variations of imaginary situations and asking in each case, What if? This is partly in the tradition of a priori speculation based on the philosophical thought experiment but partly too an attempt to locate skeptical reasoning in practical life. What would we do, how would we react, what would the consequences be if in actual life someone we believed to be a sentient, living human being turned out to be an automaton, an alien, a robot? The speculation is familiar enough. Mostly we are unsure how to answer, perhaps just to the degree that we are sure that the occasion could never arise. At one point, in *The Claim of Reason*, Cavell asks if someone could be "soul-blind," as he puts it: "If it makes sense to speak of seeing human beings as human beings, then it makes sense to imagine that a human being may lack the capacity to see human beings as human beings. It would make sense to ask whether someone may be soul-blind."[11] It is surprising, given Cavell's view of the psychological grounding of skepticism, that he never looks to the psychological literature to see how skeptical scenarios can be realized in actual pathological cases. Many such could be cited, including even autism, with its radical failures in the use of the imagination in interpersonal relations. But I want to introduce and reflect on a different, more unusual case that is rather closer to Cavell's own thought experiments on skepticism. This is an obscure and disturbing medical condition known as Capgras' syndrome, which is illuminating both because it reveals how a pathologically based skepticism can actually affect people's lives and, even more interesting, because of the pertinence of what contemporary research is suggesting about such cases.

Capgras' syndrome or Capgras' delusion was first noted in 1923.[12] As recent researchers of the syndrome put it, it "involves the belief that certain people, usually close relatives, have been replaced by 'dummies' or imposters."[13] John McCrone notes: "Patients see someone who looks and acts just like a loved one, but don't feel any sense of familiarity for them. To explain this anomaly, they begin to confabulate. They start to believe they are surrounded by wax models or robots, for example."[14] In one har-

11. Cavell, *Claim of Reason*, p. 378.

12. J. Capgras and J. Reboul-Lachaux, "L'illusion des 'sosies' dans un délire systématise chronique," *Bulletin de la Société Clinique de Médecine Mentale* 2 (1923): 6–16.

13. Andrew W. Young, Ian Reid, Simon Wright and Deborah J. Hellawell, "Face-Processing Impairments and the Capgras Delusion," *British Journal of Psychiatry* 162 (1993): 695.

14. John McCrone, "My Family and Other Strangers," *Independent on Sunday*, 1 March 1992, p. 40. This is a popular summary of recent research on Capgras' syndrome.

rowing case some years ago, a man in the English Midlands was so convinced that his father had been replaced by a robot that he slashed open his father's throat trying to find the wires. Until recently Capgras' syndrome has been explained in terms of organic brain damage, paramnesia, or even psychoanalysis. Recent research at Cardiff and Durham Universities, however, suggests a quite different explanation. The idea is that the syndrome arises from a relatively simple failure of normal recognition processes, which might be brought on by brain damage. It draws on recent work in neuropsychology which suggests that there are two neurological routes to the recognition of faces—the "ventral route" and the "dorsal route"—the former, broadly speaking, drawing on semantic and other "intellectual" data, and the latter assigning emotional or affective significance to the visual stimulus.[15]

> Patients with Capgras' syndrome seem to have an intact primary or ventral route to face recognition, but may have a disconnection along or damage within the secondary or dorsal route. This would mean that they receive a veridical image of the person they are looking at, which stimulates all the appropriate overt semantic data held about that person, but they lack another, possibly confirming, set of information which . . . may carry some sort of affective tone. When patients find themselves in such a conflict (that is, receiving some information which indicates the face in front of them belongs to X, but not receiving confirmation of this), they may adopt some sort of rationalisation strategy in which the individual before them is deemed to be an imposter, a dummy, a robot, or whatever extant technology may suggest.[16]

On this hypothesis, a connection is made with another neurological condition, prosopagnosia, under which patients lose the ability to recognize faces previously familiar to them, even their own reflection. This is now thought to be the mirror image of Capgras' syndrome, for in this case the emotional twinge of recognition is present and can be measured in changes of skin conductance and the like, but intellectual recognition is impaired. The split between the emotional and the intellectual aspects of recognition found in both syndromes shows that emotional "twinges of

15. The "ventral route" "runs from visual cortex to temporal lobes via the inferior longitudinal fasciculus . . . (and) corresponds to the system responsible for overt or conscious recognition; . . . the dorsal route runs between the visual cortex and the limbic system, via the inferior parietal lobule . . . (and) gives the face its emotional significance," according to Hadyn D. Ellis and Andrew W. Young, "Accounting for Delusional Misidentifications," *British Journal of Psychiatry* 157 (1990): 244.

16. Ibid.

familiarity" are a real psychological phenomenon, and work is well advanced in trying to identify the precise location in the brain of these twin sources of recognition.

Capgras' syndrome might be seen as a particularized instance of skepticism about other minds. The fact that it is a pathological condition should not discount it as a mode of skepticism. Philosophers such as Wittgenstein and Cavell have made a powerful case for supposing that ultimately all radical skepticism is pathological in origin. The interest, they would say, is not in the skeptical hypothesis per se—the claim or thought that knowledge of others is impossible—but in the kinds of stories which might make the skeptic's doubts intelligible. The problem, as Cavell puts it, "is to discover the specific plight of mind and circumstance within which a human being gives voice to his condition."[17] Skepticism about other minds can arise in many different individual circumstances, but one typical general feature, so Cavell argues, is a "failure to acknowledge" the other—as occurs, he suggests, in Lear's treatment of Cordelia or Gloucester's of Edgar or Othello's of Desdemona. Sufferers of Capgras' syndrome also display a radical failure of acknowledgment, but in this case an empirical explanation is forthcoming: the intellectual element of recognition is not confirmed or backed up by the emotional element, that twinge of familiarity, which makes recognition complete. I suggest that a closer look at this explanation is a good way into the problem of other minds and will help establish the connection with tragedy.

Philosophers are familiar enough with the distinction between the intellectual and the emotional or between, say, cognitive and affective attitudes, but applied to the idea of *recognition*, central both to Capgras' syndrome and to Cavell's account of skepticism, it acquires a slightly different connotation. For what is missing from the Capgras sufferers—and perhaps, if Cavell is right, from all radical other minds skeptics—is a kind of sympathy, a *Verstehen*, a failure of response which grounds their failure of recognition. To employ something like the internal/external distinction that has come up before, we might say that what recognition they have, being purely intellectual, rests on an *external* or objective perspective, whereas what is missing is an *internal* or empathetic point of view within which a sense of familiarity might reside. The relevant distinction is not unrelated, I suspect, to Cavell's own distinction between knowing and acknowledging. As he puts it: "It is not enough that I *know* . . . that

17. Stanley Cavell, *Must We Mean What We Say?* (New York, 1969), p. 240.

you suffer—I must do or reveal something. . . . In a word, I must *acknowledge* it."[18] The suggestion is that knowledge rests on an intellectual certainty, and acknowledgment, on a mode of response. Although the implication is that acknowledgment is something more than, something deeper than, knowledge, there is at least a hint in Cavell's writing that skepticism can be described as an intractable, even irrefutable, problem only under the intellectual aspect, that which demands and challenges the "best case," not under the aspect based on modes of response, which has to make do, as it were, with the best case or lapse into madness.[19]

So what is skepticism about other minds? And how might the internal perspective of one who can acknowledge others address that skepticism? Broadly—and traditionally—the so-called problem of other minds divides into two issues, which I will label *the existence question* and *the content question*. The existence question concerns knowledge that there are other minds *tout court*. More specific, it is the question, How do I know in any individual case that I am confronted by a res cogitans, a soul, an instance of humanity, not a robot or automaton or alien? This is the Capgras problem; with the familiarity gone, the doubts set in. Its philosophical archetype is solipsism, its pedigree Cartesianism. The content question is different, at least prima facie, for it concedes the other as res cogitans but doubts reliable access to the other's cogitations. Proust states that "a person . . . is a shadow, which we can never succeed in penetrating, of which there can be no such thing as direct knowledge, with respect to which we form countless beliefs, based upon his words and sometimes his actions, though neither words nor actions can give us anything but inadequate and as it proves contradictory information—a shadow beyond which we can alternately imagine, with equal justification, that there burns the flame of hatred and of love."[20]

Paradigmatic of content skepticism is the scenario represented by W. V. O. Quine and later Donald Davidson of radical translation and radical interpretation. What intentional states or propositional attitudes or meanings can be ascribed to the alien other? Quine and Davidson reply with versions of holism. Beliefs and attitudes cannot be assigned to a person one by one; as Davidson puts it, "the content of a propositional atti-

18. Ibid., p. 263.

19. Cavell writes, "I do not know that there is a confident answer to the question, 'How do I know that there are (other) human beings?' " yet he speaks of being able to "live our skepticism," in the sense of responding in all the appropriate ways: the implied contrast being between what is known intellectually and what is "lived." See *Claim of Reason*, pp. 439–440.

20. Quoted in John Wisdom, *Other Minds* (Berkeley and Los Angeles, 1968), p. 206.

tude derives from its place in the pattern," that is, the pattern of "other beliefs, . . . intentions, hopes, fears, expectations, and the rest."[21] Furthermore, the possibility of radical error is eliminated; in Davidson's words, "To the extent that we fail to discover a coherent and plausible pattern in the attitudes and actions of others we simply forego the chance of treating them as persons."[22] Yet content skepticism still lingers in Quinean and Davidsonian holism. There remains an "indeterminacy" of translation and an "inscrutability" of reference. There is no fact of the matter, Quine insists, whether the alien confronted with a rabbit stimulus has in mind rabbits or undetached rabbit parts.

But it is the strategies for confronting the existence and content aspects of other minds skepticism which bring us back to Cavell and acknowledgment. The Davidsonian strategy for content skepticism is a principle of charity. "Charity," he writes, "is forced on us: whether we like it or not, if we want to understand others, we must count them right in most matters."[23] And not just right for the most part, but rational. The presumption of rationality is the presumption of humanness, the very presumption that is withheld or questioned by existence skepticism. Yet perhaps the difference is not too stark. For something like a principle of charity lurks beneath a characteristic strategy—that exemplified by Cavell and others—on the existence question. Indeed, anxieties about misplaced charity motivate many of Cavell's skeptical narratives.

But Cavell's strategy, more broadly, is quite unlike Davidson's and, to the extent that it can be seen as an argument rather than a positioning, amounts to something more like a transcendental argument in the Kantian sense, or at least the sense attributed to Kant by P. F. Strawson. The pattern of a transcendental argument is to characterize a certain kind of experience and then ask about the conditions for the possibility of experiences of that kind. An interesting example for our purposes would be Sartre's well-known discussion of shame in *L'Etre et le néant*. In terms that anticipate Cavell's, Sartre writes: "Shame is by nature recognition. I recognize that I *am* as the other sees me."[24] He goes on: "This shame is shame of *oneself before the Other*; these two structures are inseparable. But at the same time I need the Other in order to realize fully all the structures of my being. The For-itself refers to

21. Donald Davidson, "Mental Events," in *Essays on Actions and Events* (Oxford, 1980), p. 221.

22. Ibid., pp. 221–222.

23. Davidson, "On the Very Idea of a Conceptual Scheme," in *Inquiries into Truth and Interpretation* (Oxford, 1984), p. 197.

24. J-P. Sartre, *Being and Nothingness*, trans. Hazel E. Barnes (London, 1969), p. 222.

the For-others."[25] The necessity alluded to is, I take it, the necessity of a transcendental argument. The point is that there are certain modes of self-consciousness—shame, guilt, jealousy, embarrassment, love, resentment—which presuppose or are intelligible only under the mode of being that Sartre calls Being-for-Others. Sartre's argument is part of a larger project to explain the phenomenology of apprehending another human being not merely as an object but also *as a person*. Thus, according to Sartre, when a man appears before me in an otherwise empty park, my own awareness of the space between us and the objects in it changes radically: "Suddenly an object has appeared which has stolen the world from me. Everything is in place; everything still exists for me; but everything is traversed by an invisible flight and fixed in the direction of a new object. The appearance of the Other in the world corresponds therefore to a fixed sliding of the whole universe, to a decentralization of the world which undermines the centralization which I am simultaneously effecting."[26] For Sartre the idea that the Other has "stolen the world from me" is a source of what he takes to be the inevitable conflict between conscious beings, and it has remarkable resonances of Cavell's account of Othello: "He cannot forgive Desdemona for existing, for being separate from him, outside, beyond command."[27]

Cavell's own strategy on the existence question is, I believe, a not dissimilar kind of transcendental argument. The existence of the Other shows itself in our modes of acknowledgment, our "empathetic projection," our love or avoidance of love. Cavell is tempted by the thought that our knowledge of others "can best be expressed" by the simple "radiation of relationships," the "cares and commitments" of everyday life, "expecting someone to tea, . . . returning a favor, . . . waving goodbye."[28] But also we discover the Other by discovering something about ourselves. The rejection or denial of the Other is not a vindication of skepticism but a reflection of our own failure of acknowledgment. The point comes out in Cavell's repeated insistence that to recognize others we must first recognize ourselves: a point he makes in relation to both Lear and Gloucester.[29] And he discerns in skepticism a structure "in which the question 'Who, or what, is this other?' . . . is tied to the question 'Who, or what, am

25. Ibid.
26. Ibid., p. 255.
27. Cavell, *Claim of Reason*, p. 491.
28. Ibid., p. 439.
29. For example, Cavell, *Disowning Knowledge*, pp. 45, 50.

I, that I should be called upon to testify to such a question?' How, and why, am I thrown back upon myself?"[30]

The trouble is, as Cavell and Sartre know well enough, transcendental arguments against skepticism are notoriously inconclusive. The determined skeptic would be prepared to reject the whole conceptual framework within which our explanations for experience are lodged. Only some further argument—perhaps along Davidsonian lines—against radical conceptual relativity could tackle the skeptic on this new ground. Yet surely something different is going on in Cavell and Sartre. They might be offering transcendental arguments to locate the existence of the Other within a conceptual scheme, in terms of conditions for making sense of certain kinds of experiences, but are they offering transcendental arguments *against skepticism*, particularly against global skepticism? Surely not, in both cases. Sartre simply pushes the epistemological problematic to one side in focusing on ontology. By enshrining the Other in a mode of being, he shifts the question from what I can know to what I am like. He has sidestepped the skeptic's challenge because he has changed the subject.[31]

Cavell too seeks to change the subject, but from within, so to speak. He is still an epistemologist and still takes skeptical worries seriously (he says of the "skeptical recital" that "something of the sort . . . must be true"),[32] but he has naturalized (and thus neutralized?) those worries by asking about the circumstances in which they arise, about motives, capacities, and responses. He describes what he calls the "best case" for knowledge of others in terms of a special kind of intimacy: a search for "a given other who exemplifies all others for me, humanity as such; . . . upon whom I stake my capacity for acknowledgment altogether. . . . If it fails, the remainder of the world and of my capacities in it have become irrelevant. . . . I am not removed from the world; it is dead for me. All for me is but toys; there is for me no new tomorrow; my chaos is come. . . . I shut my eyes to others."[33] What is significant about the passage is not only that he finds it intelligible to describe what would result from the best case failing but also that, as a consequence of seeing skepticism as a natural-

---

30. Cavell, *Claim of Reason*, p. 429.

31. Sartre writes of solipsism: "If [it] is presented . . . as a refusal to leave the solid ground of experience and as a positive attempt not to make use of the concept of the Other, then it is perfectly logical . . . although it is opposed to the deepest inclinations of our being, it derives its justification from the contradictions of the notion of *Others* considered in the idealist perspective," in *Being and Nothingness*, p. 229.

32. Cavell, *Claim of Reason*, p. 423.

33. Ibid., p. 430.

ized problem, the failure of the best case results not in a philosophical stance but in a pathological condition.

Let us return to acknowledgment and what I have termed the internal and external perspectives on others. Something of what I mean by this can be captured by a distinction Strawson drew long ago between two kinds of reactive attitudes we can have toward human beings: a personal attitude of "involvement or participation" and what he called an "objective attitude." Under an objective attitude we see others as objects of social policy, for example, or as cases for treatment, but not as objects of resentment, gratitude, forgiveness, or anger. In this sense, Cavell's "acknowledgment" can be seen as a personal but not an objective reactive attitude. He would no doubt agree with Strawson that "human commitment to participation in ordinary inter-personal relations is . . . too . . . deep-rooted" to make the idea that we might have only objective attitudes toward others even conceivable.[34] That is the very framework—or as Cavell might prefer, "form of life"—within which we live. The personal reactive attitude arises from an internal perspective on the Other, that of imaginative or emotional commitment, while the objective reactive attitude is that of an external perspective distanced from personal involvement.

III

It is time to return again to tragedy. How can all the strands we have identified in the problem of other minds bear on the understanding of tragedy? For Cavell, individual works of tragedy, particularly Shakespearean tragedy, reveal patterns of denial, failures of acknowledgment, which characterize or figure the skeptical predicament. But are there any more universal connections? Cavell himself offers little to ground further generalization beyond the strictly limited thematic readings of a handful of Shakespeare's plays. But I think we can take the connections between tragedy and skepticism further, indeed, into two areas: roughly distinguished, these are that relating to the tragic predicament (the content of tragedies), and that relating to human interest in tragedy (the values and pleasures of tragic drama).

It is a feature of the tragic predicament, at least as conceived by Aristotle, that a terrible and unforeseen reversal of fortune occurs to a char-

---

34. P. F. Strawson, "Freedom and Resentment," in *Freedom and Resentment* (London, 1974), p. 11.

acter of admirable, even noble disposition. In Martha Nussbaum's striking phrase, the theme of tragedy is "the fragility of goodness,"[35] that is, the subjection of the moral life to moral luck, to the fickleness of chance. Nowhere is this more clearly seen than in the fate of Oedipus, the paradigmatic Aristotelian tragic hero. From the confident, admired ruler of Thebes, the man who saved the city by solving the riddle of the Sphinx, he is transformed, after a terrifying moment of self-recognition, to an outcast, a pariah, blinded by his own hand, the very source of pollution that might have destroyed the city. No wonder the drama incites fear and pity in those who view it. The fear, as we saw in Chapter 7, is at least partly for ourselves, exposing our lack of knowledge, confronting us with the awful truth that such a sudden and unpredictable stroke of ill fortune might await us as well. The fragility of goodness, according to which humans are always susceptible to the reversals of chance, reflects, even instantiates, the fragility of the knowledge of others, whereby humans are constitutionally susceptible to radical doubts.

Observing the transformation of the tragic hero from well-being to disaster, viewers of tragedy are reminded of the insecurity of what they take for granted. Like Capgras sufferers, they see the familiar become unfamiliar. The Othello that kills Desdemona seems quite unlike the self-confident Othello who earlier had proclaimed his love for her. Yet there is another, perhaps deeper aspect of tragedy which emphasizes the inevitability of the tragic outcome. Again the parallel with skepticism is there; for the confidence with which certainty is asserted in a unreflective stance carries the very seeds of its corruption once reflection begins.

It is the inevitability, the necessity even, of the tragic outcome within the structure of a tragic plot which yields subtle ramifications in the way that audiences respond to tragedy. By exploring these responses, we can better understand the values of tragic drama. Part of what is valuable in tragedy—one connection with the other minds problem—is the access it affords, subjectively and imaginatively, to the experience of what it is to suffer a disastrous reversal of fortune; but part of the value also lies in having this experience controlled by the formal structures of an artistic representation. Such was the conclusion of the last chapter.

The cluster of distinctions invoked earlier to expand on Cavell's conception of acknowledgment—emotional versus intellectual, personal versus objective reactive attitudes, internal versus external perspectives—carry over to the response to works of art and tragedy especially. First, as I have

---

35. Martha C. Nussbaum, *The Fragility of Goodness* (Cambridge, 1986).

frequently emphasized, the possibility of internal and external perspectives on fictional worlds is fundamental in understanding the values we attribute to them.

The internal perspective is that of imaginative involvement. According to Kendall Walton, in adopting this perspective—as he puts it, I think somewhat misleadingly, "playing a game of make-believe"—a reader imagines not simply *de dicto* that a general state of affairs obtains but also *de se* that he, the reader or viewer, is part of the fictional world observing and judging its contents. Whether or not de se imagining is too strong to explain this involvement, it is clear that readers or viewers can and do project themselves into imaginary worlds. They can reflect on the characters and events "from the inside," imagining that what they are seeing or reading is the real thing, even while they know that it is not. They concern themselves with what is presented to them *as if* it were true, without affecting their intellectual belief that it is fiction. Perhaps they imagine themselves as part of the world, as participants or observers, as Walton supposes, but perhaps if the de dicto imagining is vivid enough they might lose a sense of themselves altogether and simply fill their minds with the "otherness" of the experience. Either way, the internal perspective is inescapably that of the imagination.

In contrast, the external perspective does not involve imaginative projection; it focuses instead on the fictionality or constructedness of the worlds depicted. Under the external perspective, fictional characters are viewed as mere abstractions from a narrative; under the internal perspective, they are imagined to be fellow humans in real predicaments, with whom we share empathetic feelings. We saw in the last chapter how the two perspectives can interact. When Othello kills Desdemona, viewers are appalled by the senselessness and injustice of it, internally and imaginatively. Yet externally, reflecting on the remorseless logic of the drama, they accept that there can be no other outcome. The yokel who jumps onto the stage to try to "save" Desdemona—about whom Cavell has much to say—is in every sense failing to understand the play.

We also saw further connections having to do with the *modes of representation* in drama, whereby an "external" awareness of these modes can dictate what "internal" involvement is appropriate. The difference between fantasy (including melodrama and horror) and art lies partly in the different ways in which responses are elicited: in the latter our imaginative responses are more self-consciously constrained by "external" attitudes we form about the work, for example, about its thematic structure, characterization, use of literary devices; in the former our responses tend to be manipulated *in spite of ourselves*, the product of causes rather than reasons. The minimal awareness of representational modes, which is typical of responses to fantasy, tends to let the internal perspective overwhelm the external perspective.

The value of artistic representation is in the mediation of the two perspectives, the constraining of imaginative response through what has been termed the "controlling intelligence" of the work.[36] Thus any failure in imaginative response comes also to count as a failure of understanding. The connection arises again with Cavell's notion of "acknowledgment." What tragic art reminds us is that the intimacy of being *present* (to use Cavell's term), of *Verstehen*, of familiarity, is tempered by the very "separateness" demanded by theatrical artifice.

Here we can bring in another distinction identified earlier when speaking of other minds skepticism: that between the existence question and the content question. For this too applies to tragedy. The existence question becomes a question about classification, about genre—art or fantasy, tragedy or comedy—and thus about appropriate modes of response. Just as we respond differently to a person and a robot, the differences being normative or criterial, so we respond differently to tragedy and farce. Cavell asks, "Could we imagine that there is a culture for which *Othello*, say, reads like science fiction—a group who just have no first-hand knowledge of the need for trust or of the pain of betrayal?" His reply is that "it would not be a group of humans."[37] The simple point well establishes that tragedy presupposes and demands the very kinds of human response that we seek in Strawson's personal reactive attitudes. Yet at another level—broadly speaking, a literary level—there might well be ways of reading or performing *Othello* where it ceases to be a tragedy, where such sympathy we have for Othello and Desdemona is diluted or mocked.

The issue takes us from imaginative response to interpretation and from the existence question to the content question. Just as we can ask of persons what attitudes and beliefs they hold, so we can ask of a work what content it yields. And such indeterminacy as surrounds the former has its familiar analogue in the latter. If Davidson is right, our best hedge against content skepticism is a principle of charity in interpretation. A similar constraint manifests itself in literary interpretation as a presumption of coherence. Again there is a nice interplay between imaginative re-

36. See, for example, Colin Lyas, "The Relevance of the Author's Sincerity," in *Philosophy and Fiction: Essays in Literary Aesthetics*, ed. Peter Lamarque (Aberdeen, 1983).

37. Cavell, *Claim of Reason*, p. 458.

sponse and thematic unity in that the search for a *structure* of meaning in a literary work is guided and informed by the limits of imagination. Cavell's discussions of Shakespeare are partly an attempt to understand the human motivation of the characters and the psychology of the tragic predicament but also his attempt to make sense of the plays as dramatic works. What they ably show is that making tragedy intelligible to us is not simply making sense of the actions and motives of the characters but also involves coming to terms with a whole pattern of thought, which in a well-written tragedy reinforces the inevitability of tragic events within a structure that shows the hopelessness of the imaginative craving that "things might have been different."

So what emerges from this about the value of tragic drama? Part of the answer, as argued in Chapter 8, is that in an artistic representation, as against mere fantasy, it affords controlled imaginative access to human failure and despair, an access that balances and mediates the internal and external perspectives on imaginary worlds. Being a theatrical representation, tragic drama does not call on us to *act*, to intervene, but, as Cavell shows, it invests our inactivity, our helplessness, with its own tragic poignancy. Inasmuch as we suffer in confronting the representation, we suffer for others, yet we are not responding only to a report of suffering but to an expression of suffering as well. In that lies the intimacy of tragedy.

But why should the experience of tragedy and its consequent suffering, its inducement of pity and fear, be valuable? Why do we put ourselves through it? Perhaps the only answer is that we recognize in the tragic predicament something profoundly and inescapably human. Why should that be? Cavell offers the insight: because it figures the predicament—of ignorance, uncertainty, lack of acknowledgment—we all stand in with regard both to others and to ourselves. By being led imaginatively through the suffering of another without being called on to act and under the guidance of an artist, we have a unique opportunity to exercise that "empathetic projection" without which we would not be human. What the recent scientific work on Capgras' syndrome shows is clear empirical evidence for the psychological reality of empathy through the claim that recognition of people we know rests not only on an intellectual grasp of the facts but also on empathetic stirrings of familiarity. Cavell, persuasively, identifies skepticism and tragedy with the failure to hold these two aspects together.

10

The Death of the Author

The artist is the creator of beautiful things.
To reveal art and conceal the artist is art's aim.

—Oscar Wilde, *The Picture of Dorian Gray*

Honest criticism and sensitive appreciation are directed not upon
the poet but upon the poetry.

—T. S. Eliot, "Tradition and the Individual Talent"

I

There is no more vexed topic in the debate over the humanistic view
of literature than that of "subjectivity." And as authors are usually
deemed to be the paradigm subjects in this context, that is, those unique
authoritative "selves" responsible for literary works, it is often thought
that the battleground for literary humanism must be fought over the status of authorship. The "death of the author" is linked inexorably with the
"death" of "liberal humanist" criticism, with the clear implication that a
commitment to humanistic criticism must bring with it a commitment to
authors and the authority supposedly vested in them. But what exactly
does the humanistic view of literature imply about the author? And what
is the case against the author?

It is now over twenty years since Roland Barthes proclaimed the "death
of the author," and the phrase, if not the fact, is well established in the literary critical community. Yet it remains far from clear what it means. I
suspect that many Anglo-American aestheticians have tended, consciously or otherwise, to shrug off Barthes's formulation as a mere Gallic
hyperbole for their own more sober "intentionalist fallacy" and thus have
given the matter no further attention. In fact, as I will show, the significant doctrines underlying the "death of the author" are far removed
from the convivial debate about intentions and have their sights set not
just on the humble author but on the concept of literature itself and
even the concept of meaning as well.

Death of the Author

My aim is to identify and analyze the main theses in two papers that are the seminal points of reference for the relevant doctrines: Roland Barthes's "The Death of the Author" and Michel Foucault's "What Is an Author?"[1] I will be asking what the theses mean and whether they are true. I will not be discussing in any detail the broader context of the papers either in relation to general currents of thought or with regard to other work by the two theorists. My interest is with the arguments, not the authors. I believe that the ideas as formulated in these essays—ideas about authorship, texts, writing, reading—are fundamental to the movement labeled poststructuralism yet are imprecisely expressed and often misunderstood. Submitting them to an analytical study will, I hope, be instructive not only to those skeptical of poststructuralism but also for those supporters who might be unclear about the precise implications.

I will focus on four main theses that strike me as prominent. These I will dub the Historicist Thesis, the Death Thesis, the Author Function Thesis, and the *Ecriture* Thesis. All are closely interwoven, and each has subcomponents that I will need to spell out. It is not my contention that Barthes and Foucault agree at every point—they clearly do not—but together they do present a case about authors and texts which has had a powerful influence on the development of a whole school of modern thought.

II

Barthes's own words provide a general characterization of the Historicist Thesis:

> The author is a modern figure, a product of our society. ("Death of the Author," p. 142)

Foucault speaks of the "coming into being of the notion of 'author'" at a specific "moment . . . in the history of ideas" ("What Is an Author?" p. 101). Both locate the birth of the author in postmedieval times, a manifestation of the rise of the individual from the Reformation through to the philosophical Enlightenment. I am less concerned with the historical

1. I will be using the following editions: Roland Barthes, "The Death of the Author," in *Image-Music-Text*, essays selected by and trans. Stephen Heath (London, 1977); and Michel Foucault, "What Is an Author?" in *The Foucault Reader*, ed. Paul Rabinow (Harmondsworth, England, 1986).

details than with the status (and meaning) of the Historicist Thesis. The idea that written works acquired authors only at a specific time in history clearly needs some explanation. I suggest that at least three possible explanations, not mutually exclusive, can be offered and they will have a bearing on how to interpret the other theses in the overall argument. I am going to eliminate as uninteresting a merely lexicographical interpretation of the Historicist Thesis, that is, an interpretation that sees the thesis as about the word *author*. I take it that there could be authors prior to there being a word *author* just as there can be writers before the word *writer* and thoughts before the word *thoughts*. No doubt for some even this is controversial, but I do not believe that Barthes and Foucault had lexicography in mind in their defense of the Historicist Thesis.

The first (plausible) interpretation, then, is this:

A certain conception of a writer (writer-as-author) is modern.

For Foucault this conception is highly specific; in effect it is a legal and social conception of authorship. The author is seen as an owner of property, a producer of marketable goods, as having rights over those goods, and also responsibilities: "Texts, books, and discourses really began to have authors . . . to the extent that authors became subject to punishment," Foucault states (p. 108). In a similar vein, Barthes identifies the author with "capitalist ideology" (p. 143). I will call this interpretation of the Historicist Thesis the "social conception," the point being that at a determinate stage in history, according to the thesis, writers (of certain kinds of texts) came to acquire a new social status, along with a corresponding legal and cultural recognition.

Again, I will not debate the truth of this historical claim—I suspect the actual details would not stand up to close scrutiny—but only comment on its theoretical implications. For example, it entails a distinction between an unrestricted notion of writer-per-se (any person who writes) and a more restricted notion of writer-as-author, the latter conceived in social or ideological terms. That distinction is useful in showing that the mere act of writing (writing on the sand, jottings on an envelope) does not make an author. An author so designated is a more weighty figure with legal rights and social standing, a producer of texts deemed to have value. Significantly, the thesis on this interpretation is about social conventions and a class of persons engaged in particular acts: it is not about a persona, a fictional character, or a construct of the text. Being about the personal status of authors, it can offer no direct support, as we will see, for either the Author Function Thesis or the *Ecriture* Thesis, both of which conceive the author in impersonal terms.

The second interpretation of the Historicist Thesis I will call the "criticism conception":

A certain conception of criticism (author-based criticism) is modern.

Here the idea is that at a certain stage of history, the focus of criticism turned to the personality of the author. Thus Barthes notes that "the image of literature to be found in ordinary culture is tyrannically centred on the author, his person, his life, his tastes, his passions, while criticism still consists for the most part in saying that Baudelaire's work is the failure of Baudelaire the man, Van Gogh's his madness, Tchaikovsky's his vice" (p. 143). This state of affairs arose, according to Barthes, only after the bourgeois revolution that gave prominence to the individual. We can leave it to historians to debate the historical development of author-based criticism. No doubt it is a matter of degree how much critical significance is given at different periods of history to an author's biographical background or personality. Although the author as person (writer, cause, origin, and so forth) is again evoked in this interpretation, it is nevertheless distinct from the "social conception." No direct implications about criticism follow from the fact that the author comes to be viewed as having rights over a text. Purely formalist criticism is compatible with a state of affairs where an author is accorded a secure legal and social identity.

The third interpretation is the most controversial but also the most interesting:

A certain conception of a text (the authored text) is modern.

This I will call the "text conception" of the Historicist Thesis. The idea is that at a certain point in history, (written) texts acquire significance in virtue of being "authored." "There was a time," Foucault writes, "when the texts which we today call 'literary' (narratives, stories, epics, tragedies, comedies) were accepted, put into circulation, and valorized without any question about the identity of their author" (p. 109). He contrasts this with the case of scientific discourses that, in the Middle Ages, owed their authority to a named provenance (Hippocrates, Pliny, or whomever). A radical change occurred, so Foucault claims, in the seventeenth and eighteenth centuries, when literary texts came to be viewed as essentially "authored," while scientific writing could carry authority even in anonymity.

These sweeping generalizations invite substantial qualification from the scrupulous historian of ideas. For our purposes, further clarification is in order. The text conception is itself open to different interpretations. At its simplest it is just the claim that at a specific point in history (perhaps a different point for different discourses) it became important that texts be attributed. A stronger claim is that this attribution actually changed the way texts were understood. That is, they could not be properly understood except as *by so-and-so.* The author attribution carried the meaning, perhaps as personal revelation, expression of belief, seal of authority, or whatever. Foucault probably has in mind at least this latter claim. But from the evidence of his Author Function Thesis, which we will look at later, he seems to want something stronger still for the text conception. The suggestion is that the personal aspects of author attribution disappear altogether. It is not actual causal origins that mark the difference between an authored and an unauthored text but rather certain (emergent) properties of the text itself. The authored text is viewed as the manifestation of a creative act but, importantly, what this yields or makes accessible is a distinctive kind of unity, integrity, meaning, interest, and value. And it is these qualities themselves, rather than their relation to some particular authorial performance, that are given prominence under this strengthened version of the Historicist Thesis.

Thus there is a slide in the text conception from the mere association of text and author to the much fuller conception of a text as a classifiable work of a certain kind fulfilling a purpose, expressing a meaning, and yielding a value. I suggest that the plausibility of the Historicist Thesis weakens as it progresses along this scale. In other words, the conception of certain pieces of writing as having meaning, unity, and value seems much less datable historically (was there ever a time when there was no such conception?) than the mere inclination to highlight author attribution.

III

Against this background we can now turn to the second substantive thesis, which I have called the Death Thesis. At its simplest, this merely claims:

The author is dead.

The meaning of the claim and assessment of its truth can be determined only relative to the Historicist Thesis, under its different interpretations. The underlying thought is this: if a certain conception (of an author, a text, and so on) has a definite historical beginning—if it arises under determinate historical conditions—then it can in principle come to an end when the historical conditions change.

One complication is that the Death Thesis can be read either as a statement of fact or as wishful thinking, that is, either as a description of the current state of affairs (we simply no longer *have* authors conceived in a certain way) or as a prescription for the future (we no longer *need* authors so conceived, we can now get by without them).[2] Both Barthes and Foucault seem to waver on the question of description and prescription. Barthes, for example, admits that "the sway of the Author remains powerful" (p. 143), yet in speaking of the "modern scriptor," in contrast with the Author (pp. 145, 146), he suggests that (modern) writing is no longer conceived as the product of an author. Similarly, Foucault tells us "we must locate the space left empty by the author's disappearance" (p. 105), the latter thus taken for granted, yet makes a prediction at the end of his essay that the author function, which is his own conception of the author, "will disappear," sometime in the future, "as our society changes" (p. 119).

To see what the Death Thesis amounts to, let us run briefly through the different permutations.

> The writer-as-author is dead, or should be (deriving from the social conception of the Historicist Thesis).

Does the conception of writer-as-author, with a certain social and legal status, still obtain? Surely it does. Authors are still, in Foucault's words, "subject to punishment" (they can even be sentenced to death); there are copyright laws and blasphemy laws; authors can be sued for libel or plagiarism; they attract interest from biographers and gossips. Authors under this conception are certainly not dead. But should they be killed off? Should we try and rid ourselves of this conception? The question is political and moral, not philosophical. Should we promote a society where all writing is anonymous, where writers have no legal status and no obligations? Maybe. But the point is quite independent of any theoretical

2. A similar ambiguity lies in the origin of the Death Thesis, namely, Nietzsche's proclamation that "God is dead." Was Nietzsche describing a new human consciousness already in evidence, or was he heralding a radical break with the past?

argument about *écriture* or the author function, for it is a point about the treatment of actual people in a political and legal system.

> Author-based criticism is dead, or should be (deriving from the criticism conception of the Historicist Thesis).

Here we come closest to the Intentionalist Fallacy in that anti-intentionalists can be seen as advancing some such version of the Death Thesis. But note, first, that anti-intentionalists are not committed to a version based on the social conception of authorship, or indeed to the text conception. Also, second, they are committed only to the normative element (author-based criticism should be dead) not to the descriptive element (it is in fact dead).

Although there is certainly an overlap here between the anti-intentionalists and Barthes and Foucault, it seems to be the only point of contact. If the Death Thesis simply records and endorses the decline of crude author-based criticism, then it is of only modest theoretical interest. The debate continues about the proper role of authorial intention in literary criticism, but there does seem to be a general consensus that concentration on purely biographical factors—or the so-called personality of an author—is not integral to a serious critical discipline (the point goes back at least to T. S. Eliot in 1919). In fact, as we shall see, it is quite clear that Barthes and Foucault had something more substantial in their sights when they advanced the Death Thesis. Nevertheless, much of the credibility of the thesis undoubtedly trades off the more secure intuitions within the community of literary critics that pure author-based criticism is a legitimate target. It is thus important to identify the real Death Thesis as intended by Barthes and Foucault so that we do not find ourselves forced to assent through a mistaken interpretation.

> The authored text is dead, or should be (deriving from the text conception of the Historicist Thesis).

Does the conception of the authored text still prevail, that is, the text conceived as having a determinate meaning, as the manifestation of a creative act? Certainly the qualities of unity, expressiveness, and creative imagination are still sought and valued in literary works; indeed, they are bound up with the very conception of literature. If possession of these is sufficient for something's being an authored text, then authored texts are not dead. Remember, though, that an authored text, on the strong interpretation, is defined independently of its relation to an actual author (or author-as-person). The meaning and unity of an authored text are explicable not in terms of some real act of creation, some determinate psychological origin, but only as a projection of these in the text itself. This is the import of the Author Function Thesis.

Foucault would accept that literary criticism still retains its conception of the authored text; in fact, he perceives this conception as the foundation of literary criticism. The Death Thesis, then, in this version, must be seen as a prescription, not a description. Foucault's project is to get rid of the authored text itself (along with its concomitant notions of meaning, interpretation, unity, expression, and value). The Author Function, which is the defining feature of an authored text, is, according to Foucault, "an ideological product" (p. 119), a repressive and restricting "principle of thrift in the proliferation of meaning" (p. 118). In effect, Foucault's death prescription is aimed at the very concept of a literary work that sustains the practice of literary criticism (it is also aimed, more broadly, at any class of work subject to similar interpretative and evaluative constraints). The prescription has little to do with the role or status of authors-as-persons.

Seen in this light, it is no defense against Foucault's attack to point out that the literary institution has long ceased to give prominence to an author's personality. That would be to give undue weight to the weaker versions of the Death Thesis. There is no room for the complacent thought that Foucault is just another anti-intentionalist. On the other hand, Foucault cannot find support for his attack on the authored-text merely through an appeal to the inadequacy of crude author-based criticism. He has in effect pushed the debate beyond the author altogether.

IV

The Author Function Thesis is intended to provide further support for the strong version (the "authored-text is dead" version) of the Death Thesis. Although the notion is never explicitly defined by Foucault, the central idea is that the author function is a property of a discourse (or text) and amounts to something more than its just being written or produced by a person (of whatever status): "There are a certain number of discourses that are endowed with the 'author function,' while others are deprived of it" (p. 107).

We can identify a number of separate components of the thesis which help to clarify the notion of "author function." First is the distinctness claim:

(1) The author function is distinct from the author-as-person (or writer).

Foucault makes it clear that the author function "does not refer purely and simply to a real individual" (p. 113). He complicates the exposition by often using the term interchangeably with "the author"; however, the term *author* itself is not intended as a direct designation of an individual. He says that "it would be . . . wrong to equate the author with the real writer" (p. 112), speaking of the author as "a certain functional principle" (p. 119).

What are the grounds for postulating an impersonal conception of an author as distinct from a personal conception? Foucault does not simply have in mind the literary critical notion of an "implied author," that is, a set of attitudes informing a work which might or might not be shared with the real author. For one thing, Foucault's author function is not a construct specific to individual works but may bind together a whole oeuvre; and whereas an implied author is, as it were, just one fictional character among others in a work, the author function is more broadly conceived as determining the very nature of the work itself.[3]

One of the arguments that Foucault offers for the distinctness claim (1)—it is also his justification for describing the author as an "ideological product" (p. 119)—rests on a supposed discrepancy between the way we normally conceive the author as a person (a genius, a creator, one who proliferates meaning) and the way we conceive texts that have authors (i.e., as constrained in their meaning and confined in the uses to which they can be put). But this argument is unsatisfactory simply because there is no such discrepancy. To the extent that we conceive of an author as offering "an inexhaustible world of significations" (p. 118), as a proliferator of meaning, then we expect precisely the same of the work he or she creates.

It is more promising to read Foucault as proposing a semitechnical sense of the term *author*, one that conforms to the following principle:

3. I am guided here, indeed throughout this essay, by the useful discussion in Alexander Nehamas, "Writer, Text, Work, Author," in *Literature and the Question of Philosophy*, ed. Anthony J. Cascardi (Baltimore, 1987).

(2) "Having an author" is not a relational predicate (characterizing a relation between a work and a person) but a monadic predicate (characterizing a certain kind of work).

This principle signals the move from "X has an author" to "X is authored" or, more explicitly, from "X has Y as an author" (the relational predicate) to "X is Y-authored" (the monadic predicate). The author function becomes a property of a text or discourse, not a relation between a text and a person. We need to ask what the monadic predicate "being authored" or being "Y-authored" actually means in this special sense.

First, though, it might be helpful to offer a further elaboration of (2) in terms of paraphrase or reduction:

(3) All relevant claims about the relation between an author-as-person and a text are reducible to claims about an authored text.

In this way the author disappears through a process comparable to ontological reduction by paraphrase. In place of, for example, "The work is a product of the author's creative act," we can substitute "The work is an authored text" and still retain the significant cognitive content of the former. Such a semantic maneuver is not intended to show that authors (as persons) are redundant. At best its aim is to show that *relative to critical discourse,* references to an author can be eliminated without loss of significant content. I take it that some such thesis underlies Foucault's statement that the "aspects of an individual which we designate as making him an author are only a projection, in more or less psychologizing terms, of the operations that we force texts to undergo, the connections that we make, the traits that we establish as pertinent, the continuities that we recognize, or the exclusions that we practice" (p. 110). Foucault is thinking of such aspects as an author's "design" and "creative power," as well as the meaning, unity, and expression with which the author informs the text. He believes, as we have seen, that these features can be attributed directly to an authored text without reference back to the author-as-person. This is the heart of the Author Function Thesis.

What support can be offered for propositions (2) and (3)? After all, they are not obviously true, and they depart from the more familiar meaning of "author." The main logical support that Foucault offers is an argument about authors' names. An author's name, he suggests, does not operate purely referentially; rather than picking out some individual person, it has, he says, a "classificatory function," it "serves to characterize a certain mode of being of discourse" (p. 107). I think he has something like the following in mind:

(4) (Some) author attributions (using an author's name) are nonextensional.

If we say that a play is by Shakespeare, we mean or connote more than just that the play was written by a particular man (Shakespeare). For one thing we assign a certain honorific quality to it (it is likely to be a play worthy of our attention); we also relate the play to a wider body of work—to *Hamlet, King Lear, Twelfth Night,* and so on. Being "by Shakespeare" signals not just an external relation but an internal characterization. We move from "X is a play by Shakespeare" to "X is a Shakespeare play" or even "X is Shakespearean." The latter formulations are nonextensional—or at least have nonextensional readings—in the sense that substitution of coreferential names is not always permissible (does not preserve truth); if Shakespeare turns out to be Bacon, it does not follow that the plays become Baconian, where that has its own distinctive connotations.

Let us suppose that stated like this the argument has some merit. Does it in fact support the Author Function Thesis? Certainly it provides an illustration of the move from a relational predicate to a monadic predicate, in this case from "by Shakespeare" to "Shakespearean" Is this an instance of the move from "X has Y as an author" to "X is Y-authored"? Maybe. But what it shows is that we are not obliged to make the move. "X has Shakespeare as an author" has both a nonextensional, classificatory meaning *and* a fully extensional, relational meaning. In other words, the reference to Shakespeare the person still stands. By pointing, quite rightly, to the classificatory function of authors' names, Foucault mistakenly supposes that this in itself eliminates the referential function.

What about the move in (2) from "X has an author" to "X is authored"? This move is not directly supported by the argument from authors' names but hangs on a distinctive conception of an "authored text." This takes us back to the Historicist Thesis. Foucault, as we saw, has in mind not just the attribution of an author to a text, nor in the more sophisticated version of (4) a text classified through a nonextensional attribution, but rather a notion of an authored text conceived more broadly:

(5) An authored text is one that is subject to interpretation, constrained in its meaning, exhibiting unity and coherence, and located in a system of values.

It is precisely this notion he is attacking when he attacks the author function. But now we can begin to see how uncomfortably the pieces fit together for Foucault. The author as a person—with a personality, a biography, a legal status and social standing—has no role in (5). The reductive theses (2) and (3) see to that, as does the distinctness thesis (1). In effect, Foucault has recognized, in postulating the author function and the notion of an authored text, that the qualities in (5) are *institutionally based* qualities—part of the conception of literature—and not *individualistically based*—formulated in terms of individual psychological attitudes.[4] There is no need to see the constraints on interpretation, or the source of unity and coherence or the criteria of value, as directly attributable to an individual (the author-as-person).

If that is the point of the Author Function Thesis, then it has some force, albeit reiterating a position well-established in anti-intentionalist critical theory. But Foucault cannot have it both ways: he cannot distance the authored text from the author-as-person and at the same time mount his attack on the authored text on the grounds that it perpetuates the bourgeois ideology of the individual, that it elevates the author into a position of God-like power and authority, enshrined in law. It is as if Foucault has not fully assimilated the implications of his own Author Function Thesis; he speaks as if his main target is still the author-as-person behind and beyond the work, informing it with a secret and inner meaning. Perhaps the source of the problem is the misleading invocation of the author in "author function" and "authored text." Strictly speaking, authors have nothing to do with it; the authored text, so-called, at least in its most obvious manifestation, is a literary work, defined institutionally. Literary works have authors, of course; they are the product of a creative act (a real act from a real agent), but the constraints on interpretation and the determination of coherence and value are independent of the individual author's will. That is the lesson of the Death Thesis in its more plausible versions, and it should be the lesson of the Author Function Thesis.

V

Barthes's version of the author function is what he calls the "modern scriptor" who is "born simultaneously with the text" (p. 145). But Barthes bases his move from the relational author to the nonrelational scriptor—

4. For a useful account of institutional qualities in the literary context, see Stein Haugom Olsen, "Literary Aesthetics and Literary Practice," in *The End of Literary Theory* (Cambridge, 1987).

his version of the Author Function Thesis—on a thesis about writing (*écriture*). The basic claim of what I have called the *Ecriture* Thesis is this (in Barthes's words):

Writing is the destruction of every voice, of every point of origin. (P. 142)

The implication is that the very nature of writing makes the author (the author-as-person) redundant. What arguments does Barthes offer to support this thesis?

The first is an argument from narrative: "As soon as a fact is *narrated* no longer with a view to acting directly on reality but intransitively, that is to say, finally outside of any function other than that of the very practice of the symbol itself . . . the voice loses its origin" (p. 142). It is difficult to conceive of any act of narration which satisfies the condition of having no other function than the "practice of the symbol itself." Nearly all narration has some further aim, indeed, the aim in some form or other to "act . . . directly on reality": be it to inform, entertain, persuade, instruct, or whatever. Narration is by definition an act, and no acts are truly gratuitous. Strictly speaking, the narrative argument collapses here.

Still, one might suppose, charitably, that certain kinds of fictional narrative come close to Barthes's specification: narratives where playfulness is paramount. It is a convention of some kinds of fiction that they draw attention to their own fictional status, that they point inward rather than outward, that they teasingly conceal their origin. But even if we grant that in these special cases attention focuses only on the "symbol itself," nothing here supports a general thesis about writing (or authors). For one thing, different kinds of conventions, often far removed from the tricks of fiction, govern written narratives (as with speech acts), and in many such cases narrative purpose (and thus the "voice of origin") is manifest. Also not all writing is in narrative form.

A second argument for the *Ecriture* Thesis rests on the characterization of writing as performative: "*Writing* can no longer designate an operation of recording, notation, representation, "depiction" . . . ; rather, it designates . . . a performative . . . in which the enunciation has no other content . . . than the act by which it is uttered" (pp. 145–146). But the claim that writing has the status of a performative utterance, instead of supporting the *Ecriture* Thesis, in fact directly contradicts it. A performative utterance counts as an act—a promise, a marriage, a declaration of war—only under precisely specified contextual conditions; and one of those conditions, essential in each case, is the speaker's having appropriate intentions. Far from being the destruction of a "voice of origin" the successful performative relies crucially on the disposition and authority of the speaker. The analogy, then, is unfortunate, to say the least.

Clearly what impressed Barthes about the performative utterance is another feature: self-validation. If I say "I promise," I am not reporting some external fact but, under the right conditions, bringing a fact into existence. But even if we set aside the requirement of the speaker's authority and focus only on the feature of self-validation, the analogy with performatives is still inadequate. Once again Barthes is led to an unwarranted generalization about the nature of writing by taking as a paradigm a certain kind of fictive utterance, which creates its own facts or world, and ignoring more commonplace illocutionary purposes.

The third argument is about meaning. The thought is that writing per se, in contrast to the constrained authored text, does not yield any determinate meaning: "A text is not a line of words releasing a single 'theological' meaning (the 'message' of the Author-God) but a multi-dimensional space in which a variety of writings, none of them original, blend and clash" (p. 146). We find the same idea in Foucault, even though he voices some skepticism later on about *écriture*: "today's writing has freed itself from the dimension of expression," "it is an interplay of signs," it "unfolds like a game" (p. 102). How does this support the thesis that writing has destroyed the voice of origin? The argument seems to go something like this: determinate meaning is always the product of authorial imposition, where there is no determinate meaning there is no author, writing per se (*écriture*) has no determinate meaning (it is a mere play of signs), so writing per se shows the author to be redundant. The reasoning is bizarre. Its formal validity is suspect, and it also begs the question that there is such a thing as writing per se. *Ecriture* is in effect stipulated to be authorless, to be lacking in determinate meaning, to be free of interpretative constraints. But this very conception of *écriture* needs to be challenged.

The key is the idea of a "text." A "text," as Barthes conceives it, is a specific manifestation of *écriture*. It is to be contrasted with a "work": a work belongs in a genre, its meaning is constrained, it has an author, it is subject to classification. A text, Barthes tells us, is "always *paradoxical*"; it "practises the infinite deferment of the signified";[5] "it answers not to an interpretation, even a liberal one, but to an explosion, a dissemination" ("From Work to Text," p. 159); "it cannot be contained in a hierarchy,

---

5. Roland Barthes, "From Work to Text," in *Image-Music-Text*, p. 158.

even in a simple division of genres" (p. 157); and "no vital 'respect' is due to the Text: it can be *broken*" (p. 161). This idea of a text as an explosion of unconstrained meaning, without origin and without purpose, is a theoretician's fiction. Perhaps we could, by abstraction, come to look at writing in this way, but it would be quite idle to do so. It would be like trying to hear a Mozart symphony as a mere string of unstructured sounds. More important, though, it is no part of the concept of writing (or language) that it should be so viewed. Writing, like speech, or any language "performed," is inevitably and properly conceived as purposive. To use language as meaningful discourse is to perform speech acts; to understand discourse is, minimally, to grasp what speech acts are performed. In his view of *écriture* and of texts, Barthes tries to abstract language from the very function that gives it life.

An underlying assumption in both Barthes and Foucault is that there is intrinsic merit in what Foucault calls the "proliferation of meaning." Perhaps the fundamental objection to their combined program is that this assumption is unsupported and untenable. By prescribing the death of the author and by promoting the text over the work, both writers see themselves as liberating meaning from unnatural and undesirable restrictions. They both assume that more is better. Part of the problem is that they are trapped by a gratuitous and inappropriate political vocabulary: "repression," "authority," "control." But deeper still they reveal a predilection for a peculiarly sterile form of literary criticism, exemplified perhaps by certain passages in William Empson's *Seven Types of Ambiguity* and pressed almost *ad absurdum* in Barthes's own *S/Z*, where the literary work is seen as a limitless and unrestricted source of connotation and allusion. What is objectionable is that they have set up this conception as a paradigm not only of criticism but, worse, of reading itself as well.

The critical community at large soon tired of the simplistic proliferation of meaning, and outside the literary institution, it never found a foothold. It is a nonstarter—pointless if not impossible—to conceive of scientific or historical or philosophical discourse as *écriture*. It is always more interesting, more demanding, and more rewarding for understanding to consolidate meaning, to seek structure and coherence, to locate a work in a tradition or practice. This has nothing whatsoever to do with reinstating some bullying, authoritarian author. But, then, that figure was always just a fiction anyway.

11

Psychoanalysis and Criticism

The conflict in *Hamlet* is so effectively concealed that it was left to me to unearth it.

— Sigmund Freud, "Psychopathic Characters on the Stage"

. . . the psychic disposition of the poet himself . . . presents an important problem [that] is not to be denied, but the work of art is something in its own right, and may not be conjured away.

— Carl Jung, "Psychology and Literature"

I

Open any general introductory textbook on literary theory and you will find, as likely as not, significant entries on psychoanalysis, particularly on the developments of the French psychoanalytic school including Jacques Lacan, Julia Kristeva, and Luce Irigaray. Open any standard introduction to psychology and you are likely to find psychoanalysis mentioned only in passing and no reference to the French school.[1] Psychoanalysis—as a body of theory rather than as clinical practice—has, for twenty-five years or more, been appropriated by the humanities and is increasingly relegated to the margins of science.

Since Freud's own earliest writings, it has long been thought that psychoanalysis has natural affinities with literature. The reasons for this will be explained later. What is curious, though, is that the interest modern *literary theorists* show in psychoanalysis is, for the most part, far removed from anything to do with literature or criticism. Under the inspiration of Jacques Lacan, a clinical psychoanalyst with only a marginal interest in literary criticism, the focus of discussion has been on abstruse (quasi-scientific) theories of psychosexual development, the structure of the

---

1. This judgment is based more on random sampling than on statistical study and admittedly rests on a British, not North American (or French) experience. But the general point that the humanistic interest in psychoanalysis is stronger (on the whole) than the scientific interest is one that I stand by and is worth noting.

unconscious, and the nature of subjectivity. Lacanian psychoanalytic theory has had little to say on underlying principles of criticism or creativity or indeed literature itself. Nor can Lacan's appropriation of Saussure's linguistics reestablish the connection with literature, because far from using psychoanalytic insights to illuminate linguistic (and literary) forms, Lacan draws on linguistic phenomena to try to illuminate his own psychoanalytic account of the unconscious. There are no clear implications for the understanding of literature, and the direction of explanation is, if anything, from the literary to the psychological rather than the other way.

In this chapter my concerns are simple and limited: to continue the investigation into the bounds, or "autonomy," of literary criticism. I offer no assessment of current literary theoretical aspects of psychoanalysis, for example, of the Lacanian school, except insofar as they bear on that issue. It is psychoanalysis and *criticism* that will be the focus of the discussion. I am not concerned either to pass judgment on psychoanalysis itself as a theory of human behavior or personality; I am concerned only, in a more a priori spirit, with the relevance of the theory as applied to literature and criticism, regardless of whether the theory is independently valid or well supported.

Applications of psychoanalysis to literary criticism are notable for how little attention they give to the scientific credentials of the theory. Questions of empirical support, explanatory and predictive power, or clinical efficacy are rarely debated by proponents of psychoanalysis in criticism. I take it that a characteristic attitude is one adopted by Elizabeth Wright, an advocate of psychoanalytic criticism, who describes psychoanalysis as a "science of interpretation": "The emphasis must be on the interpretative force of the theory instead of on a simplistic true/false analysis of what are highly subjective phenomena."[2] Indeed, she uses the point to brush aside objections, like those of the erstwhile Freudian literary critic Frederick Crews, to the scientific credibility of psychoanalysis.[3] Perhaps behind this thinking—though it is not made explicit—is something like

2. Elizabeth Wright, *Psychoanalytic Criticism: Theory and Practice* (London, 1984), p. 3.

3. Ibid., p. 49. Crews was once a foremost psychoanalytic critic; see Frederick Crews, *The Sins of the Fathers: Hawthorne's Psychological Themes* (New York, 1966), and Crews, *Out of My System: Psychology, Ideology, and Critical Method* (New York, 1975). He subsequently rejected psychoanalysis as both unscientific and based on mendacity; see Crews, "The American Literary Critic Frederick Crews Explains Why He Has Rejected Freud," *London Review of Books*, 4 December 1980, and Crews, "Beyond Sulloway's *Freud*," in *Mind, Psychoanalysis, and Science*, ed. P. Clark and C. Wright (Oxford, 1988).

the "hermeneutic" conception of psychoanalytic theory, as developed by Habermas and Ricoeur, which rejects altogether the "scientistic" status of the theory.[4]

A still broader tendency contributes, I think, to an uneasy tolerance within the community of literary critics toward psychoanalytic contributions, namely, the thought that whatever the scientific respectability of psychoanalytic theory, its application can often afford "insights" into literary works, and as the demands of strict verification are in any case inappropriate in criticism, the independent validity of the theory is not of crucial concern. In Geoffrey Hartmann's playful terms, "passing through psychoanalysis" is widely tolerated, even among the otherwise skeptical.[5] In the interests of open-mindedness and a desire to welcome insights from any source, psychoanalytic criticism has become established as one among a number of critical approaches in the canon of accepted methods.

Against this otherwise commendable pluralism, it will be my contention that so-called psychoanalytic criticism faces an inescapable dilemma. Where criticism simply helps itself to the vocabulary of psychoanalysis without regard to the theory from which it arises, it is not *psychoanalytic* criticism; where it makes essential use of psychoanalysis as an explanatory theory, it is not psychoanalytic *criticism*.

II

The first step is to outline the prima facie case for the relevance of psychoanalysis to literary criticism. But straight away a caveat is in order. As Murray Schwartz aptly warned some years ago, "There are psychoanalyses today; there is no psychoanalysis."[6] Indeed, the subject has become so complex that generalizations are increasingly suspect. Nevertheless, since psychoanalysis is strictly Freud's preserve, by directing the bulk of my remarks to Freud's own theories and by concentrating on matters of general principle, I believe that what I have to say will

---

4. See Jürgen Habermas, *Knowledge and Human Interests*, trans. J. J. Shapiro (Boston, 1971), and Paul Ricoeur, *Freud and Philosophy* (New Haven, Conn., 1970). Serious criticisms can be found in Adolf Grünbaum, *The Foundations of Psychoanalysis: A Philosophical Critique* (Berkeley, 1984).

5. Geoffrey Hartmann, ed., *Psychoanalysis and the Question of the Text* (Baltimore, 1978), p. viii.

6. Murray M. Schwartz, "Critic Define Thyself," in Hartmann, *Psychoanalysis*.

have implications for the whole enterprise of "psychoanalytic approaches" to literature.[7]

I suggest there are five main categories under which psychoanalysis has a claim to the attention of literary critics. In ascending order of forcefulness, they are: (1) the direct influence of Freud; (2) a shared subject matter; (3) Freudian theories of the creation and reception of literary works; (4) the attraction of psychoanalytic readings; (5) some apparently impressive analogies. At this stage my purpose is only to outline a prima facie case; my assessment of each category will follow in the next section.

The direct influence of Freud   Freud's enormous influence on both literature itself and literary criticism in the twentieth century is undeniable. Of this influence, Lionel Trilling could write in 1941 that "much of it is so pervasive that its extent is scarcely to be determined; . . . it has been infused into our life and become a component of our culture of which it is now hard to be specifically aware."[8] Trilling singles out for mention the influence on the Surrealists, Kafka, Thomas Mann, and James Joyce, but in fact, as the century advances, it becomes increasingly hard to think of any writer (of stature) who is determinately not influenced by Freudian ideas. Of course, this influence can take many forms and can be more or less self-conscious: from a superficial use of "Freudian" symbols or dreams inviting interpretation as disguised wish fulfillments to deeper thematic explorations of pathological conditions. Georg Lukács has characterized the whole of modernist literature as a "flight into psychopathology."[9]

Once again, what is striking about this influence, in both its seriousness and its extent, is its independence of the standing of Freud's theories in the scientific community. The disparity has led Joseph Margolis to the suggestion that the theories have acquired the status of a "myth," which he defines as "a schema of the imagination which, independently of the scientific status of the propositions it may subtend, is capable of effectively organising our way of viewing portions of the external world in accord

7. The association of "psychoanalysis" as such with Freud himself while other designations, such as "individual psychology" (Adler) or "analytical psychology" (Jung), are assigned to distinct and breakaway alternatives is emphasized by J. A. C. Brown in *Freud and the Post-Freudians* (Harmondsworth, England, 1964).

8. Lionel Trilling, "Freud and Literature," in *The Liberal Imagination: Essays on Literature and Society* (London, 1955), pp. 38–39.

9. Georg Lukács, "The Ideology of Modernism," in *Twentieth Century Literary Criticism*, ed. David Lodge (London, 1972).

with its distinctions."[10] Some explanation is needed for how such a "myth" gets established, but such is not primarily a philosophical inquiry.

The sheer volume of critical writing about literary works which overtly draws on Freudian ideas is further justification for calling the ideas mythic. But the exact nature of this influence on criticism takes us into later categories.

A shared subject matter We can turn again to Trilling to express the close affinities between psychoanalysis and literature with respect to subject matter: "The human nature of the Freudian psychology is exactly the stuff upon which the poet has always exercised his art."[11] Freud himself frequently acknowledged his debt to the poets, and this must contribute significantly to the lasting appeal of psychoanalysis in literary circles.

Freud believed not only that creative writers had anticipated him in the discovery of the unconscious but that their writings could provide a valuable source of *evidence* for his own scientific treatment of the same ideas. In his essay on Wilhelm Jensen's novel *Gradiva*, for example, Freud asserts that "creative writers are valuable allies and their evidence is to be prized highly" (1907, 9, p. 8).[12] This novel, with its archaeological motifs, provides a nice allegory of self-discovery; the emergence of the protagonist's memories and the enigmatic revelations in his dreams give an undoubtedly "Freudian" feel to the story. Freud insists that even though the author knew nothing of his theory (of dreams and delusions), "we have not discovered anything in his work that is not already in it." He goes on: "We probably draw from the same source and work upon the same object, each of us by another method. And the agreement of our results seems to guarantee that we have both worked correctly" (p. 92).

Similar, if less detailed, appeals to literary works for support for psychoanalytic theory occur throughout Freud's writing. For example, in his discussion of parapraxes he offers instances (1901, 1916) of (deliberate) slips of the tongue in Schiller's play *Wallenstein* and in *The Merchant of Venice*. M. A. Skura has even claimed that "the poets discovered *psychoanalysis* before Freud did."[13]

10. Joseph Margolis, *Art and Philosophy: Conceptual Issues in Aesthetics* (Atlantic Lowlands, N.J., 1980), p. 152.

11. Trilling, "Freud and Literature," p. 34.

12. All references to Freud's work will be to *The Standard Edition of the Complete Psychological Works of Sigmund Freud*, ed. James Strachey (London, 1953–74). In the text the date of the work will be given, followed by the volume in the standard edition, and the page reference.

13. Meredith Anne Skura, *The Literary Use of the Psychoanalytic Process* (New Haven, Conn., 1981), p. 4.

I suggest that at the root of all such claims, at least that psychoanalysis and poetry have drawn from the same source, is an important feature of Freudian theory, namely, its convergence with common sense or "folk psychology."[14] B. A. Farrell remarks of this common sense: "It has . . . been familiar for centuries with ideas connected with human beings having impulses, growing up to deal with the world, developing a conscience, learning and losing self-control, with feelings of guilt and shame, and so on. In other words, common sense is familiar with those aspects of human functioning which the concepts of Id, Ego and Superego cover in their low level use."[15] This goes a long way toward explaining the "mythical" grip of Freudianism. In popularized forms it is highly congenial to folk beliefs.

Finally, there is a rather different, but complementary, assimilation of psychoanalysis to literature. This comes in the increasingly widespread inclination to treat Freud's own work as a species of imaginative writing. Hence such comments as this from J. J. Spector: "His writings invite us to enter and experience his fantastic psychoanalytic universe imaginatively as we share the vision of great novelists like Dostoevsky, who make the sublime, the ridiculous, and the despicably criminal palpably human and immediately real to us."[16] No wonder questions of verification or scientific respectability get pushed to one side. Who would seek to verify Dostoevsky?

Freudian theories of the creation and reception of literary works In the first two categories I focused on what might be called psychoanalysis *in* literature. The remaining categories concern psychoanalysis *of* or *applied to* literature. The starting point here has been clearly put by Frederick Crews: "The simple fact that literature is made and enjoyed by human minds guarantees its accessibility to study in terms of broad principles of psychic and social functioning."[17] Admittedly, Crews goes on to discuss why this "simple fact" is not universally accepted by critics, but its forcefulness in the prima facie case is undeniable.

Psychoanalysis has a great deal to say, if not always consistently, about how literary works come to be "made and enjoyed." It is a legitimate and

14. For an interesting discussion in relation to the case histories, see Adam Morton, "Freudian Commonsense," in *Philosophical Essays on Freud*, ed. Richard Wollheim and James Hopkins (Cambridge, 1982).

15. B. A. Farrell, *The Standing of Psychoanalysis* (New York, 1981), p. 216.

16. J. J. Spector, *The Aesthetics of Freud: A Study in Psychoanalysis and Art* (London, 1972), p. 183.

17. Frederick Crews, ed., *Psychoanalysis and Literary Process* (Cambridge, Mass., 1970), p. 1.

fundamental question in the study of human nature why fictional and imaginative writing should have the prominence it does. In an early essay on the subject, "Creative Writers and Day-Dreaming" (1908), Freud attributes to writers only the pursuit of egotistical fantasies. This view is often thought, even by psychoanalytic critics, to have had unwelcome consequences for criticism. Freud wrote: "A strong experience in the present awakens in the creative writer a memory of an earlier experience (usually belonging to his childhood) from which there now proceeds a wish which finds its fulfilment in the creative work. The work itself exhibits elements of the recent provoking occasion as well as of the old memory" (1908, 9: 151). This assertion heralded an era of crudely reductive analyses and psychobiography. But if psychoanalytic views of creativity have become more refined, they have by no means abandoned the link with personal fantasy. In the light of Freud's suggestion that art is "a path that leads back from phantasy to reality" (1917, 16: 375), attention has come to focus on the path itself and the peculiar disguises the fantasies take.

Psychoanalytic theory also offers an explanation of our enjoyment of imaginative writing which, Freud claims, "proceeds from a liberation of tension in our minds" (1908, 9: 153), a kind of "fore pleasure" in sharing a fantasy softened by literary form. In an earlier and subtle essay "Psychopathic Characters on the Stage," Freud describes our enjoyment of tragic portrayals as "based on an illusion": the viewer's "suffering is mitigated by the certainty that, firstly, it is someone other than himself who is acting and suffering on the stage, and, secondly, that after all it is only a game" (1905, 7: 306). Psychoanalysis promises not only a general explanation of why we enjoy certain genres—tragedies, romances, even comedies (given Freud's theory of jokes)—but also why particular works have an enduring appeal. A common but perhaps disturbing fantasy in an attractive disguise will ensure a lasting interest.

What is most striking is how comfortably this psychoanalytic vocabulary—"fantasy," "fulfilment," "earlier experience," "illusion," "suffering," "game"—dovetails with antecedently *literary* concerns. Also, of course, it is a widespread folk belief that fiction can offer "escape" as well as "forbidden pleasures." Add to this the lack of alternative systematic theories of creativity and response, and psychoanalytic explanations come to seem the most natural framework for understanding the elusive *ars poetica* and its charms.

The attraction of psychoanalytic readings Psychoanalytic interpretation of literature has both encouraged and flourished in an age of virtuosity in criticism. Novelty and ingenuity are rewarded when "interpretation" becomes a preeminent mode of reading. Under pressure from critical formalism, the recovery of a writer's consciously intended meaning has come to seem a parochial, even inappropriate aim in criticism. When the acceptability of an interpretation is seen instead to reside in ingenuity and "insight," the sheer daring of some psychoanalytic readings has guaranteed them a continued attention. Freud's own suggestions, in *The Interpretation of Dreams*, about the character of Hamlet—the attempt to explain Hamlet's hesitations in terms of repressed desires, later characterized as the Oedipus complex—have acquired almost the status of orthodoxy. Unfortunately, after Ernest Jones's more sweeping claims in *Hamlet and Oedipus* (1949), it is often forgotten how modest was Freud's own view of the interpretation: "All genuinely creative writings are the product of more than a single motive and more than a single impulse in the poet's mind, and are open to more than a single interpretation" (1900, 4: 206).

Perhaps not much in general can be said about the attraction of psychoanalytic readings. I will be discussing their nature and legitimacy later. Just like Freud's own interpretations of parapraxes, dreams, and neurotic symptoms, they vary enormously with respect to plausibility. Certainly, there is a frisson to be had, even where plausibility is low, in the "revelations" of sexuality in unexpected places; Norman Holland, for example, sees phallic symbolism in Macbeth's "Out, out, brief candle."[18] More pertinent, psychoanalysis is often called on to help with problem cases in criticism. One such is Shakespeare's *Measure for Measure*, which has long eluded critical understanding. A sympathetic reading, working from the Elizabethan pun on "dying," has been proposed in an imaginative effort to make sense of the play in psychoanalytic terms.[19] In all such endeavors the psychoanalytic approach appears to stand foursquare with the alternatives. "Insights" are particularly welcome where genuine puzzles present themselves.

Some apparently impressive analogies   Perhaps the most powerful appeal of psychoanalysis to literary critics, at least from a theoretical point of view, rests on a supposed similarity of aim which revolves round the ideas of interpretation and meaning. As Skura has observed, "Psychoanalysis and criticism are both interpretive acts that have come of age during the

18. Norman Holland, *The Dynamics of Literary Response* (New York, 1968), p. 111.
19. Skura, *Literary Use of the Psychoanalytic Process*, pp. 243–270.

same century and have been influenced by the same intellectual currents."[20] Freud's claim that parapraxes, dreams, and symptoms have a sense that can be revealed through analysis certainly suggests a strong analogy with literary criticism. This impression is enhanced by the very form in which Freud presents, for example, his case histories. The fact that Freudian analyses reveal not only an underlying sense but also "tensions," "ambiguities," "associations," and "symbolic meanings" will in itself predispose even the formalist critic in their favor.

Further striking analogies include the distinction between manifest and latent content and, related to this, the "literary" mechanisms of the dream work: condensation and displacement. The mind structures and transforms a deep or hidden thought, a meaning, into an overt and often unrecognizable, form; analysis reverses the process and rediscovers the meaning. It is this that lies behind Trilling's grandiose assertion that "of all mental systems, the Freudian psychology is the one which makes poetry indigenous to the very constitution of the mind."[21]

Yet another analogy can be noted arising from Freud's thesis of psychic determinism. The idea that nothing, however seemingly "trivial," that occurs in the mind is arbitrary or undeserving of attention (1916, 15: 26–28) seems to correspond to an established maxim of criticism which attributes a "functionality" to all elements in a work.[22]

Finally, psychoanalysts have been impressed by analogies from the clinical context. The "dynamic" relation between patient and analyst involving resistance, transference, projection, concealment, and so forth—has been thought to reflect the complex interaction between a reader and a text (or author).[23]

I have said least about these last two categories because they will call for the most detailed scrutiny later on.

III

So much, then, for the prima facie case in favor of the relevance of psychoanalysis to criticism. I suggest that the main reasons why psychoanalysis has retained the attention of literary critics *without regard to its*

20. Ibid., p. 271.

21. Trilling, "Freud and Literature," p. 52.

22. For a discussion of the "principle of functionality" in criticism, see Stein Haugom Olsen, *The Structure of Literary Understanding* (Cambridge, 1978), p. 94.

23. Wright, *Psychoanalytic Criticism*, chap. 6.

status as a scientific theory lie within these five categories. Do they add up to an irresistible justification for a distinctive "psychoanalytic criticism"? I think not.

The first two categories have no implications for the appropriateness of a particular critical method. They refer only to a certain kind of subject matter in literary works. Those post-Freudian works overtly influenced by Freud's writings, in which the themes and symbols are self-consciously represented, are in fact the least amenable to psychoanalytic methods, where these seek to reveal unconscious meanings. A condition for understanding such works is certainly a *knowledge* of the theory, but not an *application* of it. By analogy, a patient who openly avows an Oedipus complex is not a promising subject for analysis.

Those pre-Freudian works that allegedly anticipate Freudian ideas, for example in "discovering" the unconscious, do so ex hypothesi in a distinctive way of their own. Their "Freudian" appearance can, I think, largely be accounted for through a combination of the folk psychological basis of Freudianism and the influence of the Freudian "myth" (in Margolis's sense). When a critic simply borrows the vocabulary from the "myth" to redescribe an independently identifiable subject matter, then psychoanalytic theory is not being engaged. When the emphasis is on the value of such works in supporting psychoanalysis, as with Jensen's *Gradiva* or Schiller's *Wallenstein*, then a purpose quite distinct from literary criticism is involved. In such cases it is not the psychoanalytic method that illuminates the works but the works that illuminate or give weight to the method. Of course, if the further claim is made that the only or the best way of making sense of the subject matter in the distinctive form that it takes in the work is by applying psychoanalytic methods, then the acceptability of the resulting interpretation becomes an issue in its own right, and we are into the considerations of the fourth category.

In discussing the third category I quoted a sentence from Crews to the effect that because literature is "made and enjoyed by human minds," it must be accessible to psychological and, in this case, psychoanalytic study. The crucial objection to this, frequently made, is that those features that are accessible to psychological study are precisely not those in virtue of which the work is *literature* or *art*. Psychological explanations for the sources or effects of literature have no bearing on literary qualities per se and thus none on the critical investigation of those qualities.

The objection, though, cannot rest there. At a time when the very concept of literature has been called into question, it is no longer possible to take a complacent view of the "autonomy" of literature or literary qualities. But enough can be said, I think, to establish that psychological causes and effects are not determining factors in critical analysis.

The first step can he found in the notion that art is somehow "depersonalized." Crews cites a version of this in Northrop Frye: "Poetry can only be made out of other poems" (in contrast to the writer's private fantasies).[24] A similar view appears in T. S. Eliot when he speaks of "a continual extinction of personality" in art: "the poet has, not a 'personality' to express, but a particular medium."[25] And in Jung the point is aimed directly at Freud: "No objection can be raised if it is admitted that this approach amounts to nothing more than the elucidation of those personal determinants without which a work of art is unthinkable. But should the claim be made that such an analysis accounts for the work of art itself, then a categorical denial is called for. The personal idiosyncrasies that creep into a work of art are not essential; in fact the more we have to cope with these peculiarities, the less is it a question of art."[26] Jung goes on to speak of the artist, *qua* artist, as "objective and impersonal."

No doubt the rationale behind these views of a "depersonalized" literature differs from case to case: Frye is concerned with the constraints on criticism; Eliot, with the priority of "tradition" over "individual talent"; and Jung, with the role of a "collective unconscious." But each argument rests on a shared assumption that to consider something as a work of art is to accord it a special status, which is incompatible with its treatment merely as a product of psychological causes.

I think we can develop this point of view a stage further. The very concepts of "art" and "literature" function in a special way. They are not straightforwardly descriptive, at least in the sense of denoting "natural" properties, either inherent features of a text (for example, its subject matter or form) or its causal relations. There is no set of "objective" defining characteristics. "Art" and "literature" are, of course, partly evaluative concepts, but more significant, they are also "institutional." Literary works are identified as such only against the background of a cultural practice and conventions.[27] Using a different terminology, they are "culturally emergent" objects.[28]

24. Crews, *Psychoanalysis and Literary Process*, p. 4.

25. T. S. Eliot, "Tradition and the Individual Talent," in *Selected Essays* (London, 1932), p. 20.

26. Carl Jung, "Psychology and Literature," in *Twentieth Century Literary Criticism*, ed. David Lodge (London, 1972), p. 185.

27. See Olsen, *Structure of Literary Understanding*, p. 94. Also Peter Lamarque and Stein Haugom Olsen, *Truth, Fiction, and Literature: A Philosophical Perspective* (Oxford, 1994), chap. 10.

28. See, for example, Margolis, *Art and Philosophy*, chap. 3.

Fictional Points of View

Here, then, lies the clue as to why so little follows from the observation that a work is "made and enjoyed by human minds." Just as no causal account of how a work came to be made or how it affects an audience can be sufficient for establishing that it is a work of art, so no psychological theory of those causes and effects makes it necessary to pursue a corresponding psychological investigation of the work when considered as a work of art. A simple parallel brings out the point. Consider the "institution" of currency. No purely causal account of the manufacture of a banknote, just as no description of its physical properties, will explain its role in a system of currency. To understand its "institutional" properties requires a quite different kind of investigation from the causal or "scientific."

Interestingly, this view of the institutional nature of literature need not be unacceptable to those who seek to eliminate the concept altogether; they simply draw different consequences from it. Thus some recent "rejections" of literature have stemmed, misguidedly I believe, from the recognition that no set of objective intrinsic properties can define "literature"; other grounds for rejection, as noted in Chapter 1, have rested on the view that the cultural practice within which literature is embedded involves an outdated or undesirable ideology.[29] But strictly speaking, none of this is a challenge to the *autonomy* of literature. We will be returning to the claim of autonomy in the next chapter.

In the meantime other ramifications of autonomy will occupy us in assessing the final two categories of the prima facie case. One well-known psychoanalytic theorist, Norman Holland, seems ready to concede the argument: "Psychoanalysis has nothing, nothing whatsoever, to tell us about literature *per se*."[30] Let us see why that must be so.

Psychoanalytic interpretations of individual works are often striking and ingenious. So why not acknowledge them as genuine contributions to literary understanding? I should emphasize that I am not attempting to legislate on what should be said about literary works. I am concerned simply to identify a distinctive class of judgments that constitute literary appreciation; these are judgments, both interpretive and evaluative, about literature per se. Psychoanalytic interpretations, in contrast to the incidental use of psychoanalytic vocabulary, cannot by their very nature belong to this class. Ultimately, psychoanalysis is concerned with properties of a person, and literary appreciation, with properties of a work of art.

29. Both arguments appear in Terry Eagleton, *Literary Theory: An Introduction* (Oxford, 1983).
30. Quoted in Wright, *Psychoanalytic Criticism*, p. 67.

Various consequences concerning these distinctive literary judgments follow from the view that literary works are not constituted by objectively given properties, either features of a text (syntactic, semantic, rhetorical, structural) or causal relations with a writer or reader. One is that the judgments cannot be purely descriptive. Their aim, rather, is to identify or assign aesthetic purposes to the given textual features. Literary interpretation attributes aesthetic significance to elements of a text by subsuming the elements into ever wider combinative and thematic patterns. It does so to establish an overall aesthetic unity in the text. The patterns of significance thus revealed can be called aesthetic, rather than textual, features of the work. They might be supervenient on but are not reducible to the textual features. They require a distinctive kind of judgment and discrimination for their identification. The literary understanding that results from such judgments can be considered as an end in itself; and the methods involved are sui generis. The validity of an interpretation on this account rests on criteria defined internally to the practice of literary criticism: a special kind of "fit" is demanded between thematic pattern and text, as well as consistency, comprehensiveness, "functionality," and so on.

In contrast, psychoanalytic interpretations are concerned with significance in a quite different sense; their validity derives from a theoretical framework independent of literary practice, and they assign to the elements in a text not an aesthetic function but a psychological one. Admittedly, psychoanalysis offers different models of literature for critical purposes, not all of which rely, like the fantasy model, on causal explanations.[31] Traditionally, psychoanalytic approaches have focused either on the causes and effects of literary works or on character studies as "case histories." An alternative approach of comparing the reading process itself and psychoanalytic "exchange" is a matter of analogy; we will return to it later.

What about the "case history" model that seeks to apply psychoanalysis directly to characters? On the face of it this seems not to infringe either the "depersonalized" view of literature (with regard to a writer's psychological states) or an autonomy based on the "institutional" definition of literature. Yet an argument from autonomy is available against this model. Skura, otherwise sympathetic to psychoanalysis, makes the first move: "For characters enmeshed in their fictional worlds, even the most sensi-

---

31. Richard Wollheim discusses different models in "Freud and the Understanding of Art," in *On Art and the Mind* (London, 1973), as does Skura, *Literary Use of the Psychoanalytic Process.*

tive and carefully descriptive psychoanalysis is out of place, though it would not be in life. My expectations about a man next door who acted like Leontes would be very different from my expectations about Leontes in *The Winter's Tale* . . . the cluster of traits can only mean what they mean in the play itself."[32] This is certainly right, yet it appeals to autonomy where it might seem at its most vulnerable: resting only on a distinction between characters and real people. A more powerful argument, I think, against psychoanalyzing fictional characters emphasizes less their fictional status and more their role within a literary context. Freud is quite right not to be too concerned with the fictionality as such of Norbert Hanold in *Gradiva*. A psychoanalyst might legitimately invent and analyze a fictional case for expository purposes; Freud simply helped himself to one already available. There is nothing wrong with that. But taken as components in a literary work, Hanold's dreams must be assumed to have a literary function. Now to say that the dreams have a sense in this context is, as we have seen, to say that they have a function within a pattern of meaning that unifies the work. That is a different kind of claim from saying that they arise from unconscious wishes in Hanold's mind.

The only complicating factor here is that we might well draw on a psychoanalytic vocabulary—repressed emotion, wish fulfillment—to enrich our understanding of a character, as with Hanold in this example. These terms have an established place in our everyday thinking, under the influence of the Freudian "myth." So what marks the literary from the psychoanalytic interpretation is no longer the vocabulary used but the purposes attributed to the features of the text under discussion. The explanations offered for what functions are being fulfilled by textual elements (like Hanold's dreams) will differ radically.

As we turn to the final category—the impressive-seeming analogies between psychoanalysis and literary criticism—we already have all the background to establish that what we have are at best only parallels. To begin with the analogies from the psychoanalytic process—the dynamics of the patient/analyst relation—although pursuit of these might be instructive, the parallels within literary criticism are in principle either purely contingent or involve independently identifiable and explicable phenomena. They are contingent where they refer to particular psychological attitudes of a reader (such as emotional attachments, self-deception, and so forth); they are independently identifiable where they refer to rhetorical "strategies" in texts, such as "invit[ing] complicity" or "ward[ing] off

32. Skura, *Literary Use of the Psychoanalytic Process*, p. 41.

understanding."[33] The devices of rhetoric are already the stock-in-trade of critics, and while the parallels might be interesting, they are not indispensable to critical method. Similarly, the analogy between psychic determinism and a principle of functionality in criticism is merely superficial, in that the former is rooted in what Freud calls the "*Weltanschauung* of science" (1916, 15: 28), whereas the latter is essentially linked to aesthetic unity.

What about the analogies with *meaning*? When Freud speaks of parapraxes, dreams and symptoms as having a *sense*, the word has very specific applications that are unlike those in literary criticism. A slip is a product of "mutually interfering purposes," the "disturbing purpose" being its sense. The sense of a dream is the "latent dream thought" in the unconscious, which is revealed in the manifest content only in a distorted form, as a result of "censorship"; the process of distortion is the "dream work." The sense of neurotic symptoms can be found in a traumatic memory repressed in the unconscious; to give the sense of the symptoms is to explain the "motives" underlying the neurotic behavior.

The difference with literary criticism is evident. We have seen it already in the two very different claims—psychoanalytic and literary—that might be made in saying that Norbert Hanold's dreams *have a sense*. In psychoanalysis, sense is essentially connected to (unconscious) states of mind. In literary criticism, sense, with its distinctive literary meaning, is essentially a complex relation, an internal connectedness, ascribed to elements in a text.

This irreconcilable difference carries over to all the seeming analogies. Interpretation in both cases involves the recovery of sense. But the aims and methods have little in common. For example, nothing comparable to "free association," Freud's favored route into the unconscious, is either possible or appropriate in literary criticism. This is another reason for the weakness of the analogy with patient and analyst.

The distinction between manifest and latent content again reflects the fundamental differences over sense. In literary criticism some meanings are indeed "hidden." But there the analogy ends. First, in the relevant sense, they are not hidden *in a mind*. This bald statement clearly confronts the issue of intentionalism in criticism. This is not the place to pursue that issue except to say that psychoanalysts can draw little support from literary intentionalism, at least in its refined forms, for example, where "intended meaning" is connected with such ideas as expression or

33. Ibid., p. 183.

"controlling intelligence."[34] Characteristically, the intentionalist critic is proposing not so much a psychological program for criticism as a certain kind of constraint on interpretation. Second, literary meanings might be "hidden" in a variety of ways. Allegory and satire, for example, present clear literary cases of a division into manifest and hidden contents, but again not in the psychoanalytic sense. Empson-type ambiguities need to be uncovered, or "teased out," but the sources are semantic and allusive rather than psychological. The favored concepts of the formalist New Critics—"tension," "ambiguity," "implicit meaning"—all have a linguistic, not a psychological, basis.[35]

As for literary themes, describing them as hidden or latent oversimplifies the complex relation they bear to a literary work. When Wilson Knight describes *Macbeth* as a "profound and mature vision of evil,"[36] it is not that he has discovered evil in the play—that has always been recognized as manifest—but that he is offering the concept of evil as an organizing principle in the play, a proposed focus for its aesthetic unity. In 1939, Edmund Wilson established the prison as a central symbol in *Little Dorrit*, identifying prison analogies throughout the work. It has been suggested that this discovery in fact occasioned a radical revaluation of the novel.[37] Seeing the prison as a unifying theme gave a particular sense and significance to the novel which had been previously unnoticed.

Psychoanalytic interpretations can have the appearance of operating in the same way: Skura writes, "In *Jane Eyre* . . . the manifest story about Jane's progress to adulthood is reinforced by a barely concealed female Oedipal fantasy in which growing up means marrying daddy."[38] But it is crucially unclear what status this alleged fantasy is supposed to have as a latent meaning. Is it a feature of Charlotte Brontë's unconscious mind? Or the reader's? Or Jane's? A latent unconscious thought must belong to some mind or other on psychoanalytic theory. The only way a fantasy can be viewed as a property of a *work* is either by treating the work as a behavioral manifestation of an unconscious state of mind or by seeing the fan-

34. See, for example, Colin Lyas, "The Relevance of the Author's Sincerity," in *Philosophy and Fiction: Essays in Literary Aesthetics*, ed. Peter Lamarque (Aberdeen, 1983), p. 20.

35. See, for example, Monroe Beardsley, *Aesthetics: Problems in the Philosophy of Criticism* (New York, 1958), chap. 3.

36. In the opening sentence of G. Wilson Knight's "*Macbeth* and the Metaphysic of Evil," in *The Wheel of Fire: Interpretations of Shakespearian Tragedy*, ed. G. Wilson Knight (London, 1949).

37. Stein Haugom Olsen, "Literary Aesthetics and Literary Practice," in *The End of Literary Theory* (Cambridge, 1987), pp. 15–19.

38. Skura, *Literary Use of the Psychoanalytic Process*, p. 91.

tasy as an abstracted theme identified through literary critical methods. If the former, the latent content is not *literary*; if the latter, it is not *psychoanalytic*. From a literary critical point of view, one significant difference between the theme of evil in *Macbeth* or the prison in *Little Dorrit* and the theme of a female Oedipal fantasy in *Jane Eyre* is that the credibility of the latter depends on the importation of a highly contentious theory, in this case about the relations of fathers and daughters. The novel on its own offers no support in folk psychology for this interpretation.

The analogy of the dream work can establish no closer a connection between psychoanalysis and literary criticism than can be found in the analogy of manifest/latent content. For the dream work is the mechanism by which a latent dream thought is transformed into a manifest dream content. Freud speaks of the main "achievements" of the dream work as condensation, displacement, and the transformation of thoughts into visual images. Although similar kinds of mechanisms can undoubtedly be found in the creation of art, once again the function they perform there will be different. There is barely even an analogy between what the unconscious does to foil an inner censor and what a poet's conscious mind does to create an aesthetic effect.

Furthermore, the suggestion by Jacques Lacan that condensation (in the dream work) is a form of metaphor and that displacement (in the dream work) a form of metonymy is of no help to the literary critic.[39] The direction of explanation is entirely the other way. The idea that the unconscious has a linguistic structure might help to cast light on psychoanalysis but it does nothing to illuminate the devices of poetry. Metaphor and metonymy as linguistic phenomena are much better understood than the Freudian dream work. This is yet another example where the debt seems to run from literature to psychoanalysis, not vice versa.

Literary criticism in the twentieth century has inevitably had to confront the overwhelming force of Freudianism. Psychoanalytic vocabulary has permeated the way we think about people's behavior and hence our perceptions of art and the artist. Modern writers endlessly dally with Freudian themes. But psychoanalysis cannot subsume literary or artistic criticism. Explaining a work of art, making sense of its aesthetic qualities, is never equivalent to explaining human behavior or states of mind. No

39. Jacques Lacan, "The Agency of the Letter in the Unconscious or Reason since Freud," in *Ecrits: A Selection*, trans. A. Sheridan (London, 1977), p. 160.

doubt there are similarities and parallels. Perhaps each enterprise can even learn from the other. But by a curious irony, the evidence seems to suggest that psychoanalysis, under the charge of "empirical groundlessness," is at its most credible when it most closely imitates the established procedures of literary criticism.

12

✶✶✶

The Literary Point of View

And how is criticism to show disinterestedness? By keeping aloof from what is called 'the practical view of things;' by resolutely following the law of its own nature, which is to be a free play of the mind on all subjects which it touches. By steadily refusing to lend itself to any of these ulterior, political, practical considerations about ideas, which plenty of people will be sure to attach to them, which perhaps ought often to be attached to them, . . . but which criticism really has nothing to do with.

—Matthew Arnold, "The Function of
Criticism at the Present Time"

The only obligation to which in advance we may hold a novel, without incurring the accusation of being arbitrary, is that it be interesting.

—Henry James, "The Art of Fiction"

I

The idea of the "autonomy" of literary criticism, or critical practice, has come up in several of the preceding chapters, notably in the last chapter in relation to the possibility of "psychoanalytic criticism," but also in the discussion of the "literary dimension" of tragedy and in the analysis of *écriture* and "the death of the author." It was foreshadowed throughout the discussion of fiction in the central argument that reading fiction *as fiction* involves adopting a distinctive point of view on descriptive content, emphasizing sense over reference, imagination over belief, internal connectedness over external truth directedness. In this final chapter I hope to bring many of these points together by addressing the question of what it might mean to read or judge a work from a "literary point of view."

We should not assume at the outset that a literary point of view is identical with a fictional point of view even when applied to the same work. Indeed, it should be apparent by now that they are not the same, either extensionally or by definition. Not all works of fiction are literary works, and perhaps not all literature is fictional (see Chapter 2). To view a work as fiction is to view it as a mode of discourse, subject to determinate conventions, involving the suspension of standard speech act conditions (associated, for example, with asserting, reporting, truth telling, questioning) and the eliciting of a complex imaginative response whereby the speech acts are pretended to be as they seem to be (assertions or reports of "fact"), even in the knowledge that they are not. This fictional perspective is value-neutral; "fiction" is a purely descriptive concept. A work can be fictional yet fail to be of any merit or interest. By contrast the literary point of view essentially involves an expectation of value: an expectation that the work has literary or aesthetic value (in a sense to be explained); that, for example, the interplay of subject matter and form has a reasonably high degree of subtlety and complexity; and above all that the work, under a process of literary interpretation, can be shown to develop *themes* of more or less general (if not universal) human interest. A work that fails to deliver on these expectations fails also as a work of literature.

Recent literary theorizing has seen considerable resistance to the idea of a "literary point of view" or the "autonomy" of critical practice. It has been thought to involve an unwarranted essentialism in literary criticism or an overformalistic conception of literature; to presuppose the existence of "literary qualities," an ineffable "literariness"; to impose arbitrary and artificial boundaries around modes of reading; to deny the embeddedness of literary works in wider social, cultural, or ideological constructions. The idea of "autonomy" is also subject to perennial confusion, especially regarding *what* is autonomous from *what*, which has made it an easy target for skeptics. Sometimes the conception is taken to involve the individual work in splendid isolation from its context, like a metaphysical substance or "windowless monad"; even here autonomy is conceived in different forms, sometimes causal, either of origin or effect, sometimes referential. Or autonomy is ascribed to the whole class of literary works whereby although interrelations are acknowledged one with another, the class itself is conceived as set gloriously apart from works of other kinds.

The autonomy I will defend is none of these; it is the autonomy of critical practice, of a mode of reading and interpretation. I will defend the view that at the core of literary criticism, as historically determined, is a distinctive interest or point of view that can be adopted toward a work, but one that does not rule out other kinds of interests or points of view on the same work. I am less concerned to give a detailed characterization of critical practice, an "anatomy of criticism"—which I believe has been adequately done by others[1]—as to explore the consequences and commitments of a defense of the literary point of view. In particular I want to address and meet the charges raised against this version of literary autonomy, especially those of essentialism, arbitrariness, and formalism.

I hope to establish the following conclusions, some of which have been anticipated in earlier chapters:

1. Reading, like writing, is a purposive activity.
2. Interpretation can proceed only relative to assumptions about what is being interpreted and to what end.
3. The distinctiveness of literary works is not established by attention to the features of individual works but to the conventions of an institution (or practice).
4. Disciplinary boundaries—for example, between philosophy and literary criticism—are real enough but do not rest on differences at any deep metaphysical level (the disciplines are not "natural kinds").
5. Appreciation of a literary work *as literature*—adopting the literary point of view on the work—does not involve an exclusive focus on formal properties.
6. The idea of "text" is logically secondary to that of "work."

II

Richard Rorty gives perhaps the clearest account of the views I seek to oppose. He rejects as "essentialist" the idea of a distinctive literary point of view which is definitive of critical practice, he sees literary criticism as the "presiding intellectual discipline," he wants to blur the distinction between philosophy and literature, and like Barthes, he supports the move away from "works" to undifferentiated "texts."

We can start with his elevation and consequent dilution of the concept of literary criticism. Rorty simply takes it as a fact (though one he welcomes) that the term *literary criticism* now covers virtually all kinds of serious reading (and writing). To account for this broadening of the term, he offers the following elaboration:

It [literary criticism] originally meant comparison and evaluation of plays, poems, and novels—with perhaps an occasional glance at the visual

---

1. For example, one fairly comprehensive account of the principles involved is Stein Haugom Olsen's *The Structure of Literary Understanding* (Cambridge, 1978).

Fictional Points of View

arts. Then it got extended to cover past criticism (for example, Dryden's, Shelley's, Arnold's, and Eliot's prose, as well as their verse). Then, quite quickly, it got extended to the books which had supplied past critics with their critical vocabulary and were supplying present critics with theirs. This meant extending it to theology, philosophy, social theory, reformist political programs, and revolutionary manifestos. In short, it meant extending it to every book likely to provide candidates for a person's final vocabulary.[2]

But a moment's reflection reveals a fundamental confusion in all this. Just because literary critics found themselves reading theology, philosophy, or revolutionary manifestos does not mean that they were ipso facto reading these as works of *literary criticism* and certainly not (there seems to be a slide here in Rorty's argument) applying methods of literary criticism in their reading or treating the works as if they were *literature*. They might well have been drawn to this wider range of works, as seems likely, through an interest in the theological, philosophical or political influences on the literary writers they were otherwise studying as literary critics. There seems no reason to suppose that they typically saw themselves as extending the bounds either of literary criticism or of literature in virtue of this further reading.

In another passage, Rorty writes: "Influential critics, the sort of people who propose new canons—people like Arnold, Pater, Leavis, Eliot, Edmund Wilson, Lionel Trilling, Frank Kermode, Harold Bloom—are not in the business of explaining the real meaning of books, nor of evaluating something called their "literary merit." Rather, they spend their time placing books in the context of other books, figures in the context of other figures."[3] Again a glaring equivocation is evident. It would be absurd to suppose that everything these writers produced must fall into a single category—literary criticism—just because the authors themselves can be broadly labeled as "literary critics." *Some* of what each of these "critics" wrote was indeed literary criticism, precisely involved in "explaining . . . meaning" and "evaluating . . . literary merit": think of Leavis on *Daniel Deronda*; or Eliot on the *Divina Commedia*; or Bloom on *The Songs of Innocence*. But much of what they wrote, again in each case, was not literary criticism: think of Leavis on C P Snow, Trilling on Freud, not to speak of Eliot's poetry or Edmund Wilson's plays. Of course, much of what these writers produced was a hybrid: part literary criticism, part

2. Richard Rorty, *Contingency, Irony, and Solidarity* (Cambridge, 1989), p. 81.
3. Ibid., p. 80.

something else. But not even that fact weakens (by diffusing) the sense of "literary criticism." The confusion—although to a philosopher it seems remarkably unproblematic—stems from the fact that the predominant *subject matter* of these writers was literary criticism, its nature, principles, and justification. But, as Stanley Fish puts it, in a robust defense of the autonomy of critical practice, "Once you turn . . . from actually performing literary criticism to examining the 'network of forces and factors' that underlie the performance, literary criticism is no longer what you are performing."[4] Perhaps Rorty might reply that to insist on these distinctions is to beg the question. Certainly more needs to be said in defense of such distinctions (for example, between theory and practice), but it seems just as accurate, at this stage, to press the charge of begging the question on Rorty himself. There is no reason why literary criticism must extend its bounds to cover all books that some critics happen to read or other critics happen to write.

With the broadening of the scope of "literary criticism" comes the broadening of "literature," according to Rorty: "The word "literature" now covers just about every sort of book which might conceivably have moral relevance—might conceivably alter one's sense of what is possible and important. The application of this term has nothing to do with the presence of "literary qualities" in a book."[5] The assertive tone in this passage is reminiscent of assertions to the effect that the author is "dead." But as we saw in Chapter 10, this is as much a statement of a wish as of a fact. Just as the author seems to linger on in critical discourse, so does a more narrowly defined "literature." Rorty's use of "scare quotes" around the term *literary qualities* is an attempt to link this supposedly discredited conception with the equally (supposedly) discredited notion of *literature* in its restrictive sense. But I will show later that a defense of literature relies on the notion of "literary qualities" only in a rather special, nonformalistic sense.

Most surprising is that Rorty is prepared to describe literary criticism, under his broad definition, as "the presiding intellectual discipline,"[6] for this seems to be just the sort of "privileging" of discourse that literary theorists have so persuasively warned us against. Just when philosophers seemed to be coming to terms with the idea, from literary theorists, that *philosophy* is not the "presiding intellectual discipline," because there is no

4. Stanley Fish, *There's No Such Thing as Free Speech, and It's a Good Thing Too* (New York, 1994), p. 240.

5. Rorty, *Contingency, Irony, and Solidarity*, p. 82.

6. Ibid., p. 83.

such thing, it is strange to find Rorty, a philosopher, elevating literary criticism to just that status. Rorty's claim is nonsense. It is difficult to make sense of the idea of a "presiding intellectual discipline," except perhaps as a university statistic, but the thought that literary criticism is paramount among disciplines—biology, physics, biochemistry, psychology, law, economics, social science, philosophy, history—is hard to take seriously.

But there is something deeper and more interesting behind this provocative banner waving. That is the extreme reductionism that Rorty promotes, no doubt with a significant following among literary theorists, in the idea of a "text" being read or interpreted. This brings us back to the conception of the literary point of view. One very clear statement of this reductionism comes in Rorty's debate with Umberto Eco, where he is criticizing Eco for supposing there to be an *intentio operis*, or an "intention of a work," which gives the work a coherence *prior to* any externally imposed interpretation. According to Rorty: "A text just has whatever coherence it happened to acquire during the last roll of the hermeneutic wheel, just as a lump of clay only has whatever coherence it happened to pick up at the last turn of the potter's wheel. . . . The coherence of the text is not something it has before it is described. . . . Its coherence is no more than the fact that somebody has found something interesting to say about a group of marks and noises—some way of describing those marks and noises which relates them to some of the other things we are interested in talking about."[7] Rorty sees the bedrock of interpretation as "texts" conceived as no more than "marks and noises," comparable in many respects to lumps of clay.[8] He rejects any clear distinction between *interpreting* and *using* a text: "All anybody ever does with anything is use it."[9] And a reader should not feel constrained in the uses to which a text might legitimately be put by "the work itself," for there is no such thing apart from the multitude of readers' uses. It is on this basis that distinctions between kinds of works (philosophical, literary, historical, autobiographical) become blurred in favor of "the idea of a seamless, undifferentiated 'general text.' "[10]

7. Richard Rorty, "The Pragmatist's Progress," in *Interpretation and Overinterpretation*, ed. Stefan Collini (Cambridge, 1992), p. 97.

8. Rorty has another essay, entitled "Texts and Lumps," in which he explicitly compares "things made" (texts) and "things found" (lumps) in the hope of showing the similarities between them, in *Objectivity, Relativism, and Truth*, vol. 1 of *Philosophical Papers* (Cambridge, 1991), pp. 78–92.

9. Rorty, "Pragmatist's Progress," p. 93.

10. Richard Rorty, *Essays on Heidegger and Others*, vol. 2 of *Philosophical Papers* (Cambridge, 1991), p. 87.

We have already seen some of the difficulties in the Barthesian move from "work" to "text." Now I want to show how fatal the move is to the very possibility of interpretation. Certainly it is possible to *use* a text in any way one likes—as a source of quotations, a way of boosting one's vocabulary, a prompter for general reflection. But interpretation cannot be thought of as just one use among others. Strictly speaking, interpretation cannot be applied to *texts* at all, only to *works* of determinate kinds. We might need to interpret newly discovered hieroglyphics, a passage from the New Testament, the State of the Nation speech, a Blake poem, or a ruling of the Supreme Court, but it is only under those classifications, minimally, that the interpretations can proceed. Texts are merely abstractions from works (conceived broadly as meaningful utterances). Without some knowledge of what they are texts *of*, no interpretation could get going, because any interpretation would be as good as any other, which would make the very process of interpretation redundant.

A number of arguments could be brought to defend the view that it is works not texts that are interpreted. The first we have seen already in discussing the idea of *écriture*: no coherent conception of "writing" can be said, in Barthes's term, to destroy the "voice of origin"; *écriture* itself is an abstraction, a theoretician's fiction; writing, properly so-called, can never be context-free; the context can be ignored but not denied. A related argument is grounded in standard speech act theory. To grasp what is *meant* in an utterance involves grasping what illocutionary act is being performed. Although it is possible to give a general semantic characterization of a sentence such as "I am cold" by specifying its truth conditions, a full interpretation of an utterance of that sentence in context requires not just this semantic knowledge but also knowledge of the speaker and occasion and especially what illocutionary intentions lie behind the utterance: perhaps the speaker is merely *stating a fact* or *requesting* that someone close the window—or *ordering* them to do so—or *quoting* or *telling a story*. The spoken "text" gives no clue in itself as to which of these interpretations is correct. Yet interpretation only begins at the speech act level; specifying the truth conditions of a sentence, apart from any occasion of use, is not a matter of interpretation.

A third argument comes from aesthetics and has the closest bearing on the literary application. Kendall Walton has decisively shown that many aesthetic properties of works of art cannot be identified solely from direct perception of the works (at a "textual" level) but require for their identification essential reference to facts about the origins of the works, in particular those bearing on what "categories" the works belong to. He develops the following well-known thought experiment to elaborate the point:

> Imagine a society which does not have an established medium of painting, but does produce a kind of work called *guernicas*. *Guernicas* are like versions of Picasso's "Guernica" done in various bas-relief dimensions. All of them are surfaces with the colors and shapes of Picasso's "Guernica," but the surfaces are molded to protrude from the wall like relief maps of different kinds of terrain. Some *guernicas* have rolling surfaces, others are sharp and jagged, still others contain several relatively flat planes at various angles to each other, and so forth. Picasso's "Guernica" would be counted as a *guernica* in this society—a perfectly flat one—rather than as a painting. Its flatness is variable and the figures on its surface are standard relative to the category of *guernicas*. Thus the flatness, which is standard for us, would be variable for members of the other society . . . , and the figures on the surface, which are variable for us, would be standard for them. This would make for a profound difference between our aesthetic reaction to "Guernica" and theirs. It seems violent, dynamic, vital, disturbing to us. But I imagine it would strike them as cold, stark, lifeless, or serene and restful, or perhaps bland, dull, boring—but in any case *not* violent, dynamic, and vital. We do not pay attention to or take note of "Guernica" 's flatness; this is a feature we take for granted in paintings, as it were. But for the other society this is "Guernica" 's most striking and noteworthy characteristic—what is *expressive* about it. Conversely, "Guernica" 's color patches, which we find noteworthy and expressive, are insignificant to them.[11]

What the example shows nicely is that judgments about a work's aesthetic properties—and I would include such judgments within the class of *interpretations*—make implicit reference to a "category" in which the work is placed. "Guernica" is dynamic as a painting, cold and bland as a *guernica*. But it would be wrong to suppose that Walton is proposing a radical relativity of interpretation. He is not saying, as perhaps Rorty might, that it is an arbitrary matter what category a work belongs to, thus how the work should be appreciated or interpreted, and thus what aesthetic properties are perceived in it. Instead he identifies a number of criteria for determining whether a work is *correctly* or *incorrectly* assigned to a particular category. These include, though defeasibly in each case, facts about what the artist intended, facts about wider social or cultural ex-

11. Kendall L. Walton, "Categories of Art," *Philosophical Review* 79 (1970): 347.

pectations with regard to the work, facts about the most rewarding way of perceiving the work, and naturally facts about the (nonaesthetic) properties of the work itself. Although he believes that the category of a work determines the aesthetic properties to be seen in the work (that the properties are *relative* to the category), he does not believe that there can be no objective fact of the matter as to which properties *do* belong to the work by virtue of its being in such and such a category.

More needs to be done to show that Walton's points about aesthetic properties in the visual arts can be carried over to the literary case. But it seems likely that strong analogies can be drawn. Indeed I will show later what sense can be given to "aesthetic properties" of literary works. The upshot so far is that powerful prima facie arguments from both philosophy of language and aesthetics exist against taking undifferentiated "texts" (the literary equivalent of uncategorized [art] objects or uncontextualized sentences) as the bedrock for interpretation. Rorty's excessive reductionism, the view that "texts" are there to be "used" in any way a reader sees fit, without real constraints from the work itself or its context, is just the mistake of supposing that we can ignore the category to which a work properly belongs or the occasion on which a sentence is used.

But might it not be objected that "works" cannot be the bedrock of interpretation, as I am proposing, because to establish what kind of work is at issue is the first task of interpretation? If that is so, then identifying a text as a text-of-a-certain-kind, that is, a work, is not a precondition of interpretation so much as an initial stage of interpretation. Then interpretation would after all have to be of texts in the first instance. But the objection does not stand. Only in the most extreme and unusual cases are we confronted with a "text"—calling for an interpretation—without any knowledge of what it is a text of, that is, merely a piece of unidentified writing, void of context. Furthermore, were we to be confronted with such a text, we would have no means of proceeding; any attempt to assign illocutionary force, discursive function, point or significance, to the "undifferentiated text" would be entirely speculative. The crucial first step, seeing it as a work of a certain kind, could not take place.

In contrast, the normal case of interpretation arises where there is no doubt as to what category of work the text belongs to: a speech, a poem, a philosophical treatise, a letter. Interpretation then has a foothold from which to move to the next, more important stage; conventions governing works of that kind are invoked, just as we know what features to take as "standard" or "variable" once we have identified "Guernica" as a painting (and an artwork) rather than a *guernica*. Of course, there might be cases where interpretation, along with other investigations, serves to dislodge a work from one category into another or to show it to fall into more than one category. Perhaps Oscar Wilde's letter from prison to Lord Alfred Douglas changed, on publication as *De Profundis*, from being (merely) a personal letter to being an essay, an apologia, a statement of personal philosophy. But it could never revert to being *just a text*. Even a string of words found floating in a bottle is likely to be interpreted, in the first instance, as a *message*, an attempt at communication.

The idea that it is not texts but works that are the objects of interpretation is of fundamental importance in the discrimination of modes of reading. For works (unlike texts) invite readings of a particular kind; they invite a specific stance or point of view. The literary point of view, whatever that turns out to be, is, trivially so, the stance appropriate to works in the category of literature. Philosophical works invite a philosophical point of view. And so on. But to the extent that all such points of view involve interpretation, it should not be supposed that this is a uniform activity following the same conventions in all cases. It clearly is not. No doubt there is a shared aim common to all interpretation: making sense of something that is puzzling.[12] But the conventions, assumptions, and procedures for "making sense of something" will differ from case to case. If I want to make sense of your remark during a conversation, I will need to determine your intentions; perhaps there is a "conversational implicature" behind what you say, in which case, if I am a Gricean, I will need to establish, among other things, whether you are adhering to conversational maxims. If I want to interpret your dreams and I am a psychoanalyst, I will follow a different strategy: I will explore your free associations, your relations with family and friends, your anxieties, the symbolism in your dreams.[13] There is no reason to suppose that I must

12. Annette Barnes has convincingly argued that we cannot speak of interpretation where no puzzle arises: we cannot interpret the obvious. As Barnes puts it, "If it is obvious to A that x is F, then A is not interpreting x as F for himself," in *On Interpretation* (Oxford, 1988), p. 26.

13. Beyond that of requiring different modes of interpretation, a further disanalogy between the conversation and the dream cases is arguable. Grasping a speaker's intentions is an *essential* feature of following (interpreting) a conversation, whereas giving a psychoanalytic interpretation of a dream is far from essential—indeed, it involves a commitment to a highly controversial theory. The difference here recalls the distinction drawn by Arthur Danto between "surface" interpretation and "deep" interpretation. The former is indispensable for the very identification of a work (in the artistic case) and relies on recognizing intentions, whereas the latter is not indispensable, can take multiple forms, and rests on some wider theoretical framework. See Danto, *The Philosophical Disenfranchisement of Art* (New York, 1986); see also Peg Brand and Myles Brand, "Surface and Deep Interpretation," in *Danto and His Critics*, ed. Mark Rollins (Oxford, 1993).

follow procedures that correspond to either of these models when I want to interpret a literary work, a poem, a passage in a novel, or the opening scene of *Macbeth*. In fact, it became clear in the last chapter that psychoanalytic and literary interpretations, for example, differ in fundamental ways.

For Rorty, the postulation of a distinctive "literary point of view" involves commitment to an unwarranted essentialism. He rejects the notion that there is such a thing as "the work itself"—giving rise to Eco's *intentio operis*—which constrains the uses to which a text might be put. I have dwelt at length on the need to see works rather than texts as primary in the determination of an appropriate response (a mode of reading), which to some extent simply acknowledges a degree of essentialism. What is Rorty's objection? He targets two kinds of essentialism: what might be called content essentialism and function essentialism. Content essentialism is "the notion that there is something a given text is *really* about";[14] function essentialism is the notion that a text has some intrinsic purpose, "the idea that the text can tell you something about what *it* wants."[15] I suggest there is a short answer and a long answer to the charges of essentialism in both cases. The long answers will rest on a more detailed examination of the literary point of view. The short answers simply show that the charges rely on false assumptions.

As for content essentialism, it is just wrong to suppose that the literary point of view requires the search for—or commitment to—a single correct interpretation of a literary work to the exclusion of all others. Critical practice has always been hospitable to interpretive pluralism, the idea that works can sustain different readings, with different emphases, with weight given to different themes. In many ways that again highlights a contrast with works of other kinds, within law or archaeology or history, for example, where more determinate meanings are sought. In the literary case, though, interpretive pluralism does not mean interpretive indifference; there are better and worse readings, more and less plausible interpretations, and objective criteria are available for making these assessments. As for function essentialism, the crucial point rests on whether the essentialism is applied to texts or works. There are no *textual* properties that determine "literariness"; there is nothing in a text per se, a string of words or sentences, that

14. Rorty, "Pragmatist's Progress," p. 102.
15. Ibid., p. 103.

dictates one type of reading to the exclusion of other types. Only when a text is identified, for different (usually "external") reasons, as the text of a literary work does the invitation arise to approach it from a "literary point of view." There is an essential connection between being a literary work and inviting a literary response, but there is no essential connection between being a text of a certain kind and being a literary work.

III

Throughout this chapter and, indeed, throughout the book, I have carefully avoided attempting to offer a general definition of literature. Partly this is because I do not believe it is possible to give such a definition that is substantive and noncircular, and partly because I believe that attempts by others to do so are nearly always prescriptive and I have no desire to prescribe a concept as against describing basic features of a practice (or practices). The term *literature* is used in many senses, "broad" and "narrow," and although I think that attempts of those such as Rorty to remove the concept altogether are misguided, I have no desire to legislate on English usage. My focus throughout has been on notions like a "literary point of view" or a "literary dimension," which shift away from properties of works themselves to attitudes taken to works (by readers); such notions allow in principle for a literary interest to be pursued in works that might otherwise (and paradigmatically) not be classed as literature.

In several places in preceding chapters I have invoked the idea of an "institution" of literature, along with the idea of a "practice" of criticism (and a practice of reading and responding to fiction). These ideas of "institution" and "practice" are now well established in the analysis of different kinds of cultural phenomena. In the context of literary phenomena they have proved especially fruitful, not least for directing attention away from the search for elusive qualities of "literariness."[16] They allow us to see that literary qualities are not "brute" facts definable in linguistic or semiotic terms but "emergent properties"—in this case "aesthetic" rather than "natural" properties—whose nature and very existence are made possible only through institutional conventions. Plenty

16. For a detailed account of the "institutional" approach to literature, see Stein Haugom Olsen, *The End of Literary Theory* (Cambridge, 1987), passim.

of analogies are at hand. One is the familiar games analogy: no purely physical description of actions or objects can adequately explain what it is to "score a goal" in soccer. The very possibility of "scoring a goal" owes its existence to the game and its rules, such that type-identical actions and objects in a world without the game of soccer (or in a context outside the game) would not, and could not in principle, possess the property "scoring a goal." Another analogy, briefly introduced in the last chapter, is with the properties of units of currency. Coins or banknotes have no intrinsic physical properties—be it of constitutive material, design, appearance, weight, color—that are necessary or sufficient to make them units of currency. These are paradigmatic "institutional objects" that get their value and status as currency through the complex functions they serve in a social practice (buying and selling). Their monetary value is conventional, not derivable from their value as objects. This is not to say that the property "being a 25¢ coin" is not a "real" property of a particular object and not determinable as such precisely and objectively. But it is not a property reducible to any intrinsic, nonrelational properties of the object itself. It requires the institution of money in general and the conventions of a specific nation's currency in particular for its very existence.

"Literary qualities" can be thought of, in some respects, as analogous, and not only because they both yield values that are dependent on broader institutional conventions. If there were no institution of literature, there would be no literary qualities. Literary value and literary interest arise out of a mode of apprehension made possible by a rule-governed institutional practice linking authors, works, and readers. Textual properties—formal properties of texts of a rhetorical, syntactic, phonological, or even semantic kind—are not sufficient in themselves to count as literary qualities, although no doubt some textual properties have a greater potential than others to fulfill a literary function (comparably, an object that weighed two tons would not be suitable as a coin). It is often supposed that textual features such as rhyme, meter, assonance, alliteration, metaphor, pun, or simile, are literary qualities that texts possess intrinsically and attention to which is the hallmark of a literary point of view. But that is wrong. Critical practice does not consist simply in the identification and cataloguing of these kinds of textual features but rather in *assigning significance* to such features within an overall conception of the text *as-a-work-of-literature*. Consider the following critical comments from Michael Riffaterre on the final lines of Wordsworth's poem "Yew-Trees":

Fictional Points of View

> . . . or in mute repose
> To lie, and listen to the mountain flood
> Murmuring from Glaramara's inmost caves.

"Listen" is not alone. The verb "lie" prepares and justifies it within the conventions of descriptiveness. And "in mute repose" functions as a hyperbole developing the semantic feature of *attentiveness* inherent in "listen". These modifiers are thus operating as verisimilitude factors, giving tangible reality to the scene. But they operate also as counters to the *troubled* semantic invariant of the subject group: listening soothes them.

As for the object, the "flood", one descriptive feature—the sound it makes—is stylistically emphasised. "Glaramara", aside from being a place name, is a phonetic variant of the onomatopoeic "murmuring" which it echoes and amplifies. This element, both phonetic and semantic, is synonymous with the soothing component of the verb group; it is the agent of that action.

The text cumulatively establishes an image of Man beset by fear and refusing hope, shutting himself against the future in tight-lipped frustration. The components of the second sequence are derived from this stylistic overloading which generates its extreme opposites: simplicity is derived from and balances complexity, and literalness is derived from and balances allegory.[17]

In this passage certain literary qualities of Wordsworth's poem are brought out, or elicited, *in interpretation*. Textual features, such as hyperbole, onomatopoeia, and "stylistic overloading," are assigned significance first by showing how they create and balance oppositions in the structure of the poem and then, as a consequence, how they contribute to and help develop a general theme or vision of "an image of Man beset by fear and refusing hope." Whether or not one agrees with the reading itself or with the pronounced structuralist methodology, there is no question that the critic is adopting a literary point of view to the work. It is from that perspective that literary qualities are being adduced. Only given the conventions of critical practice can such a focus of interest make any sense. Without the concept of a poem, as a literary work of art subject to just this kind of attention, critical passages like this would be virtually unintelligible. More significant still, there would be no such literary qualities; the very possibility of appropriating formal stylistic features to develop a vi-

17. Michael Riffaterre, "Interpretation and Descriptive Poetry: A Reading of Wordsworth's 'Yew-Trees,' " in *Untying the Text: A Post-Structuralist Reader*, ed. Robert Young (Boston, 1981), p. 125.

sion with universal interest out of particularized local description (in this case the inspiration is "a Yew-tree, pride of Lorton Vale") depends essentially on a poetic tradition and a tradition of responding to poetry as art.

Literary qualities, however, should not be thought peculiar to poetry. It is not just the condensed use of imagery or metaphor which makes literary appreciation possible. It arises too with narrative prose. Consider these comments by Elizabeth Dipple on certain passages in Iris Murdoch's novel *Nuns and Soldiers*:

> The novel is . . . using Tim and his artistic combination of the abstract and organic more simply as an illustration of its own structure. In his first conversation with the Count, Guy has described philosophical speculation irritably as "a dance of bloodless categories after all" (p. 2), and *Nuns and Soldiers* which subtly opposes intellectual disciplines to lived experience is well served by Tim's combination. At every turn in the novel, the organic gives full illustration to and is more effective than the ideological, as for example when Anne throws herself confidently into the sea only to find that she cannot cope and nearly drowns. The act had been, as she interprets it later, a kind of vanity, an abstract belief in the power she had won by leaving the convent; her defeat and near death remind her that the external world is greater than her internal thoughts and image-creating capacities.
>
> More poignant are the canal sequences in France where Tim undergoes his ordeals; indeed all the French landscape sequences are fraught with beauty and significance. The rushing canal itself invites abstract identification as an image of life: Tim's escape from the tunnel of death clearly parallels his emergence on the other side of his deadly moral failures into happiness and forgiveness with Gertrude. But the image is made stronger and connected to the old literary trick of pathetic fallacy in the presentation of the two dogs: the first dead, bloated dog, at first glance like a human being, is a terrible image of Guy, and recognition of this sends Gertrude into hysterical tears and Tim into a misery in which he wishes he were dead. The second dog, very much alive and struggling as it is swept towards the fatal tunnel is joined by Tim, whom it also symbolizes, and their emergence on the other side illustrates Tim's triumph and life as opposed to Guy's defeat and death.[18]

What is characteristic about this piece of interpretive analysis—and it should be emphasized that it is a mere fragment from an extensive, forty-

18. Elizabeth Dipple, *Iris Murdoch: Work for the Spirit* (Chicago, 1982), p. 339.

page discussion of this one novel—is the way that narrative details are linked together (for example, the dogs in the canal/the contrast between Tim and Guy) and shown to support broader themes (the opposing of "intellectual disciplines to lived experience," for instance). Such moves are utterly familiar to literary critics, for they constitute the very core of the enterprise of literary criticism, regardless, in virtually all cases, of what theoretical "school" underpins the criticism. Identifying internal connectedness of this kind is just what it means to identify literary qualities in a novel. It is also the source of aesthetic pleasure derived from literary narrative in that it invites just that controlled imaginative engagement that we examined in the case of tragedy. The "literary qualities" of narratives are not merely the formal features of the narrative, the mellifluous prose, the well-chosen epithet, the vivid descriptions, nor do they reside only in the lifelike characterizations or well-structured plots. Rather, they "emerge" in the multitude of ways that the formal features *make possible* the thought or vision of the whole.

Put simply, this way of reading (as illustrated by the *Nuns and Soldiers* example), this kind of interest we might have in literary narratives, is quite unlike the way we would standardly read or take an interest in a historical or biographical account of actual lives (unless we are self-consciously seeking the literary qualities of the factual account). The focus in the literary case is on the significance assigned (assignable) to formal features, the way that the formal features (vocabulary, structure, rhetorical device, style) help sustain an internal coherence among segments of the descriptive content, the way that universal themes can be elicited to give sense and unity to the whole work. The literary point of view is an *aesthetic* interest, and the literary qualities are aesthetic properties. But that, as we have seen, cannot be reduced to a mere aesthetic formalism. Only through the attention grounded in literary appreciation can the aesthetic properties be identified: and thus the connections forged, the imaginative reconstruction developed, and the thematic unity characterized.

Now the pieces begin to fall into place. First, by reintroducing the idea of aesthetic properties (manifested in the literary context as "literary qualities") we can see clearer parallels with the earlier Walton paradigm. The relevant aesthetic properties only emerge given the assignment of the work to the category of literature; only by *seeing* a work *as* a literary work is the presence of aesthetic properties, of the kind described, made possible. The expectation of a complex interplay between form and vision is, in Walton's terms, "standard" for the category of literature. Perhaps this is just an alternative way of making the point about the institution-dependence of literature. The conventions of the institution determine the mode of appreciation and the expectation of an aesthetic "reward." The very idea of a literary "point of view" rests on the metaphor of perception, and it is exactly a kind of perception (broadly conceived) that is invited by literary works. Internal thematic connections become salient only when the textual properties are perceived through the lens of literary appreciation.

Then, second, this yields the longer and deeper response to Rorty's charge of content and function essentialism in literary criticism (narrowly conceived). It is not that "Yew-Trees" is "intrinsically"—that is, at a textual level—about the "image of Man beset by fear" or that *Nuns and Soldiers* must, in some essential way, be about the theme that "the organic . . . is more effective than the ideological." Rather, these are ways of construing the works through the literary perspective. It might be that, on conventionally determined criteria for supporting literary interpretations, these readings cannot be sustained; it might be shown, for example, that they fail to account for a sufficient number of details in the works. But it is not an arbitrary matter that the works do invite, and reward, a literary reading, that they fall into the category of literary works. Nor is it an arbitrary matter what interpretations count as more or less plausible.

Although all literary works do, by definition, contain literary (and aesthetic) qualities, it should be clear by now that there can be no set of textual, or formal, qualities that all literary works must possess to qualify as literary. There is no property of "literariness" which can be abstracted from individual literary works. Literariness, like the value of a unit of currency or even like a move in a game, is an institutionally defined property not reducible to "natural" properties of a linguistic or psychological nature. It reveals itself through the complex relations in which authors, works, and readers stand one to another.

We can indeed distinguish, precisely and objectively, literary works from philosophical, historical, or scientific works, for certain ends. But we cannot do so by listing internal properties possessed by works of one kind and not the other. A literary point of view can often and fruitfully be adopted to, for instance, philosophical works, particularly those that employ textual features, such as dialogue, narrative form, or fictional example, which are characteristic of more paradigmatic works of literature. But a literary interest cannot be adopted *at the same time* as a philosophical interest. The two are categorially distinct. To the extent that the latter too has a concern with form and theme, it is a concern not with aesthetic significance and internal connectedness but with argument and reason and truth. Literary works differ from works of other kinds both in having as their primary purpose the adoption of a literary perspective but also in rewarding that perspective. The purposes behind philosophical, historical, or scientific works are different, as are the modes of apprehension and the expectation of "rewards." But there is no reason to think that these differences lie at a deep "metaphysical" level, that discourses fall into "natural kinds," or that they rest on profound differences in the way that truths are distributed in the objective world. They are differences in practices: in ends sought, expectations raised, conventions followed, rewards attained. This perhaps explains the seductive half-truth in Rorty's relaxed devil-may-care attitude to the "uses" to which "texts" are put. Yes, we can put any text to any use we like and see what comes of it. But it is inevitably more rewarding to identify *works* that are offered for particular ends and to see how far those ends are attained within the appropriate conventions for works of that kind.

IV

It is time to return again, in conclusion, to autonomy. The autonomy or distinctiveness or self-containedness that has concerned me in this chapter is that of critical practice or the literary point of view. The "principle of autonomy," to use Monroe Beardsley's words, used to be a central tenet of the New Criticism. It was thought to underlie the great, alleged, "fallacies" of literary criticism: the Intentional Fallacy and the Affective Fallacy. And no doubt it also underpinned Cleanth Brooks's Heresy of Paraphrase. When William Wimsatt and Beardsley sought a general characterization of their critical "fallacies," they did so in terms of "the poem itself," which they saw as being in danger of "disappearing": "The Intentional Fallacy is a confusion between the poem and its origins. . . . It begins by trying to derive the standard of criticism from the psychological *causes* of the poem and ends in biography and relativism. The Affective Fallacy is a confusion between the poem and its *results*. . . . It begins by trying to derive the standard of criticism from the psychological effects of the poem and ends in impressionism and relativism. The outcome of either Fallacy, the Intentional or the Affective, is that *the poem itself* [italics added], as an object of specifically critical judgment, tends to disappear."[19] The idea of "the poem itself," idolized as a "verbal icon" or "well-wrought urn," gave rise in the New Critical lexicon to the terminology of *inside* and *outside*—*internal* or *external* evidence (Wimsatt and Beardsley) or *intrinsic* and *extrinsic* criticism (René Wellek and Austin Warren).[20] The critic's task was to analyze only such features as were truly "within" the poem and all references to "extrinsic" matters were deemed to be beyond the proper domain of literary criticism.[21]

I hope that the preceding discussion has shown decisively that this whole approach as a defense of "autonomy" is radically misconceived. The distinction between what is "inside" and "outside" a literary work, as made by the New Critics, is virtually meaningless. (It should be clear that *this* distinction is quite different from the "internal"/"external" distinction that has figured prominently in earlier chapters, for the latter concerns different perspectives that can be adopted to the *worlds* of a work and has nothing to do with the citing of evidence in criticism or interpretive properties of the "work itself.") What the discussion of autonomy has established is that the very features supposedly "internal" to the work—its literary or aesthetic qualities—rest *essentially* on a web of relations involving the author, readers, and other works which are both manifestly "external" to the individual work itself yet constitutively "internal" to the institution that makes the work what it is. Because literary works derive their identity from the institution of literature, the boundary between what is in "the work itself" and what is brought to it from "outside" cannot be coherently drawn. Needless to say, though, we should not conclude from this that no boundary exists between *relevant* and *irrelevant* considerations (what can be said or thought) in the appreciation of literary works or that citing elements in the text of the work is not an important means of support for literary interpretation. The point, once again, is that the "intrinsic" textual properties, to which the New Critics

19. William Wimsatt and M. C. Beardsley, "The Affective Fallacy," in *The Verbal Icon: Studies in the Meaning of Poetry*, ed. W. Wimsatt (Lexington, Ky., 1954), p. 21.

20. For the latter, see René Wellek and Austin Warren, *Theory of Literature* (London, 1949).

21. It is not clear that Wellek and Warren were as committed to New Critical dogma on the matter of "autonomy" as Wimsatt and Beardsley. After all, they devote a great deal of space in their classic *Theory of Literature* to discussing what they call the "extrinsic approach to the study of literature," including literary history and the use of biography, psychology, and social science. But when they come to the "intrinsic approach," which they conceive in largely formalistic terms, they do write of a "healthy reaction" among their contemporaries to the older "extrinsic" styles of criticism and seem to endorse the more "recent" view that "the study of literature should, first and foremost, concentrate on the actual works of art themselves" (ibid., p. 139).

insisted we give our full attention, are not what make a work "literary"; aesthetic properties alone do that, and they "emerge" only from the *work* conceived *under a perspective.*

The autonomy of critical practice, with its own ends and its own procedures, has a consequence that might be unpalatable to many literary critics, particularly those under the Rortyian delusion that theirs is the "presiding intellectual discipline." The consequence is that literary criticism is just one discipline among others, with its own limited subject matter (literary works) and its own purpose-built methodology. The notion that it occupies a privileged position from which to view, and even change, the world is an illusion. Literary criticism is as impotent to bring about political or social change as any other academic discipline. Its purposes and achievements are more narrowly focused, though it is none the worse for that. The same is true of all humanistic enquiry. For those of us who recognize the central cultural importance of works of literature and a literary tradition, the intrinsic value of reading and appreciating those works is justification enough. Perhaps a case might be made for further instrumental values—relating to educational and intellectual development, for example—in learning how to read literary works and read them well. But these ancient and familiar points are often sneered at by those who expect much more from a "modern" literary education, where the emphasis is as much on literary *theory* as critical *practice.* Literary theory is sometimes thought to provide the deepest insights into what is wrong with late-twentieth-century, postindustrial society, able not only to diagnose the problems but to offer practical political solutions. Literary theorists sometimes see (or portray) themselves as at the cutting edge of social change, forging new and enlightened attitudes, exposing and sweeping away outdated ideologies. But whatever the independent merits of the diagnoses or the solutions—and whatever the (probably marginal) practical effects on social change attributable to literary theorists—none of this has anything whatever to do with literature or literary criticism.

From within the senior ranks of literary theory, no one has seen this point more clearly or argued for it more persuasively in recent years than Stanley Fish. Consider this not untypical passage in which he once again draws the demarcation lines:

> Literary critics do not traffic in wisdom, but in metrics, narrative structures, double, triple and quadruple meanings, recondite allusions, unity in the midst of apparent fragmentation, fragmentation despite surface

unity, reversals, convergences, mirror images, hidden arguments, climaxes, dénouements, stylistic registers, personae. This list goes on and on, but it does not include arms control or city management or bridge-building or judicial expertise or a thousand other things, even though many of those things find their way into the texts critics study as "topics" or "themes". While it is true that a critic can exercise his bag of tricks on any material whatsoever—on politics, war, science, religion—this does not make him an expert in the fields from which those materials are quarried.[22]

We find here an echo of Plato's own strictures about the poets themselves, who, he feared, purported to an expertise they did not really possess. Plato saw, quite rightly, that it is one thing to have as your subject matter themes that are grounded in a particular area of knowledge and to *represent* (in his terms, "imitate") practitioners in that area but another to contribute to that knowledge yourself or even share it. This, as I have argued in earlier chapters, is one reason for being wary of attributing a truth-telling role to literature or even a role in moral philosophy. Now we find just the same kind of arguments brought to bear on literary criticism. A critic can show how a theme is developed imaginatively in a novel without thereby acquiring the resources to pronounce authoritatively on a similar theme in an extraliterary context. Of course the very same person might want to go on to make such pronouncements in a different, political capacity, but that is to move beyond the literary critical task, and it calls on different skills.

Fish has repeatedly insisted on the distinctiveness of literary criticism, not only from philosophy but also from literary theory itself: "They are different games, and they remain different even when they are played by the same person."[23] The main weakness of literary theory has been its expansionism, for in seeking to colonize its neighbors, it has fatally lost touch with its home territory of literature and criticism. No doubt the first steps were innocent enough in following up genuinely *literary* concerns with fiction, reality, truth, meaning, subjectivity, but the temptation to overgeneralize the findings and move directly into philosophy, psychology, and history has resulted in a dilution of the contribution to both the new and the old realms.

22. Stanley Fish, "Why Literary Criticism Is Like Virtue," *London Review of Books*, 10 June 1993, p. 12.

23. Stanley Fish, *Doing What Comes Naturally: Change, Rhetoric, and the Practice of Theory in Literary and Legal Studies* (Oxford, 1989), p. 335.

Literary criticism should not make the same mistake. The practice of criticism is only weakened by being overextended and misapplied. It is best seen as an end in itself, not as a means to something else, although that is not to disparage it. Only those who undervalue literature will think that the trained appreciation of literature, promoted by the practice of criticism, is a secondary activity. "Literary interpretation," as Fish puts it, "like virtue, is its own reward."[24] It would be futile to suppose that adopting the literary point of view has benefits or rewards beyond the appreciation of literature. It does not need that for its justification. But it would be equally futile to infer from this that only some more politically or socially relevant point of view is desirable to reap the value of literary works. For this is self-defeating. To view the works as something other than literary is to lose sight of what makes them *literary* works in the first place. The logical connection between literary works and the literary point of view is nicely brought out by Stanley Fish and I will leave the last word to him:

> If I am interested in the moral structure of *Paradise Lost*, I will look at Satan's speeches to see whether they display contradiction, evasions, self-deceptions and hollow posturings; if I am interested in rousing my troops or rousing a nation I will accept those same speeches (no longer the same) at face value and quarry from them shamelessly so long as they lend themselves to my cause. I cannot, however, do both—perform as a literary critic and perform as political or military leader—simultaneously; for while the two performances will at some level share *Paradise Lost*, the *Paradise Lost* that emerges at the conclusion of one project will have very little resemblance to the *Paradise Lost* that emerges at the end of the other.[25]

24. Fish, "Why Literary Criticism Is Like Virtue," p. 15.
25. Ibid., p. 11.

INDEX

Index

Index

Index